GROUPS AND THE CONSTITUTION

STANFORD UNIVERSITY PUBLICATIONS
UNIVERSITY SERIES
HISTORY, ECONOMICS, AND POLITICAL SCIENCE
VOLUME XII

In the twentieth century, voluntary associations—groups—have grown to a position of great strength in the American culture. To define their rights, privileges, and obligations, the Supreme Court is slowly creating, case by case, a body of constitutional law of association. The Roman Catholic Church, the Ku Klux Klan, the CIO, Jehovah's Witnesses, and the Communist Party are only a few of the diverse groups which have come under the Court's consideration.

In this book, Robert A. Horn reviews modern political theories on the subject, from Hobbes and Locke onward, and relates them to principles which are emerging from Supreme Court decisions concerning the rights of groups. He then traces the application of these principles in Supreme Court cases concerning churches, labor unions, political parties and pressure groups, and subversive organizations. A concluding chapter relates the cases concerning these diverse kinds of groups to the general legal principles applicable to them all, and examines the creative efforts of the Court in developing the modern constitutional law of association.

Dr. Horn (A.B., Ohio Wesleyan University; M.A., Ph.D., Princeton) has taught at Harvard, the University of Chicago, Sophia University in Tokyo, at the Salzburg Seminar, and at a Fulbright conference at Cambridge University. At present he is assistant professor of political science at Stanford.

Groups and the Constitution

ROBERT A. HORN

AMS PRESS

NEW YORK

For
Edward S. Corwin

FOREWORD

The Charles R. Walgreen Foundation for the Study of American Institutions is happy to present this work by Professor Horn, initially given as a series of five lectures at the University of Chicago. Professor Horn directs his attention to freedom of association as a guaranteed liberty under the United States Constitution. His work gives thorough consideration to the development of the large body of constitutional law on freedom of association built up in the United States through decisions of the Supreme Court involving the First Amendment. The limitations placed upon this freedom in some democratic countries stand in notable contrast to both the theory and the practice in the United States. Professor Horn gives us a most complete study and analysis of the American constitutional law of association that is valuable not only in itself but especially for students who desire to compare foreign theory and practice with our own.

JEROME G. KERWIN, *Chairman*
Charles R. Walgreen Foundation

PREFACE

This book is an exploration of only part of a much larger and still incompletely mapped expanse. American law governing the rights and duties of voluntary associations is made by legislatures, administrative agencies, and courts, both state and national. The law of association laid down by the Supreme Court of the United States is only a small part of the whole legal effort to define the place of groups in our society, although a crucially important one. It is that part of the law with which this book is concerned.

Those who wrote about property rights and due process of law in the nineteenth century usually thought in terms of the rights of individuals, of natural persons. Now we see the real problem of that era as the adjustment of the laws of property to the growth of great organized economic groups, the business corporations. Today a large volume of writing about civil liberties is likewise cast in terms of the freedoms of speech, press, and assembly belonging to individuals. Yet the truth is that almost all these First Amendment and due process cases of this century deal with the rights of individuals acting as members of organized religious, political, and economic associations, acting in their behalf or in their name, and utilizing their vast resources and power. May it not be possible that some of our present hesitancy and uncertainty in delineating rights of personality stems from a confusion analogous to the earlier one? Is it any more realistic now to conceive these civil liberties primarily as if they are exerted by isolated individuals than it was then so to envision the exercise of property rights? That is the question which motivated this exploratory essay.

The late Charles E. Merriam encouraged me to set out upon it, and a preliminary sketch appears in his and Robert E. Merriam's volume, *The American Government, Democracy in Action.*

A series of Walgreen Lectures at the University of Chicago in 1953 provided an opportunity to prepare this book, which is a considerably expanded and revised version of those lectures. To the Chairman of the Walgreen Foundation, Professor Jerome G. Kerwin, I am greatly indebted for his many kindnesses.

Other friends and former colleagues at the University of Chicago have also lent their generous and valuable help. Professors David Easton and Charles Hardin each read part of the manuscript. Professors Morton Grodzins, C. Herman Pritchett, and Leonard D. White read all of it, and what their stout support and encouragement have meant I cannot even adequately express.

At Stanford, Professor Arnaud B. Leavelle has also read the manuscript and Professor James T. Watkins IV has been a warm and constant friend to the enterprise.

My assistants at Stanford, Messrs. Cary Fisher and Robb Crist, and particularly Mr. Warren Campbell and Miss Olga Sonder, have done valuable service. Miss Florence Stevens and Mrs. Robert Mozley, and Mrs. H. M. Herlihy especially, have carried the burden of secretarial assistance.

To them all my thanks, and absolution for faults, which are mine and not theirs.

ROBERT A. HORN

STANFORD, CALIFORNIA
February 8, 1956

CONTENTS

1

FREEDOM OF ASSOCIATION: THE GROWTH
OF A MODERN LIBERTY

Let us suppose that the First Amendment to the Constitution read: "Congress shall make no law abridging the freedom of speech or of the press *or of association* . . ." If the amendment protected freedom of association explicitly, our law of associations might not be much different from what it now is. But treatises on American constitutional law would have a rubric of freedom of association. Our casebooks would assemble together cases under this heading. The law reviews and learned journals in political science would carry many articles considering in those terms the legal problems of association. Freedom of association would appear as a distinct strand in the thread of civil liberty running through American constitutional history.

But the Constitution of the United States, unlike the more recent constitutions of some European nations and unlike the proposed Charter of Human Rights of the United Nations, does not speak of freedom of association.[1] In consequence, anyone interested in the constitutional protection extended to this freedom in the United States must search among the cases on labor law, study the history of religious freedom and the relations of church and state in America, examine the law regarding political parties, and explore other niches of our constitutional law. He must ask himself if the diverse problems arising from the activities of a multitude of associations so different in their forms and purposes can be brought within the unifying conception of a law of association.[2]

It is the central theme of this book that freedom of association is one of the most important civil liberties guaranteed by the Constitution of the United States, that we already have a substantial corpus of constitutional law on the freedom of association, and that the rapid creation of this body of law in the twentieth century by the United States Supreme Court is one of the most significant aspects of American constitutional development.

---

[1] See, e.g., Article 20 of the Universal Declaration of Human Rights promulgated by the General Assembly of the United Nations, December 10, 1948.

[2] Cf. Sir Ernest Barker: ". . . we may say that the acknowledgement of liberty of association should be expressed in a general law of associations, which translates the principle into detail and formulates its consequences. The historical State, as it has grown in time, has scattered its rules about associations under different heads, according to the accidents of its growth: it may even have deposited discrepant rules in different branches of its law," at page lxi of his Translator's Introduction to *Natural Law and the Theory of Society, 1500 to 1800*, by Otto Gierke.

1

Associations and the problems that they pose for law and political theory are not new. Associations have long been one of the principal means by which men have sought to achieve their material well-being and their spiritual and cultural ideals. Men work in groups, worship in groups, and in democratic states they must even seek to govern through groups. But important as group activity has long been in social life freedom of association is distinctively a problem of modern politics, for at least three reasons.

In the first place, only a society which is large and diverse has or feels a need for a large number of associations. For the Greeks the *polis* was much more than a state. If our language, like German, permitted us to string words together in one long compound we could call the *polis* a neighborhood-kin-group-church-army-state-economy. Thus we should catch the sense of all-embracing community in the Greek city-state. But in a modern state with many more people of heterogeneous stocks spread out over wide territories and working with specialized skills in an elaborate division of labor this feeling of community vanishes. A modern state's boundaries may coincide with a national culture or a "great society" but not with a community, to say nothing of a neighborhood that may be seen entire from the highest mountain on a clear day. Modern intellectuals who feel *anomie* in their bones and long for a return to that Golden Age might, if they were transported back to it, find that they had merely exchanged their present affliction for *claustrophobia* (which is also a Greek word). The glory that was Greece shone upon the city-state as this sense of close-knit community was dissolving, and perhaps because it had been dissolving.[3] Some may say that the modern state as their only common association is inadequate to the needs of so many people with diverse beliefs, interests, and customs. But is this a fault of the modern state or a virtue of modern society? If variety is the spice of life, the advantage lies with us, not the Greeks.

In the second place, freedom of association becomes an issue only when one association in a society not only asserts but establishes pre-eminent authority over all other associations. From the time that the state established this claim—in short, became sovereign—the rights of men to join in other associations and the rights of these associations vis-à-vis the state have been an ineluctable concern of political theory. It was not always so. Medieval political thought about associations was cast in quite different terms during the centuries when two great associations, the State and the Church, struggled to find a way either of sharing men's allegiance equally between them or of winning it exclusively. The crucial importance of the struggle and its outcome is shown by our dating the beginning of the modern period of Western history from the triumph of the sovereign state system.

As one result of the state's new claim, it became different from all other associations not only in the degree of its authority over men but in kind. The state became an involuntary association, as Justice Holmes put it, "the one

---

[3] Harry Elmer Barnes and Howard Becker, *Social Thought from Lore to Science* (Boston, 1938), at pp. 141–54.

club to which we all belong." All other associations remained (or became) voluntary or free associations.

Admission to membership in the state is not a matter of choice for most of its members; they are born citizens. The Fourteenth Amendment to our Constitution puts the doctrine succinctly: "All persons born or naturalized in the United States, and subject to the jurisdiction thereof, are citizens of the United States . . ." The state presents the natural-born with much the same Hobson's choice his family offers him; God gives us our relatives and fellow citizens, but we can choose our friends. But if we have no choice about accepting our parents, neither do they have any in accepting us as their children. The state as *parens patriae* is not in the same position as natural parents. It may deny citizenship to those born within its control if it chooses to do so. We have the words of the Fourteenth Amendment because the Supreme Court of the United States thought in the Dred Scott case that the country had excluded those born slaves from its citizenship.[4] Modern states only appear to renounce their power for the same reason that most of their natural-born citizens have no feeling of compulsion in their state membership: both have accepted the idea of nationality and the nation state.[5]

If nationalism has so far triumphed over sovereignty as to make choice about citizenship illusory for both the state and its natural-born citizens, it is instructive to recall John Locke's struggle with the question.[6] "It is plain," he tells us, "by the practice of governments themselves, as well as by the law of right reason, that a child is born a subject of no country nor government." From this categorical assumption Locke proceeds to difficult, and to our age, quite unreal questions: How, then, does a man become a citizen? Any man who lives within the territory of a state and enjoys its benefits is for that time subject to its law, but is not thereby a citizen. He becomes a citizen, apparently, only by ownership of property, particularly land.

The character of the state as an involuntary association is still more clearly revealed if we ask whether there is any more choice about ending membership in it than there is in entering it. Banishment in classical times and outlawry in early and medieval England suggest that the state may expel citizens against their will. But as far at least as the Constitution of the United States is concerned, the government has no power to deprive the citizen of his citizenship without his consent unless we hold that this power is "inherent in sovereignty."[7]

On the other hand, can the citizen end his citizenship against the will of the state? It is clear enough that he can expatriate himself with the state's consent. Indeed, the state decrees that certain acts by the citizen will expatriate

4 Dred Scott v. Sandford, 19 Howard 393 (1857).

5 Cf. Bertrand Russell, *Power: A New Social Analysis* (London, 1938), at pp. 219–20.

6 Cf. Sections 116–21 of the *Second Treatise of Civil Government*.

7 Deprivation of citizenship should not be confused with the deprivation of some rights of citizenship prescribed as part of the punishment for certain crimes in the various states and by the United States. See 8 United States Code 801.

him, so that persons sometimes lose their citizenship because they are unaware that the state will interpret their voting in a foreign election or serving
in a foreign army as an expression of their intent to expatriate themselves.
It is not so easy to say whether the citizen can expatriate himself against his
state's will. Our Constitution provides that as long as an American citizen
is "subject to the jurisdiction" of the United States he remains a citizen, and
as long as he is within the territory he is within the jurisdiction. He cannot
find an asylum from citizenship within his own country. But can he leave the
country at will and thus, so to speak, banish himself? Ordinarily in time
of peace, it is no crime to leave the United States without a passport, for
a passport is only a request to other governments for fair treatment for one
of its citizens. But in the contemporary world this right of expatriation by
exit is becoming more and more nugatory.

The position of the naturalized citizen is akin to that of the adopted child.
In entering the state he is both more and less free than the natural-born, for his
naturalization requires the mutual consent of the state and himself. Once a
citizen, is he on any different footing from the natural-born in keeping his
citizenship? Our law has long provided for a cancellation of naturalization,
but the grounds for this action have been such that denaturalization implied
that the original naturalization had never really been effective; it had been
void *ab initio* because procured by fraud of some sort. Denaturalization is
an annulment rather than a divorce. Or the naturalized citizen might lose
his citizenship by prolonged absence from the country; his action was taken,
not unnaturally, as an expression of intent to expatriate himself. The people
of the United States have in their Constitution explicitly denied to the naturalized citizen two rights of the natural-born: he cannot become President or
Vice President. The fair implication of this action is that he does have every
other right of the natural-born.

This, then, is the character of the state as an involuntary association. Its
closest relative among associations is the family. But in modern society the
extent to which the family approaches an involuntary association is determined by the state's laws, although they may simply confirm for the most
part pre-existing customs. All other associations are spoken of as free or
voluntary. We enter these associations only by mutual consent of both parties, but our membership ceases at the will of either party. This at least is the
general rule which distinguishes them from the state. The exceptions to this
rule are few and mostly specious. Some churches may consider membership
a birthright and charitably decline to recognize a member's declaration of his
expatriation. Such theories are relics of an earlier time, relics which the law
leaves undisturbed as long as the individual loses no rights as a result. The
officers of college fraternities, vested with the titles of ancient Greek magis-
trates, may warn their neophytes in sepulchral tones that they can never dis-
solve the bonds of brotherhood, but the middle-aged college alumnus sees the
bathos in the impressive ritual. The genuinely important exceptions to the
rule are of modern, even contemporary, origin and are the creation of the
state. They will demand our attention later.

Modern political and legal thought about the rights and functions of associations in society has developed, therefore, in the context of modern society as distinguished from classical or medieval society. It makes basic in its theories those distinctions which in fact exist in modern society between the state as a superior and involuntary association and all others as subordinate and voluntary. Our ultimate goal is some understanding of the place of associations in American law, but since our treatment of associations and our thinking about them stems from general Western thought, we will do well to recollect some of the landmarks in that thought as we start out upon our search. On our right stand Hobbes, Rousseau, and modern totalitarians; on our left, Locke, Gierke the German, and finally his English disciples Maitland, Figgis, Cole, and Laski.

HOBBES

As might be expected, Hobbes was no more inclined to allow rights against the sovereign to associations than to individuals. But if he gave groups—or systems, as he called them—little freedom, he gave them much attention. In the twenty-second chapter of the *Leviathan* he set forth a classification and analysis of these systems which is characteristically precise and logical. All systems may be divided into the regular and irregular, or in modern terms, the organized and the unorganized, the structured and the unstructured, the enduring and the ephemeral.

Thus Hobbes draws a fundamental distinction between an association and a mere assembly, a mass meeting, an audience, a crowd, a mob. With his assembly, or irregular system, we need concern ourselves no further than to notice that his division makes clear that the right to associate comprehends more than a mere right to assemble.

The most fundamental distinction between regular systems, or associations, according to Hobbes, is that between those which are absolute and those which are dependent, subject, and subordinate. Only states can be absolute associations; the preceding chapters of the *Leviathan* have been devoted to demonstrating why this must be so.

Among the subordinate, subject, dependent associations there is also a basic division into the political and the private. Hobbes's terminology sounds a little strange to modern ears, but his meaning is clear. The political system is a body politic, it is a person in law, it is a corporation. In short, it is an association which the sovereign has expressly authorized, or chartered. The two main types Hobbes discusses are the municipal corporation and the company of merchants, that ancestor of our modern business corporation which the commercial expansion of seventeenth-century England had brought into prominence. These political systems or chartered associations need have no fear of their legitimacy; the Crown's letters patent are their certificate of honorable birth. But they must have a care for the lawfulness of their conduct, for this birth certificate is also a constitution beyond their right to change or to exceed. Hobbes thus adopts for these associations what jurisprudence calls the concession theory of the source of corporate personality.[8]

The private associations are simply all those others which are not expressly authorized by the sovereign. They are finally divided into the lawful and the unlawful. Lawful private associations are those which are allowed by the sovereign; all others are unlawful. This rule on its face is a stringent enough limitation on the rights of voluntary associations, but it seems to grant some freedom if one assumes that the sovereign allows all associations that he does not expressly prohibit. Although a private association does not require a specific grant from the sovereign to be lawful, it must be able to show some "public authority"; it must be able to justify itself under the laws common to all subjects. The only example of a lawful private association that Hobbes mentions is the family. Doubtlessly he saw the common law of domestic relations as the public authority for the family. The severity of Hobbes's view is made manifest in his discussion "of the things that weaken or tend to the dissolution of a commonwealth." There he warns against "the great number of corporations which are as it were many lesser commonwealths in the body of a greater, like worms in the entrails of a natural man." *E pluribus unum?* No—out of many, chaos. That is the warning of Hobbes.

ROUSSEAU

That also appears to be the warning of Rousseau. In *The Social Contract* we find no such close analysis as Hobbes offers. The father of Romanticism is impressionistic where the mathematician is systematic. In cryptic fashion Rousseau tells us that

> when factions arise, and partial associations are formed at the expense of the great association, the will of each of these associations becomes general in relation to its members, while it remains particular in relation to the State: it may then be said that there are no longer as many votes as there are men, but only as many as there are associations. . . . It is therefore essential, if the general will is to be able to express itself, that there should be no partial society within the State, and that each citizen should think only his own thoughts . . . But if there are partial societies, it is best to have as many as possible and to prevent them from being unequal . . .[9]

Surely our perplexity is justified. His fellow countrymen after the French Revolution attempted to put Rousseau's dictum, as they understood it, into practice. The result was a stringent limitation of the legal rights of association lasting into the present century. Perhaps Rousseau has received too much credit for the turn which the French law of association took. It is hard to believe that the French version of the *Kulturkampf* under the Third Republic did not contribute to a retention of this law. Yet the effort to proscribe associations certainly did not bring about that single-mindedness in French

---

[8] For a succinct account of these theories see W. Friedmann, *Legal Theory* (2d ed., London, 1949), chap. 26.

[9] *The Social Contract*, Book Two, chap. 3.

society which Rousseau had seen as the desired result, and it may very well have exacerbated the conflicts and tensions in France. Did Rousseau intend, however, to condemn all associations? On closer reading we may doubt it. His remarks occur at the very heart of the book, in the chapter describing the *volonté générale*. The evil charged against associations is their corruption of the political process. When an association functions as a political party or as a pressure group, it leads men to mistake their selfish and particular interests for the public interest and to prefer them over the good of the whole society. In this view Rousseau was condemning, not all associations, but those which are actively involved in politics. If this view is correct, Rousseau takes his place among those eighteenth-century publicists who warned against the evils of faction and seems closer to George Washington than to Thomas Hobbes. Whereas Hobbes saw all associations as a threat to the *power* of a nonpopular sovereign, Rousseau saw parties and pressure groups as a threat to the *rectitude* of a sovereign people.

Rousseau's practical second-best solution suggests that this interpretation is the sounder. If the ideal of no associations is impossible, let there be many equal associations. (He never explains why an absolutely sovereign people cannot achieve this ideal.) In this Rousseau is closer to James Madison than to Thomas Hobbes. (The American or Englishman is likely to think that the French with their multitude of political parties have been equally unfortunate in exhibiting this side of Rousseau's idea.) At any rate, it seems fair to say that Rousseau does lie on our right, if not so far to the right as Hobbes.

TOTALITARIANISM

About the third landmark on the right little need be said, for in the theory and especially the practice of modern totalitarian states it has stood and still stands before us all. The essence of totalitarianism is determination that men have no right to associate for purposes that do not fit the plans of the government and that it is the right and, indeed, the duty of the state to make churches, labor unions, trade and professional associations, universities, political parties, and even recreational societies mere agents for carrying out state purposes and to destroy those which it cannot bend completely to its will. The practice of this conception of society in one country helped loose the scourge of the Second World War on our generation, and its practice in still another nation may help bring upon us a Third World War. In this view it does not seem too much to say that the denial of a reasonable freedom of association is the consummate frenzy in a fanatical vision of society.

LOCKE

We may take our first bearing to the left from Locke's *Letter on Toleration*. Unlike Hobbes and Rousseau, Locke did not express his thought about associations in general terms. His concern was freedom for one kind of association, the church. In this connection it is well to remember that although Hobbes and Rousseau wrote in general terms, the particular animus of each was directed against religious groups. Hobbes's *Kingdom of Darkness* and Rousseau's *Civil Religion* are evidence enough for that conclusion.[10] Since Locke is concerned with the church, we may leave an extended consideration of his thought till later. But two of his arguments have much broader implications. Most important, Locke assumes that the individual has a natural and inalienable right to associate. He needs no permission from government to exercise this right; indeed, civil society has an obligation to protect his right and to limit it only on a clear demonstration of necessity. It is this principle which is the foundation of Anglo-American thinking about freedom of association. A corollary of this principle is almost as important: the rights of a group are a derivative from the right of the individual to associate. It is this conception which significantly distinguishes Locke's view from that advanced in Gierke's doctrine of real group personality. Here, too, dominant Anglo-American thought has followed Locke.

Locke leaves us to infer his other important general doctrine about freedom for associations, although the inference is plain enough. Locke's basic argument for religious freedom rests on the distinct functions which church and state perform in society. The state is concerned with man's material welfare in this life on earth. The church is concerned with man's spiritual salvation in the life to come. Therefore, the church's business is no concern of the state, and vice versa. Let us not stop to consider the soundness of this conclusion now. An important inference from this line of thought is that other kinds of associations which, like the state, are concerned with man's material welfare here on earth cannot claim as much freedom from state control as the church can. The church is *sui generis* among the voluntary associations. It is not hard to understand why Locke did not himself draw this inference out. Labor unions, business corporations, political parties, and pressure groups did not loom so large in his society as they do in ours. According to Locke, men have an inherent right to form such groups for the promotion of their material welfare and to demand that any state interference with that right be justified in reason, but not to demand complete freedom from state control.

NINETEENTH-CENTURY INDIVIDUALISM

As J. W. Gough has said, "In his attitude to toleration, as in his political theory, Locke was no innovator, but was stating rational grounds for a case which was already nearly won."[11] The growth of religious toleration in the eighteenth and nineteenth centuries, particularly in the Anglo-American world, removed the most painful symptoms of the "church question." The minor irritations that remained could be borne by society and ceased to preoccupy political philosophers and jurists. In this period what other great associations were there to raise the challenges to the state which churches had advanced? The family we have always with us, but enough has been said to

[10] Part Fourth of *Leviathan* and Book Four, chap. 8, of *The Social Contract* respectively.
[11] At page xxxvii of the Introduction to his edition of *The Second Treatise of Civil Government and A Letter Concerning Toleration* (rev. ed., Oxford, 1948).

indicate that although we may call the family an association, it is not a voluntary association in any ordinary sense. Sociological and juristic theory about the family clearly recognizes its differences from other groups.[12]

The shift toward popular control of the nation-states did bring with it the rise of political parties. These factions were at first treated with suspicion and hostility. But time and experience brought a large measure of acceptance and even approval from thinkers. And among ordinary men it could never be more truly said that familiarity bred contempt. In prosperous and sufficiently homogeneous countries it has been a good-humored contempt nowhere better expressed than by the line of American humorists from Mark Twain through Mr. Dooley to Will Rogers.

The great business corporations which grew so rapidly in the nineteenth century could not be laughed off. Society's need or desire for the material advantages which only these great aggregates of men and money could produce dictated their toleration. The question was, toleration on what terms? The great body of corporation law which every state with a modern economy has built up shows how each state has answered this question. In sheer bulk, to say nothing of importance, it dwarfs the law regarding any other type of association. And no wonder, for corporation law deals with money, and property has always been the center of gravity in the mass of the law. Naturally this great body of law has elicited much more analysis and interpretation from lawyers, political scientists, and economists than the law of other voluntary associations.[13] It is mainly for this reason that these chapters will not consider it, and not from any misconception that it is not a part of the law of associations.

There is another reason for omitting a detailed consideration of the business corporation. The needs which have molded its form have sharply differentiated it from other voluntary associations. Advantages were sought that existing law did not offer to groups. These privileges were granted in corporate charters. Thus the most important form of business organization came to differ from other associations, almost all of which remained unincorporate. Legal personality was assured to the business corporation; limited liability could be guaranteed to its members; other privileges also accrued. In addition, a share of stock, rather than a person, became the basic unit of the corporation; that is, legal control of the corporation is in the hands of the owners of a majority of the shares, not in a majority of the shareholders. And these shares can ordinarily be transferred from one owner to another without the consent of the corporation. In this sense the corporation can

---

[12] Professor Eugen Ehrlich's description of the family, translated as a "genetic association," felicitously suggests this difference. Ehrlich's work, part of which has been translated by L. Moll as *Fundamental Principles of the Sociology of Law* (1936), powerfully emphasizes associations as the central concern of modern law. Cf. the analysis of Ehrlich's thought in Julius Stone, *The Province and Function of Law* (ed. of the Harvard University Press, 1950), *passim*.

[13] Adolph Berle and Gardner Means, *The Modern Corporation and Private Property* (New York, 1932), is a landmark in this interpretation. Cf. also Julius Stone, *op. cit.*, chap. 23, "Freedom and Control of Economic Association."

scarcely be called a voluntary association. As demands for public control of the business corporations grew, on the other hand, governments could and did make the exercise of these extraordinary privileges conditional upon the observance of special regulations. All this is a many-times-told tale.

The important aspect of this development for us is that this law of business corporations, at least in Anglo-American jurisdictions, was for a long time treated as a branch of private rather than public law, and still is for the most part so treated. This view may lend great weight to the criticism made by Professor Kelsen and other modern jurists of distinctions between private law and public law, but it does not alter the fact that this is the view that has been taken. As one result, the law of the business corporation remained for most political theorists of the nineteenth century a mere technical matter.

As a consequence nineteenth-century political thinkers focused their attention upon the problem of *The Man versus the State*, as Herbert Spencer's title reminds us so well. In this era of individualism the problems of voluntary associations receded into the background of political theory. One notable exception to this trend, as we shall see, was De Tocqueville. Another and later one was Gierke.

PLURALISM

We must stop on our way to look at pluralism without losing ourselves in this imposing edifice of thought.[14] Unlike our other landmarks, this is the work of a number of builders. Gierke provided the spacious grounds for it, but his landscape is dotted with thorny Teutonic thickets we cannot stay to explore. Maitland designed the impressive central halls and Laski and Cole each added a left wing. Figgis constructed a private chapel to provide sanctuary from Erastian English judges. Each of these architects had his own designs and each his critics. Despite the plurality of architects there is enough unity in the structure to view it as a whole. Seen so, it is a pleasing neomedieval mansion in which few have been content to dwell for long. Many lawyers and political theorists trained in the school of monistic sovereignty rejected it from a glance at the blueprints. Others, more sympathetic, adapted some of its style into their own thought.[15] Laski eventually tore down most of his own wing. The British Labour party considered making its home in Cole's wing but found it unsuitable.[16] Parliament proved less Erastian that the judges, so that neither churchmen nor trade union

[14] Resisting a similar impulse to make exhaustive or even extensive bibliographical reference, it is enough to mention the Introductions to their translations of Gierke by F. W. Maitland, *Political Theories of the Middle Age* (Cambridge, 1900), and Sir Ernest Barker, *op. cit.*; William Yandell Elliott, *The Pragmatic Revolt in Politics* (New York, 1928) and H. M. Magid, *English Political Pluralism, The Problem of Freedom and Organization* (New York, 1941), which contains a selective bibliography.

[15] Notably A. D. Lindsay, *The Modern Democratic State* (Oxford, 1943), I.

[16] Robert A. Dahl, "Workers' Control of Industry and the British Labor Party," 41 *The American Political Science Review*, 875 (October 1947). Cf. Sir Ernest Butler, "British Ideas of a Social Parliament," 44 *The American Political Science Review*, 14 (March 1950).

leaders felt the need for Figgis' sanctuary. The house of pluralism has become a hostel where students stop for a while to refresh themselves.

What precisely did the pluralists propose? What practical results were to flow from the concept of real group personality set forth by Gierke? It is not easy to say. The concept itself does not help too much in finding the answer. Even Sir Ernest Barker, one of Gierke's translators and sympathetic interpreters, was forced to conclude that it was only an analogy, a metaphor that might be dangerously misleading.[17] How shall we state the main propositions of the pluralists?

Freedom of association is important to realization of the good society; it is essential to maintenance of a modern democratic government; the state should be guided by these insights in formulating its law of association. In accepting these judgments we are all pluralists today and we are all in the debt of those who stated them so powerfully. But one can hold these views without accepting any of the other contentions of the original pluralists. They do not account for the strenuous opposition to pluralist theory.

The most obvious demand of the pluralists is that since a group is as real as a human being, the law must treat it as it treats an individual, according it the same measure of rights. This is really to turn Gierke's concept into a proposition. But even when we respect Maitland's insistence that a group is not a mere sum or collection of its individual members, this premise alone cannot prove that a group is therefore an individual, or even— to shear Gierke's metaphor of its mystical wool—that a group is so exactly like an individual that it can or should be treated as one. Even if we were to agree to this proposal, it would not in itself guarantee an association any rights but only throw us back in our search for a sound law of association upon the rights of individuals. The pluralists, it seems fair to conclude, took for granted individual rights with which they were familiar in English democracy and claimed them for groups.

A more modest version of this theory might read: a group of men is at least like an individual in this respect: the group has a right to change its mind, its purpose, without outside approval. This is, after all, no more than the state claims for itself. It is the right of the sovereign people not to be bound by its constitution. This is a call for the internal sovereignty of associations, for the right of all groups to govern themselves. Its legal result would seem to be that the state should not intervene in a dispute among the members of a group, at least that it should not do so on the allegation of a minority of the group that the majority is overriding the group constitution. The appeal of this position to the English pluralists is understandable. The common law has always been reluctant to intervene in intramural disputes of voluntary associations. The tradition of the sovereignty of the British Parliament, unhindered by judicial review of its acts under a written constitution, must have seemed analogous. The question raised in

---

[17] Cf. pages xxviii–xxx, lxxxiv–lxxxvii, of the Introduction to his translation of Gierke. When the doctrine of real group personality is applied to the state, Gierke is transplanted from the left of our road to the right.

the famous case of the Free Church of Scotland, which occasioned considerable pluralist theorizing, was, moreover, of exactly this sort.[18] This position is connected with the demand that the group be treated as an individual, for such an idea suggests that the state should not look behind the mask of corporate unity in these disputes, although the disputes themselves throw a revealing light on the weakness of the pluralist analogy between group and individual. This claim for self-government for groups has merit, but as an unqualified demand it also has serious weaknesses.

In the first place, such an absolute rule can work great hardship on the individual members of a group. Only totalitarian states insist that their members have no rights against the unified façade of the state. It is often unrealistic to tell the member of a voluntary association that if he does not like what the majority does, he may quit it, leaving behind all that he has contributed to it and surrendering his expectations of reciprocal benefits. It is equally unrealistic to suppose that the majority in a group always acts justly. It is also unrealistic to forget that many associations do not have a popular form of internal government, or that even in those which do, the governing officials of the association may sometimes violate the group's constitution to the damage of some or all of the members.

In the second place, many groups affect the rights of others outside the group. Even if a qualified plea for self-government of groups is granted, it does not solve these problems. The idea of the internal sovereignty of groups is therefore not an adequate basis for the law of associations.

The most radical claim of pluralism might be stated thus: the state cannot justly compel obedience to its commands whenever these conflict with the purposes of another association. Critics of pluralism have attacked this doctrine as little more than a restatement of anarchism certain to lead to chaos in practice. But accepting the idea for a moment, let us ask who is to decide which is right in a conflict between a state and a church or a labor union? Pluralism's answer seems to be curiously individualistic. Those individuals who are members of both groups must decide where their greater loyalty lies. But how is this decision to be registered so that it expresses a right, not simply once again superior power? It may be asked too if many individuals really care to have such onerous responsibility thrust on them in the name of freedom.

One must suspect that some of the pluralists were led to this formulation because of their belief that the purposes of the state are infected with an inherent ethical inferiority as compared with those of voluntary associations. After all, the state's purposes are not those of a group freely joined together for their achievement, and the state's monopoly of force has often been used in ways that seem brutal, excessive, and irrational to many humane minds. To a devout churchman like Figgis the very worldliness and materialism of the state's purposes may have appeared to be another blemish. Laski's pluralism may well exhibit his initial acceptance of the Marxian doctrine that the state is merely the board of directors and police force for the bour-

[18] Free Church of Scotland (General Assembly) v. Lord Overtoun (1904) A.C. 515.

geoisie, an acceptance which led him later to abandon pluralism in favor of other remedies for the ills he thought he detected. Let us attempt to state the most radical claim of pluralism less stridently. No group of individuals by calling themselves a state can justly claim unlimited obedience from all other groups, any more than they can justly make such a claim upon all men as individuals. Further, the state should be so constituted that its government cannot lawfully assert such a claim in the name of the state. Put thus modestly, pluralism appears to be a contemporary adaptation and extension of traditional Western constitutionalism, which began by saying that no individual by calling himself a king can justly claim unlimited obedience from all other individuals. If this version of pluralism is more modest, it is also more defensible, as American experience shows.

ASSOCIATIONS AND AMERICAN LAW

This is no place to labor the obvious fact that associations are important in American society and American politics. It would be both vain and tedious to parade even a selection of the great volume of literature that pours forth concerning these groups from sociologists, social psychologists, economists, political scientists, lawyers, historians, journalists, and even novelists and poets . It would be equally vain to resort to masses of statistics to prove what we all know. The Roman Catholic Church, the largest sect in the country, claims communicants roughly equal to the combined population of half the smaller states in the Union, and the largest single Protestant denomination exceeds by millions the largest state. Only four states have a larger population than the American Federation of Labor has members, and several craft and industrial unions have more members than any one of more than a dozen of the smaller states can claim as citizens. The same may be said of several fraternal orders whose names are obscure to most of us, and the American Legion and its women's auxiliary exceed in membership the populations of all but a dozen of the larger states. Finally, to vary the comparison, our two major political parties commanded between them in the election of 1952 the more or less fervid allegiance of more persons than compose the entire population of Great Britain, of France, or of Italy. These facts and figures alone are enough to suggest why it is a cliché that Americans are a nation of joiners and why students of our culture and our politics give attention to the composition, the purposes, and the activities of groups in the United States.

This concern was early expressed in the greatest political discussion America has yet produced. In what has often been called the most brilliant essay of The Federalist papers, James Madison wrote:

There are two methods of curing the mischiefs of faction: the one, by removing its causes; the other, by controlling its effects. There are again two methods of removing the causes of faction: the one, by destroying the liberty which is essential to its existence; the other, by giving to every citizen the same opinions, the same passions, and the same interests. It could never be more truly said than of the first remedy, that it was worse than the disease. . . . The second expedient is as impracticable as the first would be unwise. . . . The latent causes of faction are thus sown in the nature of man; and we see them everywhere brought into different degrees of activity, according to the different circumstances of civil society. . . . The inference to which we are brought is, that the *causes* of faction cannot be removed, and that relief is only to be sought in the means of controlling its *effects*.[19]

Madison's concern was primarily with the effects of freedom of association upon politics. It remained for the most perspicacious of all foreign observers of American society to show that association is a distinctive characteristic of every aspect of American life:[20]

In no country in the world has the principle of association been more successfully used, or more unsparingly applied to a multitude of different objects, than in America. . . . Americans of all ages, all conditions, and all dispositions, constantly form associations.

De Tocqueville saw clearly that the future of democracy in America depended upon the right of association:

Thus the most democratic country on the face of the earth is that in which men have in our time carried to the highest perfection the art of pursuing in common the object of their common desires, and have applied this new science to the greatest number of purposes. Is this the result of accident? or is there in reality any connection between the principle of association and that of equality?

After contrasting the power of leaders in aristocratic societies to compel their dependents to join in their plans, he observed:

Among democratic nations, on the contrary, all the citizens are independent and feeble; they can hardly do anything by themselves, and none of them can oblige his fellow men to lend him their assistance. They all, therefore, fall into a state of incapacity, if they do not learn voluntarily to help each other.

Without this right men in a democracy would fall victim to tyranny in politics and to barbarism in social life. Unless men exercised this right a dangerous burden would fall upon government. With remarkable clarity De Tocqueville foresaw that the problem would be even greater in the future as technology transformed the economy.

Surely associations could not have grown as they have nor flourish as they do in this country unless the law had recognized the rights upon which the existence of groups depends. What are these rights and how has the law recognized them? The answers to these questions will show us how the civil liberty of association has developed in the United States.

The right of association, like the right of property, is a bundle of rights. The right to assemble and the right to communicate by speech and writing

[19] *The Federalist*, No. 10.
[20] Alexis de Tocqueville, *Democracy in America*; cf. particularly chap. 11, "Political Associations in the United States" and chap. 25, "The Use Americans Make of Political Associations," from which the quotations are taken.

are parts of the broader right of association. These the First Amendment of the Constitution specifically guarantees. But what of the rights to admit, to discipline, and even to expel members? What of the rights to enact constitutions, by-laws, and regulations of the association, to choose officers, and, more than that, to determine how they shall be chosen and what their powers shall be? What of the rights to acquire, to hold, and to expend funds, and to enter into legal relations with individuals and groups outside the association? All these rights go to make up the power of an association to govern itself and are in some degree also indispensable to effective association. The exercise of many of them also involves, it is important to observe, the interests of others outside the group. Whatever protection for these rights the Constitution of the United States affords must be drawn from the broad language of the due process clauses that no person shall be deprived of his liberty or property without due process of law. Under the traditional interpretation of these clauses, rights are not protected by them absolutely, but if any governmental limitation upon these rights is challenged, the question is whether or not the limitation is a reasonable one. Such a standard requires that the interests of the group be compared with interests asserted by the law in question. In short, our constitutional system recognizes that freedom to exercise these rights is the rule, and that exceptions must have a rational justification acceptable to the courts.

Many lawyers will protest that the rights of groups have thus been defined in terms of public law, and of its highest component, constitutional law, at that. Surely, they will say, rights of association are also protected, defined, and regulated by ordinary statutes, and in addition by common law, and much of the law of associations falls into the province of private law. All this is quite true, but it is also true that all these other sources of law have proved increasingly inadequate to deal with all the problems of association. The reliance by the Supreme Court of the United States upon these constitutional guaranties as the basis of adjudication of cases arising out of group activities in this century makes that fact clear.

A transformation of the rights of association has been occurring in our law, a transformation from private rights to constitutional liberties. One reason for this change is probably the reluctance of the common law to intervene in associational questions, a reluctance wittily set forth by Professor Zechariah Chafee.[21] But the larger reason is surely that the profound effects of group activity in twentieth-century life raise far more important legal questions than did a protest of a gentleman expelled from a social club or a squabble between two schismatic factions of a local congregation over who got the church building. Questions of this older kind present theoretical problems similar to those with which we shall be concerned, but they present them in a social microcosm, whereas those which concern us occur in the social macrocosm. Their solution often requires application of the highest law by the highest court in that macrocosm.

[21] Zechariah Chafee, Jr., "The Internal Affairs of Associations Not for Profit," 43 *Harvard Law Review* 993 (1930).

Another important factor in this transformation has of course been the decision of the Supreme Court as recently as 1925 to incorporate the guaranties of the First Amendment in the due process clause of the Fourteenth Amendment, and thus make possible assertion of claims to free speech, press, and assembly on behalf of associations against legislation of the states.[22] But it is worth noting that the court only provided the opportunity; these cases have come in increasing volume to the courts because lawyers and their clients have come to think of rights of association in terms of constitutional liberties. It is also true that the Supreme Court since the constitutional revolution of 1937 has exercised its discretion under the writ of certiorari to bring many of these cases to itself for decision and thus manifests its conviction of their constitutional importance. Congress also by the exertion of its legislative powers over labor relations and over subversive associations has brought new kinds of cases to the courts. The whole development is not the result of isolated judicial action; the legal profession, social scientists, and the popular branches of the government have all contributed to it.

The emergence of this new constitutional liberty should not be taken to mean, however, that the Supreme Court of the United States has adopted the political theories of the pluralists. The rights of associations have been raised upon the rights of individuals to associate. Indeed, it is a rare thing to find in the judicial opinions with which we shall be concerned any overt discussion of the nature of groups or the rights of groups. The court's rhetoric is still the rhetoric of individualism, but its logic is the logic of the collectivity of our own time. The Justices focus the light of their learning upon the individual before the bar, but if one looks back at the rear wall of the courtroom, one can see, large and distinct, the shadow of the group for whom the individual litigant stands. But this will not seem strange to anyone familiar with the ways of the law. Novel questions are answered in familiar words, and almost unconsciously, absent-mindedly—or with the art that conceals art—the judge refashions old ideas to fit new problems. On the technical level, for example, the Court sometimes treats an association as a legal entity and sometimes not.[23]

[22] The leading case in this development is Gitlow v. New York, 268 U.S. 652 (1925).

[23] This technical question, like many others, is of great theoretical and practical importance, but its exploration lies outside our scope. There is no better introduction to the theoretical importance of the question than *Maitland: Selected Essays* (Cambridge, 1936). The practical question in American constitutional law involves more than the right (and liability) of an association to be treated as a juristic person, important as that right is. Aside from that general question the Supreme Court has held that although an association, corporate or incorporate, can claim constitutional protection against a deprivation of its *property* without due process of law, it is not entitled to judicial protection against deprivation of the civil liberties guaranteed by the Constitution; cf. as recent a case as Hague v. Committee for Industrial Organization, 307 U.S. 496 (1939) at pp. 514 and 527. Such a position appears both anachronistic and illogical and is now perhaps being undermined *sub silentio*; cf. Busby *et al.* v. Electric Utilities Employees Union, 323 U.S. 72 (1944) interpreting Rule 17(b) of the Rules of Civil Procedure for

Whence come these rights of the individual to associate upon which the group's rights are being built? Immediately they come from the Constitution, but why did they get into the Constitution, and how do we justify their being there? There can be little doubt that the men who drafted these constitutional provisions believed that they were only guaranteeing the natural rights of men. The sovereign people enact the natural rights of man into the constitutional rights of Americans. This concept surely goes as far to explain the paucity of political theory in America as it does to explain the practical success of our constitutional system. By linking these two quite different theories all sorts of hard questions are avoided. The rights of association, like our other constitutional rights, are both natural and the command of the state. They are the fundamental positive law of the land *because* they are natural.

James Madison himself expressed this view with specific reference to the rights of association. In 1793–94 there sprang up in the country the Democratic-Republican Societies. They were the beginnings of the political organization that later brought Jefferson to the White House, but one of their immediate purposes was to protest the federal excise tax which led to the Whisky Rebellion. President Washington was not alone in feeling that these societies bore heavy responsibility for fomenting the trouble, and in his annual message to the Congress in 1794 he said "certain self-created societies assumed the tone of condemnation" of the law. Federalists in the House of Representatives proposed to insert in their address of reply to the President a strong denunciation of the societies. Madison successfully led the opposition to this resolution. He argued that Congress had no business passing resolutions on matters over which it had no power to legislate, and that it had no power to act.

He conceived it to be a sound principle, that an action innocent in the eye of the law could not be the object of censure to a legislative body. When the people have formed a Constitution, they retain those rights which they have not expressly delegated. It is a question whether what is thus retained can be legislated upon. Opinions are not the objects of legislation. You animadvert upon the abuse of reserved rights: how far will this go? It may extend to the liberty of speech and of the press . . .

---

the District Courts of the United States, which provides that "capacity to sue or be sued shall be determined by the law of the state in which the district court is held; except that a partnership or other unincorporated association, which has no such capacity by the law of such state, may sue or be sued in its common name for the purpose of enforcing for or against it a substantive right existing under the Constitution or laws of the United States." Cf. also Grosjean v. American Press Co., 297 U.S. 233 (1936) in which the Court extended freedom of the press to a newspaper corporation. For protection of groups' rights under the federal Civil Rights Acts, cf. Collins v. Hardyman, 341 U.S. 651 (1951), and for a recent case under the equal protection clause, cf. Ellis v. Dixon, 349 U.S. 458 (1955). The present confused state of the case law reflects a still unfinished trend away from the older idea that civil liberties can be claimed only by natural persons.

Nothing could make clearer the belief of the principal author of the Bill ot Rights that it protected, in the Tenth Amendment if nowhere else, a natural right of man to associate with others.[24]

But this theory of natural rights constitutionally guaranteed does not really avoid the hard questions, for these constitutional guaranties are general and require interpretation when they are applied to concrete problems. What it does do is to reduce controversy from the justice of principles to the justice of their application and to make the Supreme Court of the United States the most continuously active and influential faculty of political theory in the country. Our purpose in the chapters to follow is to discover what political theory the Supreme Court has been developing and pronouncing as the constitutional law of associations.

PRINCIPLES OF THE LAW OF ASSOCIATION

To be able to say that there is a growing constitutional law of freedom of association, and not merely labor law and political party regulation and the law of church and state, and so forth, we must be able to discern and state some general principles which the Supreme Court is developing for all associations and which it will apply to any association. Can we do this? Already, it is suggested, five principles can be seen emerging.[25] To be sure, these principles are formal. Like other general propositions, they do not settle concrete cases. Substance must be put into them, not drawn out of them. Their worth, if they are sound, is that of any generalization. They suggest what is important in a concrete problem and how we can begin to think about it.

First: *The rights of individuals to associate must be protected from unlawful governmental infringement.* This principle is both logically and chronologically prior to all others. It is supported by the constitutional guaranties we have already noticed. The vindication of this principle is peculiarly a responsibility of the judiciary, since it assumes that legislative or executive action may sometimes violate these constitutional rights. The practical significance of this principle has been greatly enhanced in recent years by the doctrine that the due process clause of the Fourteenth Amendment requires the states and local governments to observe many of the guaranties in the national Constitution which formerly were applied only against unlawful federal action.

Second: *Government may promote the opportunities of individuals to associate by appropriate means, and may grant appropriate privileges and powers to associations when the public interest will be fostered by doing so.* The fulfillment of this principle is primarily a legislative responsibility, since it is phrased almost entirely (at least for the present and the foreseeable

---

[24] Fuller accounts of this episode may be found in E. P. Link, *Democratic-Republican Societies, 1790–1800* (New York, 1942), and in the author's unpublished dissertation, "National Control of Congressional Elections" (Princeton, 1942), pp. 69–74.

[25] These may be compared with the three set forth by Sir Ernest Barker as early as 1915; *Political Thought in England, 1848–1914* (2d ed. rev., Oxford, 1950), pp. 156–57.

future) as a public policy. Even as a discretionary principle it has already borne many fruits.

Third: *Government may when the public interest requires it forbid private persons to interfere with the rights of individuals to associate and may even require private persons to enter into legal relations with associations.* The rise of this principle is recent and is part of the movement to make certain civil liberties which in their traditional meaning have been liberties against government liberties from private coercion as well. This principle is based on the belief that it is not always enough that government be "neutral" and hold the ring while private individuals and groups exert what pressures they can against one another in the pursuit of conflicting interests.[26]

These first three principles are all designed to protect and extend the rights of individuals to associate and to foster and promote the existence of associations. The last two principles, however, are concerned with limiting the powers of associations and regulating their exercise. The two restrictive principles must in their interpretation be balanced against the first, which seeks to prevent improper governmental interference with associational freedoms. When the constitutionality of any governmental limitation upon association is challenged, the question is whether the limitation is justified on the grounds set forth in one of these limiting principles, for if it is not, it must be deemed an unlawful infringement.

Fourth: *An association must not without adequate reason infringe upon the rights of other persons; and government must define the interests entitled to legal protection of these other individuals and groups, whether they are members or nonmembers of the association.* If the injury is threatened to nonmembers, the law may have to restrain the association even though the damage is not intentional or malicious, but is an incidental result of otherwise legitimate activity. If the threat is to the association's own members, the enforcement of this principle obviously requires some state interference with the rights of self-government of associations. In those instances in which membership in an association is apparently a matter of voluntary choice for the individual but is actually becoming to a great degree involuntary because it is vital to his earthly welfare, the need for legal protection of his rights is gaining recognition.

Fifth: *Government may prevent the use of the rights of association to do serious injury to society as a whole or to the organized political institutions of the society.* This last principle indicates the essential ground for regulating "subversive" associations. More accurately, it states the criterion by which we must decide if an association has objectives of a nature which make it subversive: are its objectives a grave threat to organized society itself?

These five principles we could examine one by one by reference to the cases concerning different types of groups which give each principle sub-

[26] For valuable discussions of the idea expressed in this principle, cf. Alexander H. Pekelis, *Law and Social Action* (Ithaca and New York, 1950), particularly pp. 91–127; and Robert L. Hale, *Freedom Through Law: Public Control of Private Governing Power* (New York, 1952).

stance. The gains from such a systematic analysis must be weighed against the deadliness which always pervades a treatise. Principles do not have a life of their own. But the great associations, in Professor MacIver's apt phrase, do. All of us are familiar with some of the vicissitudes in the lives of churches, labor unions, and political parties, and with the present American concern with subversive groups. So, borrowing from Gierke's insight and Walt Disney's technique, let us first stalk each of these living creatures as they move through the American scene, recording crucial legal incidents in the struggle of each kind of group for life and fulfillment or even dominance. Then we can return to the cutting room to edit our record into a tighter continuity organized around these principles. Those who order the lives of groups by law must have regard to the ecology, the taxonomy, the analogy, and even the pathology of groups, but their grasp of these sciences will be the firmer if they are first simple naturalists familiar with their subjects in real life.

2

RELIGIOUS FREEDOM: AN OLD TRADITION
IN A NEW SETTING

The framers of the American Constitution and the Bill of Rights saw little reason to concern themselves with labor unions, business corporations, or political parties. But churches were already rooted deep in American society, for they were partly responsible for its genesis. Roger Williams, William Penn, and Lord Baltimore are among the leading characters of our colonial history. For more than a century and a half before the establishment of the new government Puritans, Baptists, Methodists, Congregationalists, Jews, Presbyterians, Quakers, Roman Catholics, and even Anglicans had sought in the New World religious freedom for themselves and in turn had all too often denied to other seekers what they had claimed for themselves. It is no wonder, then, that the men of 1787 especially provided for the one type among the great associations with which they were familiar. The provision in the original Constitution that "no religious test shall ever be required as a qualification to any office or public trust under the United States" was not deemed enough by the people. So the First Amendment to the Constitution in cryptic but comprehensive language added that "Congress shall make no law regarding an establishment of religion, or prohibiting the free exercise thereof."

We cannot tarry long over what the drafters of this language meant; that question has been canvassed and recanvassed. Our interest is to see what these words have been made to mean since they were written into the fundamental law. There is more controversy today than ever before over their meaning, but no amount of argument can obscure the fact that they were intended to provide a double assurance: that there shall be both freedom *for* religion and freedom *from* religion. Freedom for religion means freedom to worship or not, according to one's belief, but it means more than freedom to do so individually and privately. It means freedom to worship publicly and collectively. It means, in short, freedom of religious associations, freedom for churches. This aspect of religious liberty was not new in America or elsewhere in 1789, even though it may not have been fully achieved.

Freedom from religion, however, was an innovation and an almost radical one. Freedom from religion means nonestablishment, or, as it has come to be expressed, the separation of church and state. This was the American experiment in the relations of church and state. Several of the states still had established churches at the time the First Amendment was adopted. Of course the amendment forbade only Congressional establishment of reli-

21

gion; it is true that it also prohibited any effort by Congress to disestablish those state churches which still existed, but to draw from this fact the inference that the amendment was designed to favor existing establishments seems quite unsound. A sense of history demands our recognition that established churches were already on the way out in America. Those who favored this American experiment could look forward with some confidence to disestablishment of the remaining state churches by the states themselves. A few decades at the most were required to prove that their hopes were well founded.

The important question is why we should have embarked upon this novel and drastic experiment at all. We need only look to modern England, for example, to recognize that a high degree of religious toleration, of freedom for all religions, can exist in a state that maintains an established church. But it was not always so in England (indeed, it was decidedly less so in 1789 than now), and it is not so in many states with established churches even today.

In the face of some recent intemperate denunciations of the "Godless secular state" which supposedly results from separation, we will do well to recall at the outset the reasoning that led Madison and Jefferson, among others, to support it. That reasoning did not need to depend upon abstract theorizing or doctrinaire hostility to religion. It rested upon experience—vivid, extensive, and disturbing experience.

Without this principle churches would be free to gain favors from the state. The possibility of gaining these favors, or of losing out in the scramble for them, could lead the many sects in America into temptation of jealous rivalry and ultimately into attitudes of hostility and distrust that would threaten the spirit of mutual toleration. If one church were pre-eminently successful in gaining public favor, it might be further tempted to secure its position by demanding the public suppression of its rivals. Freedom from religion is in this perspective an important means of making more secure freedom for religion.

Further, what might be the fate of churches that became too reliant upon governmental favor? If the government granted privileges to churches, how could it be estopped from requiring those it favored to meet the conditions it imposed upon the recipients? Might not the withdrawal of state support be destructive to a church that lost it? If so, might not the mere threat of the state's displeasure lead that church to surrender its most cherished ideals? In this light freedom from religion may help prevent what Justice Jackson recently described as "the regime of a state-ridden church in a church-ridden state."

In addition, competition for governmental support by the churches would tend to introduce extraneous religious controversy into every aspect of politics and government. Quite irrelevant religious arguments would distort the decision of public questions. Government officials of one faith would, rightly or wrongly, be suspect by citizens of another faith. In such an atmosphere men who lost their respect for their government might go on to refuse it their obedience. Freedom from religion is in this view an important means of making government more trustworthy.

Finally, and most significantly, there cannot be more than a somewhat ridiculous, somewhat painful caricature of religious liberty without some degree of separation of church and state. What kind of religious liberty is it that would tell a man that he may give money to any church he favors provided he pays tithes to one he does not, or that he may attend his own religious services if he also goes to those he disapproves, or that he may stay outside the established church at the cost of giving up normal rights of a citizen in the state? Fortunately the enlightened men of the eighteenth century who began the American experiment with church and state had more spacious conceptions of freedom than that. They would know how to answer those in the twentieth century who seem to want to abandon the experiment. They would not have to rely upon the experience of an ancient past in doing so, for contemporary Christendom—to say nothing of the rest of the world— still supplies many examples of these very evils which they sought to avert by separation of church and state.

The freedom of religion established by our Constitutional guaranties thus includes both freedom for and freedom from religion. For purposes of analysis we can and shall examine each of these two aspects of religious liberty separately, but in doing so it is important to remember that they are only different aspects of the full concept of religious freedom in America, not independent ideas. They lend mutual support to one another.

The First Amendment was adopted in response to widespread demand so strong that it was a condition upon ratification of the original Constitution. It seems fair to say that it expressed an existing attitude of toleration growing out of American experience. It is also fair to say on the whole record that this attitude has persisted. This is not to make an unctuous claim that we have ever been perfectly free from religious prejudice or even religious persecution. The Know-Nothing party before the Civil War manifested bitter anti-Catholicism. The revived Ku Klux Klan of the 1920's brought another peak of this ever-present bigotry, as it also stirred up the prejudice, so far as it is religious prejudice, against Jews. At an early period of our history the Mormons suffered mob violence. Today one suspects that we would not have so many cases involving the Jehovah's Witnesses were it not that hatred provoked by their own bigotry often animates the drafting or the enforcement of the laws which they protest. What can be said is that although religious intolerance is a cultural fact in the United States, it is not a public policy.

On the other hand religious groups have always been active and often successful in supporting or opposing legislative proposals and candidates for public office. This activity is a natural consequence of freedom for religious associations, even though it is sometimes criticized by those who would push separation of church and state beyond what the Constitution requires. Religious groups were prominent in the abolition movement which culminated in the Thirteenth Amendment and the prohibition movement which brought

about the Eighteenth. The long-run judgment of the country has been that
the churches were right in the former cause and wrong in the latter, but
clearly they had a right to support both. To many thoughtful people, however, various sects have been most open to criticism when they have used
their freedom under the First Amendment to secure legislation that seems
to encroach upon the freedom of speech, press, and assembly guaranteed to
all under that same amendment. Such are the old laws against blasphemy,
which have fallen into desuetude, the Sunday blue laws, the law against
teaching evolutionary theory made notorious by the Scopes trial, laws against
the dissemination of information about birth control, and laws under which
censorship has been used to impose a sect's moral standards upon literature,
the theater, and the arts. Religious bigotry of this kind has sometimes been
converted into public policy, but, on the whole, with declining success.

RELIGIOUS FREEDOM AND SOCIAL MORES

The first important series of cases asserting a claim of unconstitutional
interference with freedom of worship arose out of the legislation of Congress
forbidding the practice of polygamy in the federal territories.[1] The laws
were of course aimed at members of the Mormon Church in Utah, and when
some of them were prosecuted, they contended that they were obeying a tenet
of their faith and that under the First Amendment they must be held exempt
from punishment. The Supreme Court denied these pleas in a classic application of the doctrine of John Locke's great *Letter on Toleration*.

Locke's conception of freedom for churches and their members has been
the philosophic base for the Court's decision of all cases involving the question ever since, so that it merits analysis. As we have noticed, Locke began
by drawing a fundamental distinction between the purposes of a state and a
church. The state

is a society of men constituted only for the procuring, preserving, and advancing
their own civil interests . . . life, liberty, health, and indolency of body; and the
possession of outward things . . . the whole jurisdiction of the magistrate reaches
only to these civil concernments . . . it neither can nor ought in any manner to be
extended to the salvation of souls . . .

But a church is

a voluntary society of men, joining themselves together of their own accord in
order to the public worshipping of God in such manner as they judge acceptable
to him, and effectual to the salvation of their souls. . . . All discipline ought therefore to tend to that end, and all ecclesiastical laws to be thereunto confined.

It has been rightly said that Locke's thought was secular. For he does
not distinguish between state and church by claiming that the state is a human
and the church a divine institution. A church is made by men and belongs

---

[1] The leading case is Reynolds v. U.S., 98 U.S. 145 (1879). Cf. also Davis v. Beason,
133 U.S. 333 (1890), involving a territorial law, and Late Corporation of the Church of
Jesus Christ of Latter-day Saints v. U.S., 136 U.S. 1 (1890), upholding federal revo-
cation of a state charter to the old Mormon Church.

to men as does the state. Locke saw the state as almost a voluntary association; the church was completely so. Although his thought was secular, it was not Erastian. The whole purpose of his distinction of the ends of the two associations is to create a realm of inviolable freedom for the church. He insists that

the church itself is a thing absolutely separate and distinct from the commonwealth. The boundaries on both sides are fixed and immovable. He jumbles heaven and earth together, the things most remote and opposite, who mixes these two societies, which are in their original, end, business, and in everything perfectly distinct and infinitely different from each other.

This language sounds almost like Gierke's description of the church as an association *beside* the state rather than within it. Despite these words Locke was no more a pluralist than an Erastian, as his statement of the duties of toleration which the state owes churches makes clear.

Opening his discussion of the question Locke makes a by then familiar distinction between "the outward form and rites of worship, and the doctrines and articles of faith." The secular turn of his thought is again apparent in his treatment of religious rites as the use of material objects and the performance of physical acts in worship. But on Locke's own theory it is just such material matters ("indifferent," he calls them) that the state may regulate. So far as he solves this dilemma, it is by the principle that

Whatsoever is lawful in the commonwealth cannot be prohibited by the magistrate in the church. Whatsoever is permitted unto any of his subjects for their ordinary use, neither can nor ought to be forbidden by him to any sect of people for their religious uses.

If a man can kill a calf or wash an infant or wear special vestments or eat bread and drink wine outside the church, he can do it as a part of religious worship, even though the actions have a different significance there. But suppose the state is confronted by a sect that claims the right to expose itself to being bitten by live rattlesnakes as a test of faith, as sometimes has happened in the United States? The answer is clear:

These things are not lawful in the ordinary course of life, nor in any private house; and therefore neither are they so in the worship of God, or in any religious meeting . . . Only it is to be observed that, in this case, the law is not made about a religious, but a political matter . . .

Surely the dilemma is not this easy. Who is to decide whether the matter is a religious or a political matter? Locke's almost tacit answer is that the political association has the right to draw the line between political and religious jurisdiction, but should draw it in a spirit of tolerance.

The case is not really different with doctrines and articles of faith, some of which are "speculative" and some "practical." Speculative articles of faith are those which "are required only to be believed," that is, not acted upon. These should be wholly beyond the state's prescription or proscription, for "the business of laws is not to provide for the truth of opinions, but for the safety and security of the commonwealth, and of every particular man's goods and person." Even Hobbes had agreed with this, for he said rather finely that "belief and unbelief never follow men's commands. Faith is a gift of God, which man can neither give, nor take away by promises of rewards, or menaces of torture."[2]

The practical religious doctrines and articles of faith are those which influence human conduct. However "perfectly distinct and infinitely different" the ends of church and state may be, Locke admits that their interests overlap where men's conduct is involved, for

A good life, in which consists not the least part of religion and true piety, concerns also the civil government; and in it lies the safety both of men's souls and of the commonwealth. Moral actions belong therefore to the jurisdiction both of the outward and inward court . . . both of the magistrate and conscience.

There is no disguising the great danger of conflict between these two, although Locke believed its resolution would be easy if both state and church observed the spirit of his teaching. If not easy, we may credit Locke and the earlier advocates of toleration upon whom he drew with making it easier than it had been under opposed doctrines.

If conflict does arise, Locke is resolute. Private judgment does not take away the obligation of the law or deserve dispensation. The church and its members must obey the law or accept the law's punishment for obeying their conscience. But the state's right to be wrong in such an issue is only a legal right, not a moral right. Since the care of one's soul takes precedence even over the public peace, resistance in that extreme case where only God can judge between the people and the supreme magistrate may be morally justified.

Having completed his argument Locke ends by stating those few religious doctrines which the state should not tolerate. The first of these is "opinions contrary to human society, or to those moral rules which are necessary to the preservation of civil society." Thus we come back to the case of polygamy among the Mormons. Now clearly it could not be said that polygamy is contrary to human society of any kind whatsoever. But its practice would require a radically different kind of society not only from that of the United States but of the entire modern Western world. Nor could polygamy have been permitted to continue without fundamental changes in the Constitution, for under it the Mormons were entitled to move into any state,[3] but all the states forbade polygamy and had a constitutional right to do so.[4] The Mormon claim was truly contrary to the preservation of the civil society organized by the Constitution, and it had to give way. Events proved that acceptance of monogamy did not require such radical change in the Mormon

---

[2] *Leviathan*, chap. 42, "Of Power Ecclesiastical."

[3] Crandall v. Nevada, 6 Wallace 36 (1867).

[4] Even if the Court had decided that the First Amendment forbade Congress to prohibit polygamy among the Mormons, for at that time the First Amendment was not held applicable to the states.

Church as acceptance of polygamy would have demanded of the American state.[5]

Two general principles justifying limitation upon the rights of association have been suggested: first, that these rights must not injure other persons or groups, and second, that they must not threaten the whole society or its political organization. The decision of the polygamy cases is an application of the latter. A considerable number of other cases have come to the Supreme Court in which this same principle has been applied. Unlike the polygamy cases they have all been collisions of religious freedom, not with the sexual mores of society, but with the need for military security or domestic tranquillity.

RELIGIOUS FREEDOM AND NATIONAL SECURITY

In no less than twelve cases the demands of military security have clashed with those of religious conscience in the Supreme Court. Of these, all but four have involved the obligations of citizens or would-be citizens to perform military service. Congress in the draft act in the First World War gave an absolute exemption from compulsory military service to ministers of religion and students in theological schools and also provided alternatives to military or combat service for those conscientious objectors to war who were members of religious sects holding this tenet. These provisions were attacked as making an establishment of religion.[6]

Nothing could better illustrate the relation between the free exercise of religion and an establishment thereof. Plainly Congress had gone further than the Constitution required in an effort to accommodate a free exercise of religion. Ministers and theological students could scarcely have complained if they had been authorized occupational deferments conditional upon the availability of older men to fill their pulpits instead of an absolute exemption. But that course, by imposing upon the draft boards the invidious task of choosing among ministers, would have exposed them to the suspicion of discriminating among sects. In respecting, as a matter of humane grace and common sense, conscientious objection to war, Congress might well have extended the privilege to all who could establish their bona fide belief, whether it stemmed from religious or nontheistic ethical conviction and without regard to membership in a pacifistic denomination. But Congress believed, with some reason, that such church membership gives a relatively simple

---

[5] John Stuart Mill, writing *On Liberty* in 1859, might understandably plead for no legal interference with the Mormons, viewing them then as "chased into a solitary recess in the midst of a desert" (Everyman ed., London and New York, 1936), pp. 147–49. But when the late Professor Harold Laski labored to show himself a true disciple of Mill on this point as late as 1937, refusing to take account of what Mill could not have foreseen, his effort seems quixotic; *Liberty in the Modern State* (Penguin ed., London, 1937), pp. 123–25. At any rate, Laski no more succeeded in changing the Supreme Court's opinion than Mill; cf. Cleveland v. United States, 329 U.S. 14 (1946), applying the Mann Act to a member of a schismatic Mormon sect still practicing polygamy who had made the mistake of crossing a state line with his wives.

[6] Arver v. U.S., 245 U.S. 366 (1918).

and applicable standard, whereas a broader one may indulge slackers. Had Congress by thus going further than the Constitution required gone further than it allowed? The Court thought not.

The provisions of the Selective Service Act in World War II were similar. The Jehovah's Witnesses do not observe the familiar religious distinction between clergy and laity. In that sect's view every member is a minister of the gospel. Some members of that faith refused to obey the law when draft boards declined to classify them as "regular or duly ordained ministers" under the act.[7] In ordinary understanding this definition applies to those who devote substantially all of their time to religious endeavors. Most of Jehovah's Witnesses give what time they can to evangelism while earning their livelihood at other vocations. Were the draft boards obliged to accept their definition instead of that which Congress presumably intended? The Supreme Court did not pass upon this question, except inferentially. It was rightly concerned where it appeared that hostile draft boards or unsympathetic military authorities had not accorded these men full procedural rights, but it never suggested that they had a substantive right to be classified as ministers according to their own conceptions.

Related problems arose between the two wars. One concerned the right of aliens to become American citizens if they refused to state that they were willing to bear arms. The naturalization laws require an applicant to take an oath of allegiance to "support and *defend* the Constitution of the United States." The question about willingness to bear arms was administratively prescribed on the ground that unless an applicant answered it affirmatively, he could not take the oath without mental reservation.

In three cases the Supreme Court upheld this administrative requirement over eloquent dissents by Chief Justice Hughes and Justice Holmes, who urged that Congress had not laid down this requirement and that since it had in the draft law itself relieved conscientious objectors, it was unsound and narrow-minded for the administrative authorities to impute a contrary attitude to Congress in the naturalization laws.[8] Despite repeated proposals, however, Congress did not amend the law to do away with this decision. In 1940, in fact, after careful study Congress re-enacted the law, leaving the administrative officials free to continue the practice. In 1942 Congress provided for easier naturalization for aliens who served in the armed forces, although requiring of them the same oath. Of course it was possible for an alien to serve in the armed forces as a noncombatant, whether because of religious conviction or physical handicap. Did Congress intend to authorize naturalization of aliens who because of religious conviction performed only noncombatant service in the armed forces, exempting them from the rigor of the general rule? Very possibly it did. It is quite impossible to say with assurance.

[7] Falbo v. U.S., 320 U.S. 549 (1944), and Estep v. U.S., 327 U.S. 114 (1946).

[8] U.S. v. Schwimmer, 279 U.S. 644 (1929) ; U.S. v. MacIntosh, 283 U.S. 605 (1931) ; U.S. v. Bland, 283 U.S. 636 (1931). Cf. discussion of these cases in Zechariah Chafee, Jr., *Free Speech in the United States* (Cambridge, 1941), pp. 367–75.

That, however, was not the case before the Court in *Girouard* v. *United States*.[9] There an alien unwilling to bear arms who had not served in the military forces sought naturalization. The Court might have overruled its earlier decisions without any suggestion of impropriety except for the Congressional action of 1940. For it is a well-established and sensible canon of statutory construction that if Congress re-enacts without change a law that the Court has interpreted, Congress thereby indicates its approval of that construction and its intention that the law shall have the same meaning on that point in the future. Mr. Justice Douglas, for a majority of the Court, found that Congress by its act for aliens in military service had indicated that it had changed its mind about the general rule! This was judicial activism near its disingenuous worst, for it was an effort to cover with shoddy logic a high-handed judicial act, however desirable the goal. Chief Justice Stone had dissented from the original decisions, but he did not feel at liberty to repudiate what he considered the plain purpose of Congress to retain them, much as he disagreed with their wisdom. It is notable that no Justice in any of these cases ever declared that the First Amendment required Congress to make this concession to religious belief.

California and Illinois have both pursued principle with grim logic to harsh conclusions. Congress in granting lands to certain state universities had provided that they should offer courses in military science given by the Army or Navy, but it did not require that all male students in these schools should be obliged to take them. The state of California did, however, and refused exemption to conscientious objectors. The Supreme Court unanimously recognized the right of the state to demand this.[10] It is tempting to justify this result by saying that the state can require these courses as a condition upon enjoying the benefits of attending an excellent university at little or no tuition cost. But this is a variant of the lazy man's excuse in the law. A student unable to observe the requirement might not be able to attend so excellent a school, or perhaps any. Justification must rest on the right to exact military service of all, in or out of school.

The Illinois case *In re Summers* arose when the authorized committee of the state bar association refused to give the necessary certificate of good character required for admission to the bar, and the judges of the Illinois Supreme Court upheld their refusal.[11] The applicant did not believe in the use of force; it was argued, therefore, that since the state constitution made him liable for militia service, he could not take the oath to support the state constitution required for admission to the bar. By a vote of five to four the United States Supreme Court sustained this action. For the dissenters Mr. Justice Black seemed to assert that the right of conscience was entitled to absolute protection.[12] Sound reasons for reversing the state court's action exist without reliance on this absolute claim. Mr. Justice Black himself went

[9] 328 U.S. 61 (1946).
[10] Hamilton *et al.* v. Regents of the University of California, 293 U.S. 245 (1934).
[11] 325 U.S. 561 (1945).
[12] 325 U.S. 561 at 575.

on to observe that "The Illinois Constitution itself prohibits the draft of conscientious objectors except in time of war and also excepts from military duty persons who are 'exempted by the laws of the United States.'" He thought that the probability of the petitioner's liability to state militia service "has little more reality than an imaginary quantity in mathematics." There is a stronger argument than this metaphor. Under the Illinois Constitution Summers had no possible liability to serve except in time of war. But under any realistic view of the Constitution of the United States today, the state of Illinois, let alone a state bar association committee or even the state judges, could not finally determine his liability in time of war. When war or the national security demands compulsory military service, Congress has power to say who shall serve, and that power is clearly paramount over any state program. If Illinois attempted to resort to the archaic and chaotic device of a universal draft for its state militia in time of war, experience makes as clear as possible that Congress would have to forbid it in order to protect its own national program of military security from disastrous confusion, and further, that Congress would have unquestionable power to do so.

The action of the authorities here was officious, presumptuous, meddlesome interference in matters in which they had no real competence. It could have been appropriately dealt with as such without asserting any absolute right of religion over national security. The case, incidentally, involves another principle of the law of association : that the state may grant privileges to an association if the public interest is served thereby. The state bar association had been given considerable privilege to determine admission to the bar. The result suggests how carefully such grants of privilege need to be examined.

These cases involving claims of exemption from actual military service should help put the famous flag salute cases in proper perspective.[13] The opinions in those cases are so thorough, many of the commentaries upon them so excellent, that it would be supererogatory to dwell upon them at length. Let us cut to the heart of the matter as quickly as we can. We must begin by asking what is the purpose of compelling all school children to participate in the secular ritual of the flag salute. The purpose is to inculcate certain beliefs and attitudes favorable to the state among all children. The intensity of these attitudes in each individual sums up to high morale. The extent of their existence among the individuals in the state sums up to national unity. These cases came on during a total war which demonstrated beyond question that high morale and national unity are vital to national security. The purpose of the law was therefore not trivial, nor one which the state is forbidden to effect.

What was the demand of Jehovah's Witnesses? Mr. Justice Frankfurter was quite correct in insisting in both cases that it was a demand to be exempt from the general requirement on the grounds of religious belief. But Justice

---

[13] Minersville School District *et al.* v. Gobitis *et al.*, 310 U.S. 586 (1940) ; West Virginia State Board of Education *et al.* v. Barnette *et al.*, 319 U.S. 624 (1943).

Jackson was also correct in his opinion for the court in the second case when he said of the decision in the first :[14]

The Gobitis decision, however, *assumed* . . . that power exists in the State to impose the flag salute discipline upon school children in general. The Court only examined and rejected a claim based on religious beliefs of immunity from an unquestioned general rule.

We have already seen enough of the outworking of Locke's theory to sense the difficulty. When we say that a law is justified we have thereby answered in the negative the question whether or not anyone can claim exemption on religious grounds. As Locke put it, if "the law is not made about a religious, but a political matter," no religious protest is valid. But who is to decide which it is? We do not permit the Jehovah's Witnesses to decide for themselves. Neither do we allow a legislature to make the final authoritative decision. The First Amendment's guaranty of a free exercise of religion means that there are "religious matters" on which the state is forbidden to act, and our theory and practice of judicial review mean that the Supreme Court of the United States has the final authoritative power to decide whether a challenged law is about a religious or a political matter, subject only to revision by the people. Locke did not invent this institutional amelioration of his dilemma, but it is hard to believe that he would not have welcomed it and thought its value worth its price.

How did the Court resolve Locke's dilemma? By asking two questions. First, was the purpose of the law—national security—rationally one that fell within the state's domain? Only a very saintly or a very shallow mind could deny that it was. Second, did the means it employed—a compulsory flag salute—hold out a reasonable enough promise of achieving this important purpose to justify restraint upon religious freedom? This was a question of policy. The Court changed its mind about the answer and finally reached the sounder one. The reasons for supposing that the salute would increase national security seemed too remote, vague, ambivalent, and trivial. On the other hand, the dispute itself presented clear, immediate, and important evidence that it would not. It seems improbable that any member of the Court ever thought otherwise.

Why, then, were Mr. Justice Frankfurter and others so unwilling to reverse a local school board and a state legislature? The answer lies in their belief in judicial restraint. As Mr. Justice Frankfurter explained in his dissent :[15]

It can never be emphasized *too much* that one's own opinion about the wisdom or evil of a law should be excluded *altogether* when one is doing one's duty on the bench. The only opinion of our own even looking in that direction that is material is our opinion whether legislators could in reason have enacted such a law.

This is familiar and yet strange language from so close a student of Holmes, the jurist who, at least as much as any other in the English-speaking world,

14 319 U.S. 624 at 635.   15 319 U.S. 624 at 647.

is responsible for teaching us all that every judge in every case decides according to his view of the consequences of the policy he lays down. If this is correct, it is no use to emphasize at all that a judge should do something that he cannot do. This criticism may, however, be deemed unfair, for the question to decide was not, for Mr. Justice Frankfurter, the wisdom of compelling a flag salute, but the wisdom of using his judicial power to forbid compelling it.

What are the consequences of this use of judicial power? Again he tells us that[16]

Our constant preoccupation with the constitutionality of legislation rather than with its wisdom tends to preoccupation of the American mind with a false value. The tendency of focussing attention on constitutionality is to make constitutionality synonymous with wisdom, to regard a law as all right if it is constitutional. Such an attitude is a great enemy of liberalism.

The trouble with this theory is that it takes as an obvious fact what our history suggests is at best a hypothesis, and probably an untenable one. Granting that constitutionality and wisdom are not synonymous, can they be absolutely distinct, and just as significantly, do we customarily discuss them as if they were? It is at least as tenable a hypothesis that American concern with questions of constitutionality is one of our typical modes of discussing wisdom, and that this concern with constitutionality leads us to think not much less carefully about the wisdom of a law than we otherwise might, but much more. If the existence of judicial review did decrease our interest in the wisdom of legislation, it would indeed be a "great enemy of liberalism." One can adduce a great deal of evidence that many exercises of judicial review have produced evil results of various kinds, but where is the credible evidence that one of these results has been the dulling of men's sense of right?[17]

The doctrine of judicial restraint as a practical matter admonishes judges not to think that they are God, not to assume that their views of wise policy are absolutely right or to act as if they were; in short, not to be bull-headed or heavy-handed. No one who reads his opinions will doubt that Mr. Justice Frankfurter observes this admonition. The doctrine of judicial restraint carried to its absolute logical extreme, however, is a declaration that there should be no judicial review whatsoever. Because judicial review is "itself a limitation on popular government,"[18] or at least on absolute majority rule, if a judge finds that however careless, shortsighted, or vindictive the legislators were, he cannot quite say that they were idiotic in the technical sense, he must sustain what they did. But legislators are politicians, and politicians of all people are unlikely to be so thin-skinned that they will not abide being told that they were wrong. One must criticize absolute views too often not

16 319 U.S. 624 at 670.
17 Mr. Justice Frankfurter's thesis here is also developed in Henry Steele Commager, *Majority Rule and Minority Rights* (New York, 1943).
18 310 U.S. 586 at 600. Cf. 319 U.S. 624 at 650.

to protest against turning judicial restraint, which is a useful antidote against them, into an absolute itself.

The last of these cases in which national security was asserted against religious freedom suggests that absolute judicial confidence in legislative reasonableness may be misplaced.[19] In 1942 the legislature of Mississippi declared war—on Jehovah's Witnesses. It is best to let this remarkable statute speak for itself :[20]

> That any person who individually, or as a member of any organization, association, or otherwise, shall intentionally preach, teach, or disseminate any teaching, creed, theory, or set of alleged principles, orally, or by means of a phonograph . . . or by any sort of literature, or written or printed matter . . . which reasonably tends to create an attitude of stubborn refusal to salute, honor or respect the flag or government of the United States, or of the state of Mississippi, shall be guilty of a felony and punished by imprisonment in the state penitentiary until treaty of peace be declared by the United States but such imprisonment shall not exceed ten years.

Under this provision three of the Witnesses were indicted, convicted, and their convictions were sustained by an evenly divided state supreme court. Their chief offense had been expression of the sect's views of the sinful idolatry of saluting a flag. On the basis of the second flag salute case the United States Supreme Court unanimously reversed the decisions.

RELIGIOUS FREEDOM AND PUBLIC ORDER

In states that are free from embittered ideological division preservation of the public peace is not likely to stir emotions as much as protecting the national security against foreign attack. Yet domestic tranquillity is a basic need of the entire society, as the Preamble to our Constitution suggests. Fortunately we do not have to deal with threats of religiously inspired insurrection or rebellion. At most the Supreme Court has dealt with a few examples of local and isolated breaches of the peace charged against individual members of Jehovah's Witnesses.[21] They need not detain us. The reason is not simply that such cases turn so sharply on their precise, particular facts. Although the sect believes in and practices militant and often exasperating methods of proselyting, there is no reason to suppose that it teaches its members to commit breaches of the peace in the traditional sense of that term. Those that have occurred appear to be the consequence of overexcitement of individual members and, sometimes also, of overzealousness of biased police officers.

A related and more difficult problem concerns the use of public places by the Witnesses for their religious activities. These cases are on the border-

---

[19] Taylor v. State of Mississippi, 319 U.S. 583.

[20] It is set out in full at 319 U.S. 584. It is execrable even in its grammar and syntax. The condensed version quoted above may sacrifice some of its meaning—or confusion—to readability.

[21] The best known is Chaplinsky v. State of New Hampshire, 315 U.S. 568 (1942). But cf. Justice Jackson's description of the Witnesses' tactics at 319 U.S. 166–70.

line between the state's interest in maintaining the public peace for the entire society and preserving the rights of individuals against unwarranted encroachment by an association's activities. The Witnesses are a fanatical, theocratic, bigoted, chiliastic sect which frequently provokes understandable though almost equally extreme intolerance among those they attack. Too often local public authorities in regulating the use of public places have catered to the prejudices of those who paint an exaggerated picture of the sect as an enemy of society, when at most its activities in public places have sometimes been insupportable nuisances.

On the other hand, it is a mark of libertarian sentimentality to see in every effort to preserve safety in the streets and peace and quiet in the parks a malevolent and omnipotent state trampling upon the free exercise of religion. It is not pointless to note that public places are supported by public taxes, and that opening them to religious activities provides some public aid to religious groups. Any parade, and especially one that the police are not prepared for, creates traffic hazards. Bigoted street preaching holds a danger of breach of the peace. The roar of loud-speakers at a religious meeting in a park may be just as frustrating to the peace and quiet of others as that created by amplifiers broadcasting a secular assembly there. Does the free exercise of religion guaranteed by the First Amendment mean that government may take no steps to lay down regulations in advance for religious group activities in public places to control these results?

In the first of these cases Chief Justice Hughes declared for a unanimous court that it did not.[22] Several sizable groups of Jehovah's Witnesses had marched in single file carrying placards along the sidewalks of Manchester, New Hampshire, through the business district on a crowded Saturday night without even deigning to apply for the license required under state law. The law provided for a fee up to three hundred dollars as set by the licensing board. The statute itself laid down no standards to determine the grant or refusal of a license, but the supreme court of New Hampshire had construed it to require "uniformity of method of treatment upon the facts of each application, free from improper or inappropriate considerations and from unfair discrimination."

A licensing or permit system of this kind does, however, hold the possibility of discrimination against an unpopular group. This possibility—and actuality—aroused the Supreme Court's concern later. Discriminatory treatment of some churches does amount to a preference among them and may properly be considered a violation of the nonestablishment clause. Most, although not all, of the later cases had the Witnesses as one of the protagonists. In some of these later cases some members of the Court, in order to scotch any possibility of discriminatory application of controls, have been tempted to assert virtually absolute religious freedom, with rather confusing results.

The next of these cases decided is also probably the most criticized,

[22] Cox v. State of New Hampshire, 312 U.S. 569 (1941).

because the permit required was not for merely speaking in the city park, but for the use of a sound amplifier.[23] A member of Jehovah's Witnesses after using a sound truck in a small park on several Sundays with a permit was denied further permits, because of complaints about excessive noise. Mr. Justice Douglas for a bare majority of the Court held the ordinance "unconstitutional on its face," referring to previous restraints and to the Hague case, of which more later. He insisted that "Any abuses which loud-speakers create can be controlled by narrowly drawn statutes" which, he admitted, might regulate the hours and places for their use, and the permissible volume of sound.

A dissenting opinion of Mr. Justice Frankfurter was persuasive and that of Justice Jackson was piquant. They emphasized what the majority could not deny but chose to ignore—that there was no evidence of discrimination against this religious sect. So far as the record showed, no other group had been granted a permit or even sought one. Nor was the refusal of additional permits shown to be arbitrary in the sense that it was based on disapproval of the content of Saia's amplified remarks, as distinguished from the annoyance caused by the loud noise to others who had come to the park to rest or play or picnic on their day off. The general rule that public officials are presumed to act lawfully until there is evidence to the contrary, they insisted, was entitled to respect here. Lack of standards was an insufficient reason for invalidating the ordinance itself, for if their lack did lead to an abuse, courts could correct it. (It must be admitted that going clear to the United States Supreme Court to right such a wrong is a pretty expensive remedy.) Justice Jackson thoughtfully asked why, if it was admitted the decibels of sound could be limited, the limit could not be set at zero in a place dedicated to rest and recreation.

It was not so much the majority holding that provoked criticism as dicta that seemed to hint that in the name of free speech and religion sound trucks must be allowed wide scope in public places no matter how almost everyone else felt about noise *qua* noise there.[24] The minority might have added that there is scarcely a right to build a church or a private hall in a public park, and that that principle might cover the erection of sound amplifiers. In a later case not involving a religious group the Saia case's doctrine on freedom for sound trucks was sharply qualified.[25]

[23] Saia v. People of the State of New York, 334 U.S. 558 (1948).

[24] Notable among these was the application of the doctrine of no previous restraint of the *press*. No effort was made to examine the assumption that this principle is equally applicable to speech either in this case or in Thomas v. Collins, 323 U.S. 516 (1945), where it first appears to have been used.

[25] Kovacs v. Cooper, 336 U.S. 77 (1949). An ordinance of the city of Trenton, New Jersey, banning sound trucks emitting "loud and raucous noises" on the city streets was upheld by a bare majority of the Court six months after the Saia decision. The Chief Justice was the only member of the Court in the majority in both decisions. He, along with Justices Burton and Reed, who wrote the opinion, thought an absolute prohibition of sound trucks would be unconstitutional. The dissenting Justices charged, with much reason, that the ordinance was meant to apply to all sound trucks as loud and raucous and

In four later cases the Supreme Court has struck down municipal ordinances or customs by which religious groups or ministers, like any other person or group, were required to obtain a permit in advance to hold a meeting in a public park or street. In each the Court's clearest objection has been that the ordinance or custom did not specify adequate standards to forestall the possibility of an abuse of discretion by the administrative officials authorized to grant the permits. But the Court's general disapproval of any prior restraint upon the press has been carried over into these cases.

Another case in which prior restraint had been imposed on a religious speaker admittedly because of the results produced by the *content* of his speech is of more fundamental importance than the Saia case.[26] An ordinance of the City of New York punished persons who assembled others to worship or who denounced or ridiculed religion or expounded atheism or agnosticism on public streets. But the law also authorized the police commissioner to grant permits to representatives of religious or irreligious groups to make street speeches; he was required to grant an initial permit to any qualified applicant. One Kunz, an ordained Baptist minister, had obtained an annual permit which the commissioner canceled because Kunz's scurrilous and insulting remarks against Catholics and Jews had provoked many complaints and, by Kunz's own admission, led to street fights unless a policeman was provided. In later years Kunz was refused a permit, as the state courts explained, because of the belief that he would provoke further disorders. He spoke anyway and was arrested and convicted. With only Justice Jackson dissenting, the Supreme Court reversed this conviction.

Chief Justice Vinson observed for the Court:[27]

It is noteworthy that there is no mention in the ordinance of reasons for which such a permit application can be refused. . . . We have here, then, an ordinance which gives an administrative official discretionary power to control in advance the right of citizens to speak on religious matters on the streets of New York. As such, the ordinance is clearly invalid as a prior restraint on the exercise of First Amendment rights.

Unfortunately this language left unclear precisely what the Court considered the vice of the ordinance: the existence of any prior restraint at all, or the lack of standards by which a previous restraint was to be exercised. Justice Jackson clearly thought that the Court was forbidding any licensing system at all. Impressed perhaps by his special familiarity with Nazi street-fighting tactics, he objected on grounds that lose much of their force if this was not what the Court intended. That it was not is strongly suggested by the Chief Justice's closing sentence: "It is sufficient to say that New York cannot vest restraining control over the right to speak on religious subjects in an admin-

had been so applied. Justices Frankfurter and Jackson, concurring separately, seemed to agree and to consider an absolute prohibition valid for that reason. The effect of the ordinance sustained in this case seems a more severe limitation on the use of sound trucks than the one invalidated in the Saia case, even though it involves no prior restraint.

[26] Kunz v. People of State of New York, 340 U.S. 290 (1951).
[27] 340 U.S. 290 at 293.

istrative official where there are no appropriate standards to guide his action."[28] It is sufficient perhaps to say further that public officials in a city like New York who are attempting in good faith to find a just and effective way to deal with social disturbance created by hate-mongers like Kunz are entitled to clearer guidance than they received in this opinion.

The next two cases are simpler. The city of Havre de Grace in Lord Baltimore's state made no ordinance, but by custom persons wishing to hold assemblies in the city park sought a permit from the park commissioner. Jehovah's Witnesses were denied a permit and on the Mayor's advice appealed to the city council. That body questioned them about their views on the flag salute, the Catholic Church, their willingness to bear arms, and the like. Receiving unsatisfactory answers it too denied the permit. The group held a peaceable meeting in the park and some were arrested. The Supreme Court unanimously reversed their conviction on this patent evidence of discrimination on the grounds of religious belief.[29]

In the next case no permits could open a park.[30] The city of Pawtucket in Roger Williams' state provided:

No person shall address any political or religious meeting in any public park; but this section shall not be construed to prohibit any political or religious club or society from visiting any public park in a body, provided that no public address shall be made under the auspices of such club or society in such park.

For addressing a peaceful meeting of Jehovah's Witnesses over a public address system (apparently suitably modulated) in a city park one Fowler was convicted and fined five dollars. The city conceded that, strange as it might seem, "the ordinance, as construed and applied, did not prohibit church services in the park. Catholics could hold mass . . . and Protestants could hold their church services there without violating the ordinance." Again Mr. Justice Douglas spoke, as he had in Saia's case, but this time for a unanimous Court. He did not, however, hold this ordinance void on its face. Nor did he cite his Saia decision. He did not even say that the Pawtucket ordinance was an invalid interference with the free exercise of religion. Instead he termed the city's admission of discrimination "fatal."

To call the words which one minister speaks to his congregation a sermon, immune from regulation, and the words of another an address, subject to regulation, is merely an indirect way of preferring one religion over another.

So here, it seems, discriminatory administration of an absolute prohibition upon religious use of a public place violates the constitutional prohibition on an establishment of religion. The Court thought that the Rhode Island case was "on all fours" with the Maryland case. With all respect, this seems odd. There we had a custom which allowed use of the park with a permit and an instance of flagrant discriminatory denial of a permit. Here we have an ordinance which in terms forbids anyone to speak to any religious group

[28] 340 U.S. 290 at 295.   [29] Niemotko v. State of Maryland, 340 U.S. 268 (1951).
[30] Fowler v. Rhode Island, 345 U.S. 67 (1953).

in the park, with discriminatory informal exemptions granted some sects through refusal to enforce the law. Mr. Justice Frankfurter, concurring, said that the case should be disposed of as a denial of the equal protection of the laws without reference to the First Amendment. It is worthy of note that there is not a word in Mr. Justice Douglas' opinion which suggests that if Pawtucket had equally and absolutely denied use of its parks for any religious meeting whatsoever, it would not have been within its rights.

Of making many Supreme Court decisions, like the books of which the preacher speaks, there is no end; and much study is a weariness of the flesh.[31] So it shall be on this subject until the Court is ready frankly to admit that as a matter of policy there is a wider range of constitutional choices open to government than it has been willing to concede. Certainly a city if it sees fit may leave its public places open to religious meetings without any restriction so long as they are open to all. It is even arguable that no city is obligated to provide this form of public aid to any religious group and may rightfully close its public places to religious meetings, so long as it closes them to all. But if it makes a choice more prudent than the first alternative and more generous than the second, why may it not open its public places to religious meetings on whatever terms it thinks proper, so long as it applies these conditions impartially to all sects?

In another group of cases involving use of public places for religious purposes there has been much less perplexity. Some of these were raised by conviction of members of Jehovah's Witnesses for passing out handbills or other religious literature on the streets.[32] Why should a city wish to pro-

---

[31] How truly prophetic these words of Ecclesiastes were to be I could only surmise when I quoted him. But in 1953 the Supreme Court decided the case of Poulos v. State of New Hampshire, 345 U.S. 395. Poulos, a Jehovah's Witness, had been denied a permit by the city council of Portsmouth, New Hampshire—arbitrarily, as the state courts held—to sermonize in a small park in the heart of the city. The city council's licensing authority was based on the same statute which Chief Justice Hughes had sustained in Cox v. New Hampshire, *supra*. The city had apparently decided to exclude any preaching in this park but would presumably have permitted religious meetings in any of several other parks in the city. Apparently, however, no permits had been granted (or, for that matter, refused, so far as one can tell) for religious meetings in any of the city parks. At any rate, Poulos preached in Goodwin Park without the required permit, was arrested, convicted, and fined twenty dollars. The state supreme court upheld his conviction even though he had been arbitrarily denied a permit because, it held, his proper recourse would have been a civil action in the nature of mandamus or certiorari to require the city council to grant the permit. Having failed or refused to exercise this legal right to obtain a permit, he could not ignore the law and escape punishment for preaching in the park without a permit. The United States Supreme Court, through Mr. Justice Reed, affirmed Poulos' conviction. Mr. Justice Reed, however, proceeded to find that the city of Portsmouth was required to grant a permit to preach in this particular park, in short, that one park in the city could not be reserved for quiet. Mr. Justice Frankfurter persuasively insisted that this was gratuitous dictum. Justices Douglas and Black each wrote dissents. Mr. Justice Douglas' position seems to have changed from that he expressed in the Fowler case, *supra*. Now he declared: ". . . even a reasonable regulation of the right to free speech is not compatible with the First Amendment."

[32] Lovell v. City of Griffin, Ga., 303 U.S. 444 (1938), and Schneider v. State of New Jersey (Town of Irvington), 308 U.S. 147 (1939). Cf. Largent v. Texas, 318 U.S. 418 (1943) and Jamison v. Texas, 318 U.S. 413 (1943).

hibit entirely or require a permit for passing out handbills on the street? This activity will almost never draw a crowd, with the attendant policing problems, that street preaching or religious meetings in public places do create. About the only excuse offered was that a city should be able to prevent the littering of its streets with discarded handbills. To this it has been retorted that the city should punish those who threw away the handbills, not those who passed them out. This is hardly sufficient. If clean streets are a compelling social need, it might be said that both parties should properly be punished, but it is not unusual for the state to reach a desired end with an economy of effort and a minimum of public irritation. The aim of Prohibition was to decrease alcoholic consumption, but we punished the liquor sellers, not the buyers. It might well be that prohibiting the distribution of handbills was the easiest way to prevent their discard.

Clean streets are pleasant but not so important as preservation of the opportunity to communicate religious and other ideas. Besides, it is a little silly to protest that unless handbill distribution can be prevented, a city's streets will be ankle-deep in paper like Broadway after a ticker-tape parade for a national hero. The coincidence should not go unnoticed that all the cases in which the Supreme Court invalidated such ordinances arose out of their application to members of groups which, like Jehovah's Witnesses, were likely to be unpopular with the powers that be.

From distributing literature on the streets it is literally and figuratively but a few steps to go to the householder's front door, ring his bell, hand him a pamphlet when he answers, and perhaps harangue him as well. These cases bring us to efforts by the state to prevent a religious association's activities from injuring the rights of individuals. The householder brought to the door from his bed, his bath, or even his TV program may feel that a man's house ought to be his castle and wish that his evangelical caller were in the inferno that the Witnesses seem to think will be the fate of the rest of us. Somebody, he may say, ought to do something to protect him from these unwelcome pests. As public officials know, when the citizen refers to "somebody" in that context, he means them. What can they do to protect the householder without interfering too much with the Witnesses' religious freedom?

The city council of a small town in Ohio thought that they had the answer. They enacted that

It is unlawful for any person distributing handbills, circulars or other advertisements to ring the doorbell, sound the door knocker, or otherwise summon the inmate or inmates of any residence to the door for the purpose of receiving such handbills, circulars or other advertisements they or any person with them may be distributing.

When such laws are on the books, Jehovah's Witnesses are likely to bring the inevitable to pass. When the case[33] reached the United States Supreme Court, in vain did counsel for the city fathers plead that many citizens of

---

[33] Martin v. City of Struthers, Ohio, 319 U.S. 141 (1943).

the town were warworkers on night shifts who needed undisturbed sleep during the day, or that housebreakers sometimes found the disguise of a handbill passer useful for their criminal activities. The Court perceived that the ordinance did not apply to sellers of pots or brushes or magazine subscriptions. Their unwanted visits might be equally annoying, and their occupation an equally good disguise for a criminal. We may be more candid than the Court could properly be and wonder out loud if this omission might indicate an intent to thwart the Witnesses.

At any rate Mr. Justice Black for a majority of the Court disposed of the case and the ordinance with persuasive reasoning:

The ordinance does not control anything but the distribution of literature, and in that respect it substitutes the judgment of the community for the judgment of the individual householder. It submits the distributor to criminal punishment for annoying the person on whom he calls, even though the recipient of the literature distributed is in fact glad to receive it. . . . Traditionally the American law punishes persons who enter onto the property of another after having been warned by the owner to keep off. . . . The National Institute of Municipal Law Officers has proposed a form of regulation . . . which would make it an offence for any person to ring the bell of a householder who has appropriately indicated that he is unwilling to be disturbed. This or any similar regulation leaves the decision as to whether distributors of literature may lawfully call at a home where it belongs—with the homeowner himself. A city can punish those who call at a home in defiance of the previously expressed will of the occupant and, in addition, can by identification devices control the abuse of the privilege by criminals posing as canvassers.

In short, the state can help those who want help and will help themselves, but it cannot lawfully protect some men's right to privacy by depriving other men of their right to receive information at their front doors and still other men of their right to impart that information to willing listeners.[34]

In the United States a considerable number of people live in company towns. Company towns are private property, although their streets may be considered so dedicated to a public use that persons upon them cannot be treated as mere trespassers. The owners of a company town in Alabama posted notices that "This Is Private Property, and Without Written Permission, No Street, or House Vendor, Agent or Solicitation of Any Kind Will Be Permitted." Alabama law gave private property owners who thus warned off trespassers the kind of protection against them which the Court had described as traditionally American. Nevertheless a Witness insisted

[34] In Breard v. City of Alexandria, 341 U.S. 622 (1951), the Court destroyed for all practical purposes the effect of its holding in Martin v. Struthers. The case involved an ordinance which forbade canvassing a household without having obtained the *prior consent* of the occupant. (Of course a canvasser might telephone the occupant—if he had a telephone—and make an appointment to call.) The ordinance was upheld against commercial canvassers for magazine subscriptions. The Court did not indicate clearly whether it would give more protection against such laws to religious evangelists than to young men "working their way through college."

that she had a constitutional right to distribute literature on a street in the company town without a permit.

The United States Supreme Court agreed with her.[35] The owners of a company town could not accurately be compared with householders warning canvassers not to ring the doorbell. The more significant analogy is with the public authorities of an ordinary town forbidding handbill distribution on the public streets. As Mr. Justice Frankfurter said, concurring, ". . . a company-owned town is a town. In its community aspects it does not differ from other towns. These community aspects are decisive in adjusting the relations now before us. . . ."[36] The case illustrates another principle of the constitutional law of association. The state may under certain circumstances need to restrain private persons from exercising their customary rights so as to interfere with rights of association, and even compel private persons to enter into legal relations with the association or some of its members carrying out the group's work. Both aspects of the principle are illustrated here, for when a person was lawfully on a street of the company town, the owners had different legal duties toward him than they would if he were an unlicensed trespasser.[37]

One other case presents a significant example of the adjustment of the rights of association and the protection of rights of individuals injured by the association's activities.[38] As part of its laws limiting child labor Massachusetts had ordained that: "No boy under twelve and no girl under eighteen shall sell . . . any newspapers, magazines, periodicals or any other articles . . . or exercise the trade of bootblack or scavenger, or any other trade, in any street or public place." To make the law effective the state also punished anyone who set a child up in such business or any parent or guardian who allowed a child to work in violation of the law.

Mrs. Prince, her two small sons, and her nine-year-old niece and ward, Betty Simmons, were all members of Jehovah's Witnesses. Mrs. Prince sold publications of the sect on the streets and sometimes took the children with her and allowed them to do so. At their plea to go with her one night and do what they believed to be their religious duty, she again took them with her, although a truant officer had warned her against the practice. This time he caused her to be indicted for violation of the law. The Massachusetts courts in interpreting the law might reasonably have doubted that the legislature had intended the law to apply to this situation, and followed what they thought was the spirit of the law rather than its letter, leaving the legislature free to amend the law to make it apply explicitly to such cases if it desired. It should be noticed that if Betty Simmons had stood near her

[35] Marsh v. State of Alabama, 326 U.S. 501 (1946).

[36] 326 U.S. 501 at 510–11.

[37] See also the companion case of Tucker v. State of Texas, 326 U.S. 517 (1946). For an interesting application of a similar concept in requiring an employer to furnish premises owned by him for a union meeting, cf. National Labor Relations Board v. Stowe Spinning Co. *et al.*, 336 U.S. 226 (1949).

[38] Prince v. Commonwealth of Massachusetts, 321 U.S. 158 (1944).

aunt on the street, as she did, but without handling any papers, or if she had given them away instead of selling them at five cents each, the law would not have been violated. But they construed the law to cover what Mrs. Prince had done and convicted her. Under our federal system the United States Supreme Court did not possess this same freedom of interpretation when the case came there on appeal; it was bound to accept the meaning which the state court had given the state statute.

The Supreme Court, with only Justice Murphy dissenting, sustained the conviction. Justice Rutledge thought it clear and easily demonstrable that the state could protect children from harm, even against their will or that of their parents. The rights of a group's members to freedom of the press or to free exercise of religion is not an absolute bar to such protection. Since, he said, "the validity of such a prohibition applied to children unaccompanied by an older person hardly would seem open to question" (although the Witnesses insisted that it was), one must simply ask "whether the presence of the child's guardian puts a limit to the state's power. That fact," he said,

may lessen the likelihood that some evils the legislation seeks to avert will occur. But it cannot forestall all of them. The zealous though lawful exercise of the right to engage in propagandizing the community, whether in religious, political or other matters, may and at times does create situations difficult enough for adults to cope with and wholly inappropriate for children, especially of tender years, to face. Other harmful possibilities could be stated. . . .[39]

In short, although Massachusetts could reasonably choose not to go so far, it could also quite reasonably go as far as it did.

Justice Murphy, who had a strong inclination to treat the religious guaranties of the First Amendment as unqualified absolutes, demanded application of the clear and present danger test in the most absolute fashion possible. "The dangers," he contended,

are thus exceedingly remote, to say the least. And the fact that the zealous exercise of the right to propagandize the community may result in violent or disorderly situations difficult for children to face is no excuse for prohibiting the free exercise of that right.[40]

To which one might reply that it is no "excuse" in the pejorative connotation of that word, but a sound and sensible reason. But Justice Murphy held that another important issue was involved. He said:[41]

The reasonableness that justifies the prohibition of the ordinary distribution of literature in the public streets by children is not necessarily the reasonableness that justifies such a drastic restriction when the distribution is part of their religious faith. . . . The vital freedom of religion . . . cannot be erased by slender references to the state's power to restrict the more secular activities of children.

[39] 321 U.S. 158 at 169–70.
[40] 321 U.S. 158 at 175.
[41] 321 U.S. 158 at 173–74.

To this argument Justice Rutledge replied that[42]

If by this position appellant seeks for freedom of conscience a broader protection than for freedom of mind, it may be doubted that any of the great liberties insured by the First Article can be given higher place than the others. . . . All are interwoven there together.

It seems unfortunate that he did not press the argument more explicitly and ask what would be the meaning of preferring the rights of a religious group to communicate their views over the general freedom of speech and press of other persons and groups. To do so, it may well be urged, would establish the rights of a religious group in a higher position than any others'—in the First Amendment's own words, to provide for "an establishment of religion." More than once in examining the issues that must be faced in preserving freedom for religion we have seen how imminently the principle of freedom from religion confronts us. To a consideration of that latter principle, of measures taken to preserve it and acts that seem to threaten it, we must next devote our attention.

[42] 321 U.S. 158 at 164.

3

CHURCH AND STATE: AN AMERICAN EXPERIMENT

The provision in the First Amendment against an establishment of religion was, when it was adopted, an American experiment. Even today it is more experimental and more distinctively American than is sometimes recognized. Like most if not all of our experiments, however, it was not conceived in isolation from the thought and experience of the rest of the Western world. This American experiment set under way in 1789 was a logical extension of the position summarized so forcefully by the English philosopher of the Glorious Revolution a century before. In his great *Letter on Toleration* John Locke was pleading for the free exercise of religion. Prudent as he was, he did not see fit in this epistle designed for the persuasion of all his fellow countrymen to allow himself to go as far as his argument led him. To go as far as he did seemed to many devout men of his time impious and atheistic.

Locke's argument for freedom for religion is suggestive of his attitude toward freedom from religion. It is hard to believe that he looked upon any establishment of religion with enthusiasm. It is clear that he did not look with favor on the degree of establishment still existing after the Revolution in England. But he did not attack it except by implication. For the degree of establishment that England has today he did offer this much justification:

It may indeed be alleged that the magistrate may make use of arguments, and thereby draw the heterodox into the way of truth, and procure their salvation. I grant it; but this is common to him with other men. In teaching, instructing, and redressing the erroneous by reason, he may certainly do what becomes any good man to do . . . but it is one thing to persuade, another to command; one thing to press with arguments, another with penalties.

Throughout the essay he was at pains to repudiate the idea that a king is better qualified to know the true religion than each man for himself and that any religion gains added spiritual authority because the sovereign has established it. He qualified his mild defense of a mild establishment by adding drily:

. . . to speak the truth, we must acknowledge that the church (if a convention of clergymen, making canons, must be called by that name) is for the most part more apt to be influenced by the court than the court by the church.

The American Revolution declared independence from both court and church. We went further than Locke cared or, more likely, thought he dared to go.

44

Some of the reasons why we did so have already been suggested. The fullest achievement of freedom for religion, our founders thought, demands freedom from religion. Their realization of the logical and practical connections between the old and the new ideas was sound, as some of the cases in the preceding chapter have demonstrated. To begin our examination of the responsibilities which separation of church and state places upon governments in the United States we can do no better than to scrutinize a recent case in which the Supreme Court has interpreted that responsibility.[1]

In 1952 the United States Supreme Court decided a case which is likely to loom as importantly in the law and political theory of association as the Free Church of Scotland case in Great Britain in 1904. It is difficult to give any adequate brief summary of *Kedroff* v. *St. Nicholas Cathedral of Russian Orthodox Church in North America* without "wallow[ing] through the complex, obscure and fragmentary details of secular and ecclesiastical history, theology, and canon law in which this case is smothered." The suit was to determine whether Benjamin, appointed Archbishop of the Archdiocese of North America and the Aleutian Islands by one of the three Russian bishops *locum tenens* for the Patriarch of Moscow in 1933, should possess and use St. Nicholas Cathedral of the Russian Orthodox Church in North America, in New York City, or whether Leonty, chosen Metropolitan of All America and Canada by the Russian Church in America, a church organized by a convention in Detroit in 1924, should do so.

The salient facts are these. At least until 1917 Russian Orthodox congregations in America were in an archdiocese of the Russian Orthodox Church ruled under church law by the Patriarch and Holy Synod of Moscow. From the onset of the Bolshevist Revolution in 1917 until at least 1943 the Communist government made it impossible for administration of the church in Russia to be carried on in the normal way. In 1920 the Patriarch of Moscow issued a decision granting a wide measure of administrative autonomy to the American archdiocese as long as the Moscow Patriarchate was unable to function. In 1924 most of the Russian Orthodox churches in this country through a *sobor*, or general church convention, in Detroit declared, first, the former American archdiocese to be the self-governed "Russian Church in America," and, second, that it would leave future relations with the mother church in Russia to be decided in a *sobor* of the entire Orthodox Church when such a *sobor* could be legally invoked, legally elected, and could act in political freedom.

During World War II the Russian government changed its position toward the Orthodox Church, and in 1945 a *sobor* was held in Moscow which, it is said, the Americans recognized as legal under church law and to which they attempted to send delegates. Their delegates arrived too late to participate but did present to the Moscow Patriarch and Synod "a written report on the condition of the American Church, with a *request* for autonomy." Shortly thereafter the Moscow Patriarch issued a ukase "covering require-

[1] Kedroff *et al.* v. St. Nicholas Cathedral of Russian Orthodox Church in North America, 344 U.S. 94 (1952).

ments for *reunion*" of the Russian and American Orthodox churches. He required the American diocese to hold a *sobor* at which it should, first, express its decision "to *reunite*" with the Russian Mother Church; second, declare that it would "abstain 'from political activities against the U.S.S.R.' "; and, third, elect an American Metropolitan subject to his confirmation. At an American *sobor* in Cleveland in 1946 the American church refused these terms and resolved that "*any* administrative recognition" of the Russian church "is hereby *terminated.*"

New York State has a Religious Corporations Law under which a church may if it desires acquire a corporate charter. The Russian Church in America in 1925 incorporated under this law and holds legal title to St. Nicholas Cathedral in trust for use "as a residence and central place of worship" of the ruling archbishop. That law, like most general incorporation laws, carries a provision which made the legislature's right to amend or repeal the law at any time a part of each corporate charter granted under it. In 1946 the New York legislature amended the act to define the Russian Church in America as that organized in Detroit in 1924 and to require every Russian Orthodox church in the state, incorporated under the law at any time, to recognize and remain subject to this American church. Of course this amendment did not forbid the existence of any unincorporated orthodox churches in New York which wished to be governed by the Patriarch of Moscow. It did seek to ensure the American church of possession and control of St. Nicholas Cathedral as well as legal title to it.

At the time the suit commenced, Archbishop Benjamin, appointed in Moscow in 1933, actually had possession of the Cathedral. The action was one of ejectment by the corporation holding legal title to force him out so that Archbishop Leonty of the American church could take over the Cathedral. The New York Court of Appeals by divided vote gave control to the American archbishop. The United States Supreme Court reversed the highest court of New York and left the "Soviet faction" in control. Justice Jackson dissented alone.

Mr. Justice Reed in his opinion for the Court was necessarily burdened with a long statement of the complicated facts and an analysis of the New York statute and the New York court's decision. Mr. Justice Frankfurter was joined in a concurring opinion by Justices Black and Douglas. He much more briefly concentrated on the constitutional theory which guided the court. His views provide an enlightening supplement to Mr. Justice Reed's difficult task.

The New York court had sustained the legislative amendment of 1946 and based its decision for the American group squarely on that. All members of the Supreme Court majority considered the New York statute a violation of the First Amendment as incorporated into the Fourteenth, because it both interfered with the free exercise of religion and with required separation of church and state. The governing law was the constitutional law of religious association, not the concepts of the private law of real property or of trusts. Significantly for our general thesis that association is being raised from a question of private law to that of a constitutional question, the lone dissent proceeded from a premise that the matter should be decided simply as a question of property law. Justice Jackson said :[2]

New York courts have decided an *ordinary* ejectment action. . . . If the Fourteenth Amendment is to be interpreted to leave anything to the courts of a state to decide without our interference, I should suppose it would be claims to ownership or possession of real estate within its borders and the vexing technical questions pertaining to the creation, interpretation, termination, and enforcement of uses and trusts, even though they are for religious and charitable purposes. . . . The fact that property is dedicated to a religious use cannot, in my opinion, justify the Court in *sublimating* an issue over property rights into one of deprivation of religious liberty. . . . I do not see how one can *spell out* of the principles of separation of church and state a doctrine that a state submit property rights to settlement by canon law.

To this reasoning Mr. Justice Frankfurter replied :[3]

St. Nicholas Cathedral is not just a piece of real estate. . . . A cathedral is the seat and center of ecclesiastical authority. . . . What is at stake here is the power to exercise religious authority. That is the essence of this controversy. It is that even though the religious authority becomes manifest and is exerted through authority over the Cathedral as the outward symbol of a religious faith.

At various points in his dissent Justice Jackson conceded as much, and enough to impair the basis of his reasoning :[4]

The American Cathedral group . . . refused *submission* to the Patriarch, whom it regarded as an arm of the Soviet government. . . . I do not think New York law must yield to the *authority* of a foreign and unfriendly state masquerading as a spiritual institution.

Taking the view of the constitutional question that they did, why did the majority consider the New York statute bad? Mr. Justice Frankfurter explained :[5]

The judiciary has heeded, naturally enough, the menace to a society like ours of attempting to settle such religious struggles by state action. And so, when courts are called upon to adjudicate disputes which, though generated by conflicts of faith, may fairly be isolated as controversies over property and therefore within judicial competence, *the authority of courts is in strict subordination to the ecclesiastical law of a particular church prior to a schism.* . . . This very limited right of resort to courts for determination of claims, civil in their nature, between rival parties among the communicants of a religious faith is merely one aspect of a duty to enforce the rights of members in an association, temporal or religious, according to the laws of that association. . . . Legislatures have no such obligation to adjudicate and no such power.

2 344 U.S. 94 at 126–32; italics mine.
3 344 U.S. 94 at 121.
4 344 U.S. 94 at 127 and 131; italics mine.
5 344 U.S. 94 at 122; italics mine.

Quite aside from its lack of power to adjudicate, the New York legislature had not attempted, in the opinion of the majority, simply to discover which archbishop was by the ecclesiastical law of the Russian Orthodox Church prior to the schism the head of the church in America. It had apparently tried to give effect to the will of "an impressive majority both of the laity and of the priesthood" of the Orthodox Church in New York. But "it is not a function of civil government under our constitutional system to assure rule to any religious body by a counting of heads."[6] Further, the New York legislature seems to have been motivated by a fear of the subversive activity of an American Orthodox hierarchy dominated by Moscow. "If such action should be actually attempted by a cleric, neither his robe nor his pulpit would be a defense."[7] But this law was not a proper way to deal with threatened subversion.

Assuming that the only proper way to decide this controversy was to enforce church law, the majority expressed their opinion on this law. Mr. Justice Reed thought that the record showed no schism over faith or doctrine between the Russian and American churches and also showed Russian administrative control of the American diocese until the Russian Revolution. "We find," he concluded, "nothing that indicates a relinquishment of this power by the Russian Orthodox Church." The present Patriarch of Moscow was admitted by the American church to hold his office legitimately, Mr. Justice Frankfurter added. Yet strictly speaking, this is only dicta. The New York Court of Appeals had not made the decision that it could judicially make, because it did not think the evidence clear enough to enable it to decide the case on the basis of church law.

One may agree with the Supreme Court majority that if a state attempted to establish one of two competing heads of a church as the lawful one simply on the basis of the state's own purposes and preferences, it would violate the constitutional rule for separation of church and state. One may agree further with Mr. Justice Frankfurter that where it is possible to do so, courts must decide such controversies only by giving effect to the association's fundamental law. But on a realistic view of the facts, could that be done here, or would the attempt be a mere fiction? If this case is to be decided on the basis of the fundamental law of the Russian Orthodox Church, as the majority seemed to hold, then one must be able to find as a fact that that church had not perished during the years from 1917 to 1945, for surely a group's fundamental law does not continue a disembodied existence when the group itself has ceased to be. Yet when one looks for that church in Russia during much of that period, one finds only a shadow of a substance. Even if one finds that such a church continued its unbroken existence, one must admit that out of harsh necessity it could not carry on in accordance with its own fundamental canon law, and whether or not it claimed any administrative authority over the American church, for more than twenty

[6] 344 U.S. 94 at 122.
[7] 344 U.S. 94 at 109.

years it had not been able to exercise any. The question then arises, under such a state of facts did the American church remain under any legal bond of subordination to a Russian church authority of doubtful legitimacy and of undoubted lack of power? The facts may offer a more realistic understanding of the question than any words of either party.

The decisive question on this view is whether in 1924, when the American diocese declared its independence of Moscow, it was attempting a rebellion which was illegal under church law, or whether at that time the disorder in the Russian church had extinguished the sovereignty of the Moscow Patriarch, as Hobbes would put it, and had left the Americans free to form a new church and choose a new sovereign in America. Had the Russian and the American churches from 1924 to 1946 really been living together in schism? So far as the Court's opinion reveals, it would appear that the Russian church in 1945 was uncertain that it had any authority over the American church, for it had laid down terms for "reuniting." On the other hand, the American church at the same time did not seem certain that it had in 1924 made a full declaration of independence, for it continued to hope for unity and in 1945 it reported to the Moscow Patriach and made a "request for autonomy." When it heard the terms for actual resumption of close administrative relations, it rejected them and, so to speak, reaffirmed its independence. It would be strange if Americans who established their independence reluctantly and haltingly would not feel sympathetic toward the problems of the American Orthodox Church. This case was not the beginning of litigation nor is it likely to be the end. While reversing the New York court, the Supreme Court remanded the case to it for further appropriate proceedings.

Maitland described the Scottish Church case as one in which the dead hand of the law had come down with a resounding slap on the living body of the church. From one point of view our decision might be described as one in which the strong arm of the Supreme Court stopped the live hand of the New York legislature from coming down with a resounding slap on the head of the Patriarch of Moscow. Or it might be described as one in which the Supreme Court brought down the dead hand of cannon law upon the living bodies of both the State of New York and the American Orthodox Church. New York and Justice Jackson may yet prove to have sought the right result for the wrong reasons.

The constitutional mandate that Congress shall make no law respecting an establishment of religion has been invoked much less frequently than its complement. But a few recent cases have provoked a deal of excitement. The Constitution requires nonestablishment, the opposite of establishment. But logic cannot make the concept *not-x* more exact than the concept *x* upon which it depends. Our search for an intelligible meaning of the negative must begin with the positive. The most casual survey of states with established churches shows an immense variety of relations subsisting between them. Elizabeth II of England may style herself Defender of the Faith as did Elizabeth I, but the title should not blind us to the great changes in the

50   GROUPS AND THE CONSTITUTION

duties and the prerogatives of the sovereign toward the established Church of England that have occurred between the two queens.[8]

To postulate establishment and nonestablishment as precise contradictories in the mode of Aristotelian logic is jejune conceptualism. A decent regard for historical experience and present phenomena requires us to acknowledge that establishment and nonestablishment is a continuum, or, to put it another way, that separation or union of church and state is a matter of degree. It we go too far along this continuum, in either direction, we arrive at a state in which there is little or no religious freedom.

These admissions should be accorded their full weight in interpreting the First Amendment. Their over-all consequence is that the Constitution ordains a policy of separation of church and state but leaves government free to determine according to its own views of wise policy the precise degree of separation that it will maintain. The constitutional phraseology leaves reasonable latitude, without doing violence to its meaning, initially to legislatures and ultimately to courts to prescribe relations between the separate entities of church and state.

The policy of separation of church and state was a drastic one when adopted, and Americans have never been inclined to carry it to a "drily logical extreme." They have not been so inclined because, as Justice Brewer once said for the Court, "this is a Christian nation."[9] That remark is not only sound common sense; it is good anthropology. Many statutes and judicial decisions, including the one which occasioned this dictum, attest to that cultural fact. The First Amendment itself does. In his dissent in the McCollum case Mr. Justice Reed collected some examples of legislative and judicial policy falling short of the greatest possible degree of separation. He could have found more.[10] But Justice Brewer intended his dictum to describe our culture, not to prescribe our policy.

Justice Story much earlier had made the difference clear.[11] When Stephen Girard left his bequest to found a school and home for orphan boys in Philadelphia on the condition that no minister of religion should have any part in its management or even set foot on its grounds, his will was challenged in the courts. In the Supreme Court of the United States an argument against its validity was added as an afterthought. Christianity was said to be part of the common law of Pennsylvania, and therefore, somehow, the bequest was void. Daniel Webster made up in histrionics for what his argument lacked in logic in support of this contention. But the Court

[8] For the state of the church under Elizabeth II cf. O. Hood Phillips, *The Constitutional Law of Great Britain and the Commonwealth* (London, 1952), chap. 26. The Archbishop of York has recently discussed some of the disadvantages to the church in the modern establishment: Cyril F. Garbett, *Church and State in England* (London, 1950).
[9] Church of the Holy Trinity v. United States, 143 U.S. 457 (1893).
[10] For example, we learn from Chief Justice Marshall's opinion in Worcester v. Georgia, 6 Peters 515 (1832), that the missionaries sent to the Cherokee Indians were also appointed Indian agents by and received pay from the federal government.
[11] Vidal v. Girard's Executors, 2 Howard 127 (1844).

was not impressed. Christianity might well be part of the common law of Pennsylvania, whatever that might mean, said Justice Story, but whatever it meant, it did not mean Girard's design was illegal. Many people thought Webster must have been angling for a Presidential nomination in his flights of pious rhetoric.[12]

If the dictum that this is a Christian nation cannot settle concrete questions of the admissible relation of church and state, neither can a collection of illustrations such as Mr. Justice Reed offers us. Probably it was set forth in the spirit of Justice Holmes's remark that in many matters "a page of history is worth a volume of logic." But this is so only in the sense that concrete facts are often better raw materials for judicial reasoning than logical abstractions. The *fact*, for example, that the United States employs chaplains for its military forces cannot prove that a public school board *ought* to be permitted to use its employees, its revenues, and its buildings to support a program of religious instruction.

FINANCIAL AID TO RELIGION

With few exceptions the Supreme Court in interpreting the provision against religious establishment has been concerned with public aid to religious groups. In the New Jersey bus case Mr. Justice Black said for the majority that the state cannot "pass laws which aid one religion, aid all religions, or prefer one religion over another."[13] For the minority Justice Rutledge agreed that: "The prohibition broadly forbids any state support, financial or other, of any religion in any guise, form or degree. It outlaws all use of public funds for religious purposes."[14] Mr. Justice Black's use of Thomas Jefferson's metaphor was suggestive of the absolutist conceptions with which both Justices approached the question: "The First Amendment has erected a wall between church and state." It might seem presumptuous to assert that neither side meant what it said, were it not that each admitted the practical inapplicability of these words. The majority attempted to escape from the ineluctable logical implications of their principle by carving out an exception for "public welfare legislation," the minority by referring to legislation for "protection against disorder or the ordinary accidental incidents of community life." With all respect, this is playing with words. Let us see why the idea that the First Amendment absolutely prohibits any aid to religion affronts earthly common sense when it descends from the "heaven of juristic conceptions."

The metaphor of the wall betrays the whole case. It suggests that churches and the state are different societies; each exists on its own territory with its own population and between them there is a wall. Of course we all recognize that this is legal poetic license, but shall we be forgiven for unseemly levity

---

[12] Cf. Charles Warren, *The Supreme Court in United States History* (rev. ed., Boston, 1947), II, 124–33.
[13] Everson v. Board of Education of Ewing Township *et al.*, 330 U.S. 1 (1947), at 15.
[14] 330 U.S. 1 at 33.

if we paraphrase the warning of that doughty jurist, the Lord Chancellor in
Iolanthe:

> In other professions in which men engage,
> The Army, the Navy, the Church and the Stage ...
> Professional license, if carried too far
> Your chance of sound thinking may certainly mar,
> And I fancy the rule might apply to the Bar,
> Said I to myself, said I.

How can the state ignore churches that exist in the same society? True,
it might leave them to maintain their own fire departments, employ their
own guards, and provide many other services at their own expense, instead
of according them services supported by public taxes, and any religious sect
wealthy enough to do so might survive. But how could the churches defend
themselves against arsonists, thieves, embezzlers, or mobs of bigoted adver-
saries if they were denied access to the courts maintained at public expense?
Perhaps they could manage if they were permitted to establish ecclesiastical
courts in which they tried offenders under canon law and punished them in
church prisons. Needless to say, such a system would be the establishment
of religion with a vengeance. The judges need not have pondered the public
support which firemen and policemen assure the churches. The public pays
the judges' salaries when they sit to uphold the rights of a church just as it
does the rest of the time. Is this public aid? Is it public support? No other
name you choose to apply can change the fact, nor avert the necessity for it.

We reach one principle, then, in defiance of some judicial dicta, but not
of actual decisions. If the state withheld what it alone can provide, it would
deprive churches not only of their liberty, but their life. A state which
refused to give churches certain minimal public aid would in fact be passing
upon them the dread sentence of outlawry. So to interpret the freedom from
religion that the First Amendment guarantees would pervert it from its object
of strengthening freedom for religion to destroying that freedom.

Beyond this minimum of public aid essential to survival of religious
groups there is, plainly, a range of additional public assistance which makes
life easier for the churches or, if you will, enhances their liberty, and which
may also increase their dependence. How far, as a matter of wise policy,
should legislatures go or courts permit them to go in extending these public
privileges? This was the question that the Supreme Court had to answer
when it decided whether or not the state should be allowed to pay the bus
fare for children attending a Catholic parochial school. Five members of
the Court agreed with the highest state court and a majority of the state
legislature that this was not too far. Four Justices agreed with a lower state
court and presumably with a minority of the legislature that it was. Over
questions of policy reasonable men may differ. Unfortunately, nothing is
gained when we search for wisdom and find absolutes—nothing except confusion and, all too probably, increased bitterness in the relations between
religious groups.

Now it cannot be denied, though it may be glossed over, that when public aid is furnished churches a taxpayer may be thus compelled to make a contribution in aid of a religious group against his own will, although his representatives have committed him to it. The glosses of the courts to explain this away can be quickly dismissed.

One refers to the legal principle of *de minimis*—the law does not concern itself with trifles. For the ordinary taxpayer no doubt the portion of his total taxes devoted to churches is a trifling amount. The number of taxpayers begrudging this use of their money may also be trifling. But neither assumption will always necessarily be true. And it would hardly seem just to deny to small taxpayers or a small number of them what would be accorded to large taxpayers or a large number of them. The plea of *de minimis* is here, as it often is, expediency, perhaps better than nothing, but not much better.

Another gloss, one which sufficed for the majority in the Everson case, is at first glance more satisfactory. There the state reimbursed parents for the bus fares that they paid to send their children to parochial schools. This, the majority reasoned, was welfare legislation in aid of the individuals concerned. And so it was, "directly," although no one denied that "indirectly" it also aided the church schools. Governmental provision of textbooks for pupils in church schools has been similarly justified.[15] But suppose that under this reasoning parochial schools, instead of accepting pupils free or at low tuition, charged them the full cost of their education and that the state then reimbursed the parents for the tuition fees they paid? Since the majority in this case thought that payment of bus fares went to the verge of constitutional power, it would presumably have found that tuition payments went too far, though scarcely without considerable embarrassment.

In sober fact, the famous New Jersey bus case itself approaches *de minimis*. At the time it was decided the United States government's educational program for World War II veterans under the GI Bill was in full swing. Under its terms tens of thousands, perhaps hundreds of thousands, of veterans were attending private colleges and universities. Many of these schools are "church-connected." Many are governed by boards of trustees appointed by religious sects, many require students to attend religious services, many require them to take courses in religion to obtain a degree. The national government not only paid these veteran students a personal subsistence allowance but also paid the tuition fees directly to the schools.

Fortunately for the equanimity of the Supreme Court, its rules make it much more difficult to use a taxpayer's suit to challenge the constitutionality of an act of Congress than it is in many states to test the validity of a state law. If a billion-dollar-a-year federal taxpayer like the General Motors Corporation had been able and willing to challenge the GI Bill in this way, these glosses would have gone up like balloons filled with hot air.

We must also note that another gloss favored by some commentators would suffer the same fate in any crucial test. It is sometimes said that the

15 Cf. Cochran v. Louisiana Board of Education, 281 U.S. 370 (1930).

54   GROUPS AND THE CONSTITUTION

vice lies in "positive" public aid through tax support, and especially through "specific" appropriations. "General" aid, that is, aid such as police or fire protection the cost of which is difficult or impossible to apportion among potential beneficiaries, or "negative" aid in the form of tax exemption of church property and income is excusable. The answer surely is that aid is aid, whatever its form. Doubtless by far the most important public aid to religion is precisely the extension of "general" public services and "negative" tax exemptions. Both have always been extended to churches in varying degree in the United States.[16]

The question of religious tax exemptions needs a further word. These exemptions leave us only two alternatives: either some citizens will suffer a deprivation of some public services because there is less money to furnish them, or some citizens will have to bear the tax burden that the churches escape. Justification cannot rest on a quibble over negative and positive aid. Because this is a Christian nation it holds churches to be institutions devoted to a social use; it assimilates them to the concept of charitable or philanthropic institutions. As a matter of policy we exempt them from taxation because we believe that they make a valuable contribution to our culture.

Now we must return to our taxpaying fellow citizen whom we have so far left defenseless against governmental compulsion to help provide aid to religion. There can be no doubt that James Madison in framing his Grand Remonstrance in Virginia and the First Amendment to the Constitution of the United States regarded this kind of compulsion as a serious threat to men's freedom from religion and sought to guard against its abusive use.[17] Intellectual honesty requires us to admit that every penny which the state takes from the citizen for the support of religion, even with his implied consent and with his real approval, is so far a limitation upon that freedom, and if against his real wishes it is likely to be an especially hateful exaction. Of course if we abandoned the American experiment of separation of church and state, that argument would cease to matter, but so long as that experiment is a part of our Constitution, this principle is entitled to the weightiest consideration whenever we are called upon to decide how far we may prudently go in extending public aid to religious groups. All that has been said before amounts to no more than this—that the principle of separation cannot consistently with the maintenance of freedom for religion be made absolute.

We should also pay our respects to one of the glosses sometimes used to justify inroads upon the principle that Madison emphasized. This is the claim that the amendment merely forbids giving aid to some churches and

[16] On this point, as on many others regarding church and state in America, the literature is extensive. Cf. Anson Phelps Stokes, *Church and State in the United States* (New York, 1950); A. W. Johnson and F. H. Yost, *Separation of Church and State in the United States* (Minneapolis, 1948); W. G. Torpey, *Judicial Doctrines of Religious Rights in America* (Chapel Hill, 1948).

[17] Justice Rutledge's dissent in the Everson case gives a concise account of Madison's views.

denying it to others or distributing aid unequally among them. Equal aid to all religions is pronounced unobjectionable. In the first place, this was not the difficulty that led to adoption of the amendment. Aside from this objection, what is equal aid to all religions? Should each sect receive an equal sum from the government? Or should each denomination receive a sum computed on the number of its members? Or on the number of ministers it supports? Or should each church receive a certain amount per congregation? Or should government's contribution be based on the average attendance on Sundays, rather than on membership? Would it be equality if government gave as much, or more, to a large, rich, and popular church as to one that was small, poor, and struggling? Should aid be extended to those churches which maintain church schools on the theory that other churches which desired to establish their own schools could do so and claim equal aid, even though most churches in fact had no schools and received no aid? If aid were to be extended equally to all churches, how could the state deny funds even to the most outrageously fraudulent claimant without setting itself up as a judge of the good faith and genuineness of any church? Could the state grant aid to all sects without laying down some conditions about the use of its funds, for example, to forbid a church to use the money to lobby for still larger grants? To ask these questions is to dispose of the gloss that the First Amendment merely forbids aid to one church or aid on a discriminatory basis. There is no conception of equal aid to all churches on which all churches would agree.

The difficulties and embarrassments in which the state can flounder from even appearing to grant aid unequally are vividly portrayed in the series of cases arising out of the imposition of municipal license taxes on members of Jehovah's Witnesses who go from house to house selling the sect's publications.[18] So troublesome were the questions raised that the Supreme Court, after a slight change in membership, vacated its original decision of a few months earlier and reversed its stand.[19] The problem may seem simple. If freedom of press and religion are absolute, then the taxes are taxes on press and religion and must be invalid. Or one may say that a municipal license tax on the privilege of going from door to door peddling articles for sale, whether pots and pans, fresh vegetables, magazine subscriptions, or copies of the *Watchtower*, is a traditional kind of tax levied indiscriminately on a commercial activity and is not a tax on press or religion at all. Perhaps framing the question as primarily one of a group's right to the free exercise of religion accounts for some of the Court's difficulty. For the heart of the question is, I think, discriminatory aid to religion.

What the Witnesses sought was exemption from a tax. Tax exemptions

[18] The leading case is Jones v. City of Opelika, 316 U.S. 584 (1942) and 319 U.S. 103 (1943). Other cases appear with it in each of these volumes of the reports. Cf. also Follett v. Town of McCormick, S.C., 321 U.S. 573 (1944).

[19] Mr. Justice Byrnes participated in the first decision upholding the taxes; his place in the second decision was filled by Justice Rutledge, who voted against the taxes and thus shifted the stand of a bare majority of the Court.

have been widely given to other sects. Practice varies considerably. The buildings and furnishings used by denominations are quite generally exempted from the real and personal property taxes that would otherwise fall upon them . But some churches own property producing income which helps support their activities. Such property and the income from it, although it goes to a nonprofit association, is not so commonly exempt from tax. Neither is a minister's salary exempt from income tax. All of these exemptions have been considered a matter of grace, that is, of policy. Governments can and do make what exemptions they think fit, as long as they apply them to all sects in the same fashion.

The Witnesses were doing the act upon which the tax was laid : they were selling something house to house. It is true that sometimes some of them gave copies of their periodicals to persons who evinced an interest but could not pay for them, or took what they were offered instead of the full price. Some members who spent full time at this work paid the sect a wholesale price for the publications and marked up the retail price to their customers as suggested by the sect, thus earning their livelihood from the profits. So we can describe in the language of trade the Witnesses' commercial activities.

But in the language of religion the whole matter appears rather differently. Mr. Justice Douglas in his opinion gave a learned survey of the traditional work of the colporteur that made his ancient vocation of carrying religious tracts to the people, while supporting himself from the proceeds, seem much more like that of the missionary or the evangelist than of the peddler of pots and pans.[20] As Justice Murphy said, "The mind rebels at the thought that a minister of any of the old established [sic, and the word is suggestive] churches could be made to pay fees to the community before entering the pulpit."[21]

Trying to decide whether the Witnesses' activities were commercial enterprise or a form of religious teaching, the Justices were badly divided, because they had aspects of both. Yet the final weight of the Court's authority seems to accord with the weight of reason : that for the purpose of deciding this issue they were best understood as an exercise of a church's right of communication. The Witnesses might have saved the Court this trouble had they been willing to take freewill offerings for their tracts instead of setting a price for them. This they were understandably unwilling to do and were not obligated to do. Nor in fact could affixing a label of commercialism or of religious communication in itself settle the issue of tax exemption.

Tax exemptions are also granted to secular enterprises like symphony orchestras and private hospitals. Nor is the press, whether or not religious and whether or not operated for profit, exempt from all taxation. And the commercial press, secular and religious, like other enterprises, may receive public aid akin to tax exemption, as the special low book and periodical rates in our postal system show. Through many pages of opinions the Jus-

20 319 U.S. 105 at 108–9.
21 316 U.S. 584 at 621.

tices struggled in vain to find a touchstone for decision in such indistinct distinctions.

Failing to find it, those who opposed the tax stressed the burdensome nature of some of the levies, particularly those which were heavy and those which were fixed at a flat rate regardless of return from the sales.[22] But this was itself an admission of the commercial form of the activity, of dubious help to their case. Those who opposed exemption, on the other hand, emphasized that the cities had special policing expenses consequent upon the activity, which they were entitled to recoup.[23] They did not stop to ask if all the public services furnished the year around to other ordinary or, as Justice Murphy called them, "old established" churches which received tax exemption might not cost the state far more.

The truth of the matter almost certainly is that both the governmental expenditures that the Witnesses necessitated and the exemptions which they claimed were paltry compared with those for other churches. Under these circumstances to have denied the Witnesses exemption from this tax, though it was of a different type from the taxes from which other churches are exempt, would not only have been, over-all, discriminatory, but would have fulfilled the Biblical prophecy, "Unto everyone that hath shall be given, and he shall have abundance; but from him that hath not shall be taken away even that which he hath."[24] To the credit of the Court, it refused to abide this pharisaical result. Yet no one was willing to take his stand upon this ground in requiring exemption for the Witnesses.

We can only speculate about the reasons why the Court declined to view the case as one involving discrimination among churches in the incidence of tax exemption. Those members of the Court who have frequently expressed their belief that the nonestablishment clause absolutely prevents any aid to any religion would have been forced, once they looked at the problem as one of discriminatory aid, to face squarely the whole array of religious tax exemptions, which in their total effect can hardly be dismissed as inconsequential. The meaning which they have been inclined to give to separation would have pressed them strongly to take the stand that the entire system of religious tax exemptions, quite apart from any discrimination, was invalid. What would have been the public reaction to such a holding? It is fair to assume that the Court would have been widely denounced as a bench of atheists and worse, that there would have been a storm of protest like that after the Dred Scott decision or the Great Income Tax case, and agitation for a constitutional amendment with a genuine possibility of success.

The Justices who have been more inclined toward judicial restraint in passing upon the policy choices open to legislatures would not be in quite so embarrassing a position, but it would be bad enough. If they took the view that as a matter of policy legislatures had considerable legitimate freedom in granting exemptions, they could still insist that exemptions could not be

[22] See e.g., 316 U.S. 584 at 616 and 319 U.S. 105 at 112–15.
[23] See 319 U.S. 105 at 138–40.
[24] Matthew 25 : 29.

discriminatory. In considering whether or not any exemption or refusal of exemption had a discriminatory bearing, they could hardly avoid an examination of the different forms and rates of taxes and exemptions from them. Yet for these Justices questions about tax policy are peculiarly questions for legislatures alone. As a practical matter, there might have been no flood of suits challenging these exemptions. Still, Mr. Everson, the New Jersey taxpayer who challenged "public rides to private schools," might not stand alone.[25] Even if there were only a trickle of challenges, rather than a flood, the Court might dam up most, if not all of it, by refusing to grant certiorari. But after these peddlers' tax cases this kind of solution might make the Court appear to be running down the hill after it had marched to the top and been dismayed by what it saw there. Judges no more than soldiers want to be derelict in their duty or even to appear to be.

DISCRIMINATION AMONG RELIGIOUS SECTS

The difficulties confronting the state when it attempts to differentiate among religious faiths may also be seen in a series of cases in which no question of financial aid is involved. Once again we begin with Jehovah's Witnesses and a unanimous Court.[26] The state of Connecticut had provided that

No person shall solicit money, services, subscriptions or any valuable thing for any alleged religious, charitable or philanthropic cause, from other than a member of the organization for whose benefit such person is soliciting or within the county in which such person or organization is located unless such cause shall have been approved by the secretary of the public welfare council. Upon application of any person in behalf of such cause, the secretary shall determine whether such cause is a religious one or is a bona fide object of charity or philanthropy and conforms to reasonable standards of efficiency and integrity, and, if he shall so find, shall approve the same and issue to the authority in charge a certificate to that effect. . . . Any person violating any provision of this section shall be fined not more than one hundred dollars or imprisoned not more than thirty days or both.

It seems appropriate that this case should come from a state of Yankee traders who had made the wooden nutmeg famous. What shall we say about such a law? It may be approved as a laudable effort to prevent men's altruistic instincts from being imposed upon by fraud. A rugged individualist might condemn it as paternalistic interference with about as private and individual a matter as can be conceived—one man's willingness to give something to another. A cynic might shrug it off as a futile attempt to keep a fool and his money from being parted as soon as they otherwise might be.

At any rate, one Newton Cantwell and his two sons, all Jehovah's Witnesses, were caught in the toils of this statute for soliciting money for the sect's pamphlets without the required permit. From these toils Justice Roberts freed them. The statute was bad, he and the rest of the Court

[25] As another recent case from New Jersey indicates: Doremus et al. v. Board of Education of Borough of Hawthorne et al., 342 U.S. 429 (1952).
[26] Cantwell et al. v. State of Connecticut, 310 U.S. 296 (1940).

thought, because it gave too much authority to decide whether an alleged religious cause was "really" religious and because it imposed a previous restraint. The law might punish a fraudulent solicitor after he had duped his victims (although this might be cold comfort for them) and it might also require a solicitor strange to the community to establish his identity and prove his authority to act for the cause.

Southern California provided a more troublesome incident.[27] That land where Luther Burbank once performed his wonders is now a breeding ground where other wizards by crossing the whimsical with the supernatural create hybrids as dazzling as anything the plant wizard ever brought forth. Of these one of the most skillful was one Guy W. Ballard, "alias Saint Germain, Jesus, George Washington, and Godfrey Ray King." His gift to the world he called the "I Am" movement. If we may shift the metaphor to another of southern California's great industries, this cult had box office appeal. After the hierophant's death his widow and a son carried on his work and solicited funds through the United States mails. They were indicted and convicted for using and conspiring to use the mails to defraud by false and fraudulent representations. Among these representations were claims of power to cure medically incurable diseases, claims that Saint Germain had made a visitation to Ballard in San Francisco, that Jesus and the forenamed saint had dictated to them some of the religious works sold through the mails, and other such-like claims of a kind familiar to any reader of the Bible.

The federal district judge who tried the case charged the jury that they could not consider whether or not these claims were true, that the only question was the good faith of defendants in making them, that is, whether or not the accused believed them to be true. The Court of Appeals reversed the conviction, holding that it was necessary to prove that some of the claims were false as well as to prove that the Ballards did not believe them. A bare majority of the Supreme Court, through Mr. Justice Douglas, reversed the appellate court. They agreed with the trial judge that it would be an invalid encroachment on the free exercise of religion to inquire into the truth of religious beliefs. Chief Justice Stone, joined by Justices Roberts and Frankfurter, dissented on the grounds that "The state of one's mind is a fact as capable of fraudulent misrepresentation as is one's physical condition or the state of his bodily health." They thought that the issue was simply one of the defendants' good faith, that the truth or falsity of the claims was not the issue, and that the jury has rightly disbelieved their good faith.

Justice Jackson also dissented, but for a quite different reason. Quoting William James, he insisted that the whole prosecution was improper and that the indictment should be dismissed. His words deserve quotation :[28]

I do not see how we can separate an issue as to what is believed from the considerations as to what is believable. . . . If religious liberty includes, as it must, the right to communicate such experiences to others, it seems to me an impossible task for juries to separate fancied ones from real ones, dreams from happenings,

27 United States v. Ballard *et al.*, 322 U.S. 78 (1944).
28 322 U.S. 78 at 92–95.

and hallucinations from true clairvoyance. . . . And then I do not know what degree of skepticism or disbelief in a religious representation amounts to actionable fraud. . . . Religious symbolism is even used by some with the same mental reservations one has in teaching of Santa Claus or Uncle Sam or Easter bunnies or dispassionate judges. It is hard in matters so mystical to say how literally one is bound to believe the doctrine he teaches and even more difficult to say how far it is reliance upon a teacher's literal belief which induces followers to give him money. . . . If the members of the sect get comfort . . . it is hard to say that they do not get what they pay for. . . . The chief wrong which false prophets do to their following is not financial. . . . There are those who hunger and thirst after higher values which they feel wanting in their humdrum lives. . . . When they are deluded and then disillusioned, cynicism and confusion follow. The wrong of these things, as I see it, is not in the money the victims part with half so much as in the mental and spiritual poison they get. But that is precisely the thing the Constitution put beyond the reach of the prosecutor . . .

To which one may reply generally that however telling the argument, the result proposed is disturbing, and specifically that the prosecutor was not trying to punish the Ballards for putting out "mental and spiritual poison" but for taking in money fraudulently. Even so, one is perplexed by these cases. One may think of them as involving the free exercise of religion. But what is also involved is a governmental effort to establish the truth of a religion. If possible it would seem to be preferable to leave the exposure of religious frauds to the Better Business Bureaus and the newspapers. The Connecticut statute exempted solicitation for a local cause or among members of the organization, doubtless in the belief that common neighborhood report could pretty well prevent abuse. Yet private persons undertaking to expose fraud may face difficult and expensive libel suits and also lack governmental subpoena powers. In the Ballard case, even neighborhood report cannot be relied upon to alert people about a nation-wide campaign.

Perhaps the only adequate answer to Justice Jackson's acute questions is that even the government's power to "dis-prefer" religions cannot safely be construed so absolutely as to disable it to deal with a problem like this. But as a wise compromise it might be better if the state instead of employing penal sanctions would limit itself to publicizing widely, after careful investigation, an official and of course privileged statement of its reasons for believing a religious appeal is fraudulent. That would leave the decision where possibly it better belongs—to the individual.

RELIGION AND PUBLIC EDUCATION

In discussing the New Jersey bus case we have already lightly palpated the sorest spot in American church-state relations today. Churches have long sensed that an opportunity to reach the minds of youth is essential to their vitality. Until a hundred years ago American society was indebted to churches for most of the educational opportunity that existed. The establishment of compulsory educational requirements coupled with the growth of free public education has been one of the major cultural changes in our history and a manifestation of democratic nationalism of which we can justly be proud. Although some of the founders of the American republic, notably Thomas Jefferson, believed in and hoped for this great experiment in equal opportunity, they did not, when they proposed the First Amendment, have to consider its bearing upon public support of religious education, either in church schools or in the public schools of the future. We do. Unfortunately our perplexities are our own; we cannot rest on the authority of the founders, for they had little or nothing to say on the question, and we delude ourselves if we think to settle the question automatically by invoking the broad phrases of the Constitution.

This is not the place to argue the desirability of all children receiving a common education in the public schools or maintaining the cultural diversity afforded by private schools, religious or otherwise. As a constitutional question that issue was settled by the Supreme Court thirty years ago.[29] The voters of Oregon, under the urging of the Ku Klux Klan, by initiative adopted a law which required, in effect, that all children in that state must attend only the public schools through the primary grades. In 1925 the Supreme Court unanimously invalidated this law.

The opinion is a curious one. It teaches us again how recent is the growth of freedom of association as a constitutional liberty. Two schools, one a private secular military academy and the other operated by an order of Roman Catholic nuns, sought to enjoin enforcement of the act. The Court found the act invalid on two grounds. First, it was an infringement of the liberty of parents to control the education of their children and choose other than public schools so long as they met the state's requirement that the child receive education of an adequate standard.[30] Sound as this view is, it is hard to see how the schools had standing to seek an injunction to protect someone else's rights. Second, the Court found that the act destroyed the school's property rights—they had a right to engage in the business of education.[31] So far at least as the Society of Sisters was concerned, this idea was a travesty of their Christian charity in their selfless efforts to maintain schools for orphans.

The real question they clearly raised was the right of a religious association to maintain schools for education of the children of their faith. Why did the Court not treat it as such? For one thing, only one week later the Court took its momentous first step in applying the First Amendment to the states; it was apparently unsure how far it wished to go.[32] For another, the Court held to the doctrine, with some justifiable embarrassment, that an

[29] Pierce et al. v. Society of Sisters of the Holy Names of Jesus and Mary, 268 U.S. 510 (1925).
[30] 268 U.S. 510 at 534–35.
[31] 268 U.S. 510 at 534.
[32] The Gitlow case had been reargued November 23, 1924, and was not decided until June 8, 1925. The Pierce case was argued March 16–17, 1925, and decided June 1, 1925.

association, whether or not a corporate person, could not claim the rights guaranteed by the First Amendment.[33] But the result of the case is clearly, and wisely, to hold that the right of a church to maintain its own schools is a part of the free exercise of religion that the Constitution guarantees.

The recognition of that right leads on to the present state of the problem. To what extent, if any, can the state aid these religious schools with public funds? This is not the place, either, to canvass the arguments brought forth for and against tax support, save as the constitutional command of separation of church and state affects them. In that respect only one defense of tax support demands our attention. This argument runs that although the state cannot support the religious portion of the church schools' programs, it can support any or all of their curriculum and activities that can be equated with secular education in the public schools. This argument does not seem candid. Religion in church schools (at least below the college level) is pervasive and is meant to be. Otherwise there would be little if any reason for their existence today. The distinction is even more evanescent than the one attempted in the Everson case. And of course if the state were to support a substantial part of the expenses of the parochial schools, it certainly could not be said that the added burdens on the taxpayer were a mere trifle which the law should dismiss as beneath its concern.

In practice the question is complicated by our federal system. In most states, cities, and school districts the adherents of churches which desire religious schools are a minority of the population, unlikely to win tax support at the polls. But in some areas they constitute a majority. Should tax support ever be voted there we are certain to have a painful demonstration of Madison's insight that no other public measure is likely to be more productive of communal bitterness. Yet it cannot be gainsaid that many citizens feel a need for some public aid to religious education, nor that denial of the felt need also produces bitterness. Perhaps some compromise can be found in communities where a majority desire public support of the church schools. A tax rate for religious schools might be set, with the provision that all taxpayers who requested it must be excused from payment of that portion of their tax. The state would thus act as a collection agency for a freewill fund for the parochial schools. It may be that some taxpayers of other religious faiths would be willing to contribute; this might be especially true of some large business taxpayers, who would wish to show this mark of respect for the religious belief of a large number of their employees. No doubt such a plan would entail additional effort on the part of the government. But extra effort on the part of the government is often the means by which we achieve those compromises which make the community viable.

Up to the present, however, the question of tax support has arisen in regard to what might be called "fringe benefits"—transportation, school books, the federal free school-lunch program, and the like. As long as the issue is so confined the courts will probably continue to offer the justifica-

---

[33] 268 U.S. 510 at 535.

tions now relied upon. These benefits have been granted and, when challenged, have been allowed by the courts precisely because they have been relatively modest in amount, can be conceived as social welfare measures in aid of students, and do not appear to support religious education as directly, immediately, or substantially as would a general grant to the schools. There are, as we have discovered, logical flaws in these justifications; nevertheless they may be judicial compromises which also contribute to the viability of the community. Prudence is not infrequently a greater gift in a statesman than flawless logic.

The other aspect of the question which has come before the courts is religious instruction in the public schools. As long as Justice Brewer's description of us as a Christian nation remains true, it is unlikely that courts will go on a crusade to root out every evidence of religious teaching in the public schools, particularly that which, like reading a few verses from the Bible, expounds no sectarian dogma and demands no expression of faith from students or teachers.[34] If separation of church and state were really a taboo upon any religious reference in the public schools, they would be forced to teach an impoverished literature, a truncated history, and a drabber music and art. Even the delights of Greek and Norse mythology would fall under the ban. An intelligent unbeliever would agree that so narrow-minded a denial of the riches of our cultural heritage to children would be worse than silly. These reflections should provide a needed perspective upon the two cases in which the Supreme Court has passed upon a form of religious instruction carried on with the assistance of the public school system.

Several decades ago religious leaders, Protestant, Jewish, and Catholic, devised plans different in detail but providing generally for the release of pupils from their regular classes in the public schools for an hour or two a week to attend classes in religious education, on the request of their parents. Those children whose parents did not request their release remained in school during this time, when regular classes were often suspended and replaced by "study halls." Those conducting the religious classes reported to the public school authorities the attendance at these classes, and presumably the truancy laws would apply to those who had been released for religious classes but failed to attend them.

This program of released-time religious education, as it has generally been called, was widely adopted both in rural and urban communities in many sections of the country . In many places the religious classes were held in available classrooms of the public schools. In some the public school authorities took an active part in endorsing and encouraging the program. In some they went beyond this to help supervise the program and to pay for some minor incidental expenses (such as supplying the request forms for use of parents and attendance report forms for the religious classes).

---

[34] Cf. Doremus *et al.* v. Board of Education of Borough of Hawthorne, 342 U.S. 429 (1952), in which the Court dismissed an appeal in a taxpayer's suit to obtain a declaratory judgment on this question.

64   GROUPS AND THE CONSTITUTION

In 1948 the United States Supreme Court invalidated a form of this plan in use in the public schools of Champaign, Illinois.[35] Mr. Justice Black delivered the opinion of the Court, with only Mr. Justice Reed dissenting. In Champaign the religious classes were held in the public school buildings. Mr. Justice Black mentioned this fact as one of the reasons for holding that the plan violated the requisite separation of church and state, since it did mean that a certain, although not clearly measurable, amount of tax money supported the plan. Of course in other cases the Court had held that it was proper or even necessary for municipalities to allow religious groups to use the parks and streets. Since these open public places, or spaces, are supported from taxes as are public school buildings, it would have been strange indeed to rest a holding in this case simply on the use of the public classrooms. Mr. Justice Black said: "The state also affords sectarian groups an invaluable aid in that it helps to provide pupils for their religious classes through use of the state's compulsory public school machinery. This is not separation of Church and State."[36]

Mr. Justice Reed in his dissent indicated that that was his understanding of the Court's holding, but his statement does bring out what, after all, the case came down to: "Under it, as I understand its language, children cannot be released or dismissed from school to attend classes in religion while other children must remain to pursue secular education."[37]

In other words, does it violate the principle of separate church and state to offer children a choice of an hour in school or an hour at a religious class? Certainly the state compelled no child to take religious instruction. Just as certainly it did compel him to stay in school if he did not. That element of governmental compulsion or coercion is, I think, an adequate justification for the Court's decision. But the analogy between a school and a jail ought not be pushed too far, nor should the opportunity for free public education be likened to a penalty.[38] That was not the serious penalty here. The worst pressure came not from the state but from society. A student or his parents might fear social disapproval, the pressure of public opinion, the tyranny of the majority, for not attending religious classes. The reluctance of the sponsors of released-time programs to rely on attracting children to their classes if their alternative were something else than sitting in lonely solitude in school hints that there is much truth in this analysis. In today's secular world some churchmen may be tempted to read Christ's plea, "Suffer little children to come unto Me" as "Herd little children unto Me if you must, just so you get them there." One does not have to be an atheist to feel that such clerical zeal is testy and distasteful, and to regret its triumph.

[35] People of State of Illinois *ex rel.* McCollum v. Board of Education of School Dist. No. 71, Champaign County, Ill. *et al.*, 333 U.S. 203 (1948).
[36] 333 U.S. 203 at 212.
[37] 333 U.S. 203 at 252.
[38] Cf. the remarks of Justice Jackson in Zorach *et al.* v. Clauson *et al.*, 343 U.S. 306 (1952) at 324.

But can the constitutional guaranty of freedom from religion wisely be used to protect men not only from governmental coercion but from having to stand up to unfavorable public opinion if they think their cause is right? The Court might well have pondered Justice Cardozo's earlier words before so concluding :[39]

To hold that motive or temptation is equivalent to coercion is to plunge the law in endless difficulties. . . . Till now the law has been guided by a robust common sense which assumes the freedom of the will as a working hypothesis in the solution of its problems.

On that view it is hard to deny that it would have been better for the Court not to have taken quite so absolute a stand and to have admitted that support of a released-time program was within the allowable area of public choice.

The concurring Justices were hesitant about the step they took. Mr. Justice Frankfurter emphasized that they were passing only upon the program before them, not on released time in the abstract; some other plans, he thought, might be valid.[40] Justice Jackson, on the other hand, was appalled by the prospect of an endless series of such cases, to decide which, he frankly admitted, "we can find no law but our own prepossessions."[41] Although he concurred, it is difficult from his opinion to understand why. He had actually written a thoughtful dissent.

This apprehension was borne out by events. Many gentlemen of the cloth forgot their Christian charity for an erring sinner in their denunciations of the Court. Even worse, many of the two thousand communities which had released-time programs went on a sit-down strike against the decision. Finding trivial distinctions between their programs and that condemned in the McCollum case, they kept their pupils sitting down to religious instruction.

In 1952 the Court decided the case of *Zorach* v. *Clauson* and upheld the released-time program of New York City.[42] Two of President Truman's recent appointees, Justices Clark and Minton, helped make up the new majority. His other appointees, Chief Justice Vinson and Mr. Justice Burton, switched sides to swell it. Mr. Justice Reed's view became the law, but he did not announce it. That was left to Mr. Justice Douglas, who also changed sides. He said, "We follow the McCollum case." He should have added, "to the ash heap." There was no important difference in the two plans except that in New York City the religious classes were not held in the public school buildings. He seized upon Mr. Justice Black's remark in the McCollum case about use of the classrooms as the holding, despite the protest of the author of that opinion that he had "attempted to make categorically clear" that that was not the basis of the earlier decision.

[39] Chas. C. Steward Mach. Co. v. Davis, 301 U.S. 548 (1937) at 589–90.
[40] 333 U.S. 203 at 225.
[41] 333 U.S. 203 at 237–38.
[42] 343 U.S. 306.

There might have been another important difference in the two cases. The opponents of the New York plan alleged and offered to prove that New York public school teachers used their official positions to bring coercive pressure on pupils to attend religious classes. The state court had not allowed them to offer this evidence, so, said Mr. Justice Douglas, there was no evidence to support the charge.[43] The opinion's rodomontade fully merits Justice Jackson's caustic reference to the "epithetical jurisprudence" of his "evangelistic brethren." What leads a Justice of the United States Supreme Court to that bland disregard of both facts and logic often attributed to men corrupted by power? Sometimes, if Mr. Justice Douglas's words in this case offer a clue, the answer may be—intellectual confusion:[44]

. . . the separation must be *complete and unequivocal.* The First Amendment within the scope of its coverage permits no exception; the *prohibition is absolute.* The First Amendment, however, does not say that in every and all respects there shall be a separation of Church and State. Rather, it *studiously defines the manner, the specific ways,* in which there shall be no concert or union or dependency one on the other.

To avoid such confusion we should all take careful thought.

The First Amendment is a compass pointing the way, not a code from which a mechanical jurisprudence can deduce with absolute certitude one and only one correct solution to each problem of church and state. It is an expression rather than the cause of the spirit of religious tolerance which is part of our heritage. That spirit characterizes American society as a "multanimity" which Professor Crane Brinton has described and has cogently argued a modern democracy must be.[45] The interpretation of the Amendment ought always to have as its end the preservation of the spirit of tolerance in our society.

[43] 343 U.S. 306 at 311; cf. Mr. Justice Frankfurter at 322.
[44] 343 U.S. 306 at 312; italics mine.
[45] Crane Brinton, *The Shaping of the Modern Mind* (New York, 1953), pp. 13–17, 257–58.

4

THE LESSON OF LABOR: IN UNION THERE IS STRENGTH

A student of American constitutional law today must approach a discussion of the constitutional law of association as it is applied to labor unions with a diffidence that his teachers and predecessors only one generation earlier scarcely felt or needed to feel. They could have read in a single day, with reasonable thoroughness, every important opinion of the United States Supreme Court upon the subject. It was not until 1895, after the birth of most of the present members of that Court, that the Supreme Court decided a labor case of first-rate importance.[1] After the Debs case, in which the Court denied habeas corpus to the leader of the great Pullman Strike, thirteen years elapsed before the next two labor opinions were handed down. In 1908 the Court invalidated a Congressional effort to forbid yellow-dog contracts in the Adair case[2] and also held the Danbury Hatters liable for triple damages under the Sherman Act.[3] Seven years later the Court reaffirmed its decision in the Adair case in *Coppage* v. *Kansas*[4] and in 1917 enjoined breaches of yellow-dog contracts.[5] In 1911 it had held Samuel Gompers in contempt for carrying on a secondary boycott in violation of the Sherman Act.[6] As the 1920's opened there were thus only six major labor cases in the Supreme Court's reports. In that decade ten more were added—an average of just one a year. Of these ten, half arose under the Sherman Act or the Clayton Act,[7] two under national railway labor legislation,[8] and three under state law.[9] As the troubled 'thirties began there were only sixteen cases, not all of which, strictly speaking, involved constitutional issues. Strange as it may at first seem, none was to be added to this list for another seven years, for in a period

---

[1] In re Debs, 158 U.S. 564 (1895).
[2] Adair v. United States, 208 U.S. 161 (1908).
[3] Loewe v. Lawlor, 208 U.S. 274 (1908). [4] 263 U.S. 1 (1915).
[5] Hitchman Coal and Coke Co. v. Mitchell, 245 U.S. 229 (1917).
[6] Gompers v. Bucks Stove and Range Co., 221 U.S. 418 (1911).
[7] Duplex Printing Press Co. v. Deering, 254 U.S. 443 (1921); American Steel Foundries v. Tri-City Central Trades Council, 257 U.S. 184 (1921); the two Coronado Coal decisions, at 259 U.S. 344 and 268 U.S. 295 in 1922 and 1925 respectively; United States v. Brims, 272 U.S. 549 (1926); Bedford Cut Stone Co. v. Journeymen Stone Cutters' Association, 274 U.S. 37 (1927).
[8] Pennsylvania Railroad System & Allied Lines Federation No. 90 v. Pennsylvania Railroad Co., 267 U.S. 203 (1925) and Texas & N. O. R. Co. *et al.* v. Brotherhood of Railway and Steamship Clerks, etc., *et al.*, 281 U.S. 548 (1930).
[9] Truax v. Corrigan, 257 U.S. 312 (1921); Wolff Packing Co. v. Court of Industrial Relations, 262 U.S. 522 (1923); Dorchy v. Kansas, 272 U.S. 306 (1926).

of severe unemployment labor unions can hardly be militant. As recently as 1937 these sixteen opinions of the Supreme Court, together with some accompanying dissents, contained just about everything of importance that our highest tribunal had had occasion to say about labor unions and the Constitution.

In some of its annual terms since that year the Court has decided more cases of major importance to labor unions than in all its history previous to the constitutional revolution of 1937, a revolution, be it noted, which was heralded by the Jones-Laughlin case upholding the National Labor Relations Act. Something portentous has happened, as today's constitutional scholar quickly discovers when he tries to fit this new matter into a crowded text or lecture.

What has happened is not simply an increase in the size or number of labor unions or in the scope of their activities. That increase, as a matter of fact, has followed upon these decisions. We have come to believe that the relations of labor unions with other persons in the community, many of them great corporate persons, and with the community at large, and even with their own members are questions of fundamental law. Before 1937 there were many judicial decisions on labor questions, but generally, if we may put it so, they were considered to belong to a subconstitutional order of problems. In terms familiar to the common lawyer they were described simply as cases of tort and of contract and sometimes of the criminal law.

As we have already noticed, the frequent appearance of religious cases in the Supreme Court reports is also a twentieth-century development. Later we shall see that this holds true for political parties as well. It is this phenomenon that warrants reference to the growth of a contemporary civil liberty. To the student of politics, however, these new cases on the churches and the parties, quite aside from the fact that there are not nearly so many of them for him to ponder, are much more familiar. The relations of church and state have been a principal theme of the political theorists he is accustomed to read at least as far back as St. Augustine's life, sixteen centuries ago. As for political parties, they are the stuff of his discipline. In grappling with the problems of labor union law he has few comparable resources of his own to fall back on.

He finds, moreover, that specialization has bred a host of specialists. Not only are there labor lawyers. There are labor economists, labor sociologists, labor psychologists, and even that new man, the public relations expert specializing in labor relations. Each brings his own insights. The student of constitutional law feels somewhat as his predecessors must have felt at the turn of the century when industrialism and due process spawned such specialties as tax law, corporation law, patent law, antitrust law, and administrative law. He may dislike being an amateur among professionals. Yet as befits a poor relation he must learn to be humble when, dressed in his thin and threadbare concepts, he approaches those whom the generosity of the research foundations or the opulence of an advocate's fee enable to wear richer garb. If he is wise he will not be resentful of his heavier work or his modest station. The reason for his diffidence lies in a remark addressed by Justice Holmes to his fellow jurists many years ago warning them sometimes to "hesitate where now they are confident, and see that really they were taking sides upon debatable and often burning questions."

Still and all, labor unions are associations; a distinct species of the genus we should readily grant, but scarcely *sui generis*. Sir Ernest Barker, no enemy of labor, was protesting against such an exaggerated claim when he asserted that under a sound political theory[10]

The State will proceed as far as possible on the principle of the equality of associations; it will not readily tolerate the possession by one association of a privileged and exceptional position which other associations do not enjoy.

The hypothesis advanced in the opening chapter is another way of expressing the same thought: that general principles can be formulated to serve as a just foundation for the constitutional law of associations, whether churches, unions, political parties, or, for that matter, sewing circles or business corporations.

The magnitude of the subject and a proper diffidence therefore set sharp limits to this chapter. It seems best to illustrate, from an abundance of materials, the application of each of these general principles to labor unions.

FREEDOM FROM GOVERNMENTAL RESTRAINTS

The first, the longest, and the hardest legal struggle for labor unions in the United States was to establish their claim to benefit from the principle that the rights of individuals to associate must be protected from governmental infringement. For almost a century that struggle was carried on to gain recognition of this right in the common law rather than in constitutional law. For many years common law judges in America as in England inclined to look at the early unions not under this principle but as groups who should not be allowed to use rights of association to the injury of society. They were treated as groups subversive of the economic interests of society because of their monopolistic purposes. To restrain them the judges applied the common law of criminal conspiracy. But in 1842 in the famous case of *Commonwealth* v. *Hunt*, Chief Justice Shaw of Massachusetts declined to hold that men were guilty of criminal conspiracy for merely belonging to a union. He admitted that the power of a union "might be used for useful and honorable purposes as well as for dangerous and pernicious ones." He said: "Such an association might be used to afford each other assistance in times of poverty, sickness and distress; or to raise their intellectual, moral and social condition; or to make improvement in their art; or for other purposes." As the years passed this view gained support and most courts ceased to punish men as common criminals merely for forming or joining a union.

The recognition by the courts of the workingman's right of association was, however, grudgingly made and precarious in practice. In many states throughout the nineteenth century and well into the twentieth unions and their members found that once they were organized, there was very little

[10] *Political Thought in England, 1848–1914*, p. 156.

self-help they could undertake through strikes or boycotts without falling foul of common or statute law in the states. State courts developed doctrines under which many union activities were held to be carried on for illegal objectives and were treated as civil conspiracies subjecting union members and leaders to damage suits instead of criminal punishment.

Far more effective as a restraint upon labor union activities than any common law or statutory remedies was the ancient and benign relief provided by equity, the injunction. Toward the end of the nineteenth century courts began to fashion it into a weapon in labor disputes. The ancient shield became a "terrible swift sword." The injunction became the "labor injunction." "Government by injunction" became a commonplace, if one-sided method of controlling industrial warfare. Courts have been severely criticized for this intervention, but what is not so often added is that for many years, for all that appears, the legislatures seemed largely content to allow the courts to govern. Indeed, many of the state judges who imposed injunctions upon labor were themselves elective officials.

The details of the history of labor in the United States lie outside our scope.[11] What is important to note is that by the time the United States Supreme Court entered the arena of labor disputes the doctrine that labor unions were illegal per se had already been dropped. The first great case in which the Supreme Court upheld a labor injunction, it should not be forgotten, was one in which the injunction had been obtained not by the employers but by the government of the United States in a critical situation and with the full approval of the President (nor did members of Congress stint their approbation). After the Debs case in 1895 the federal courts rapidly put the labor injunction at the behest of private employers also. The results were, in Justice Brandeis' words: ". . . to endow property with active, militant power which would make it dominant over men ; in other words, that under the guise of protecting property the employer was seeking sovereign power."[12]

Labor's chief effort to secure its rights of association against improper infringement by the national government had therefore to be directed to curbing the use of the labor injunction by the federal courts. Those who have a sense of history will find ground for reflection in the fact that in less than twenty years after the Debs decision Congress made an unsuccessful and probably half-hearted attempt to limit abuses in the Clayton Act, and that within a generation after that decision the battle was won with the Norris-LaGuardia Act of 1932. To a significant extent the states followed the Congressional lead.

By the time the Supreme Court passed upon either state or federal anti-injunction acts President Roosevelt had begun his second term, and events had far outrun the decisions which only a few years before would have seemed epoch-making in labor law and constitutional law. It was appro-

[11] For a concise account of this history cf. Charles O. Gregory, *Labor and the Law* (New York, 1946), particularly chaps. 3–8.

[12] In Truax v. Corrigan, 257 U.S. 312 at 368.

priate but almost anticlimactic that Justice Brandeis, who had written a classic
dissent in 1921 in *Truax* v. *Corrigan*, when the Court had held that Arizona
had violated the Fourteenth Amendment by restricting her courts in the
granting of labor injunctions, should in 1937 uphold for the Court the validity
of Wisconsin's "little Norris-LaGuardia act."[13] The following year the
Court sustained the federal act.[14] Curiously enough the case did not involve
a labor union. The Court held that the act's definition of a labor dispute
included the picketing of stores in Washington, D.C., by an association of
Negroes to induce employers to hire members of their race, and that their
efforts could not be enjoined by the federal courts. The fight for economic
justice had produced an unexpected victory in the struggle against racial
discrimination.

With this legislation and these decisions the rights of labor to associate
and to act in concert were fairly admitted by the national government and
many of the states. In those jurisdictions courts were limited in their use of
injunctions in labor disputes to those cases in which they found that by no
other course could another principle of the law of association be vindicated.
That principle holds that the rights of association should be limited when
the effect of their use is to work undue injury to the interests of other persons. Of course there is no magic formula by which either legislatures, courts,
or philosopher-kings can resolve clashes between these two principles in
all concrete situations, but the Norris-LaGuardia Act makes an impressive
effort to provide as just a guidance to the courts as can be set forth in general
terms and holds the courts and the parties to a careful procedure designed
to ensure attention to them.[15] More cannot reasonably be demanded of a
statute.

Not all of the states enacted such a law. Alabama was one which did
not. Should she and some of her sister states be allowed to continue to deny
rights of association to labor that Congress had recognized? Or could there
be drawn from the Constitution itself a guaranty of these rights which made
them no mere matter of legislative grace, state or national, and raised them
to fundamental commands which no state in the Union could disregard?
These questions frame the great constitutional issue which the Supreme
Court of its own volition undertook to settle in the series of picketing cases
beginning with *Thornhill* v. *Alabama* in 1940.[16] The supremacy of the
national Constitution interpreted by a national judiciary was asserted in
behalf of the rights of association for labor by a Court unanimous except
for Justice McReynolds, who dissented, as by then was his habit, and without opinion. The heart of Justice Murphy's opinion deserves quotation:[17]

In the circumstances of our times the dissemination of information concerning
the facts of a labor dispute must be regarded as within that area of free discussion

---

[13] Senn v. Tile Layers' Protective Union, 301 U.S. 468 (1937).
[14] New Negro Alliance v. Sanitary Grocery Co., 303 U.S. 552 (1938).
[15] Cf. Gregory, *op. cit.*, chap. 7.
[16] 310 U.S. 88 (1940) ; cf. the companion case of Carlson v. People of State of California, 310 U.S. 106 (1940).
[17] 310 U.S. 88 at 102–3.

that is guaranteed by the Constitution. . . . Free discussion concerning the conditions in industry and the causes of labor disputes appears to us indispensable to the effective and intelligent use of the processes of popular government to shape the destiny of modern industrial society.

The rule announced in Thornhill's case has been severely criticized by some experts in labor law.[18] Many of these attacks are misdirected. Picketing, it is urged, is not "*just* speech" and should not be protected under the First Amendment. But the Court had not said or even implied in the Thornhill case that it was, and subsequent cases made clear that picketing involves other action than speech.[19] It is the critics, not the Court, who have been inconsistent, for they imply that picketing is "*just* something else," although they can hardly deny what anyone's eyes and ears inform him—that oral or written communication does occur on the picket line. At any rate, they next say, the speech involved in picketing should not be brought under the First Amendment because that must result in giving it absolute freedom from any regulation, and some of them have gleefully pointed to later cases in which the Court has sustained regulation or prohibition of some picketing as proof of the unsoundness of the doctrine, of the Court's inconsistency, and of its retreat from the Thornhill case. All this, of course, is battering down a straw man, for these critics must be aware that long before the Thornhill case it was a commonplace that not all speech is given absolute protection by the First Amendment, and that in the Thornhill opinion itself the Court indicated that circumstances might justify limitation of speech on the picket line as elsewhere.[20] Finally, they say, there was no need for the new doctrine, for picketing could be perfectly well handled under the rules of tort law formerly employed. Needless to say, the strident tone of some of these protests suggests that the new concept in contrast to the former rules has made a substantial difference in the way in which these cases are decided—a difference, which these critics dislike, in favor of labor.

A legitimate criticism of the Thornhill case is less important. Justice Murphy there asserted that any limitations on picketing would have to be tested by the clear and present danger standard. This is not the place to enter into a critique of "clear and present danger." It is true that in later picketing cases the Court has not used that test. The problem generally posed by picketing is whether it injures the economic interests of others who are so indirectly involved in the labor dispute that they should be given relief.[21] The clear and present danger test can offer little analytical insight into this problem, just as it can offer little in some other free speech problems

[18] Notably by Ludwig Teller; cf. his articles "Picketing and Free Speech," 56 *Harvard Law Review* 180, and "Picketing and Free Speech: A Reply," 56 *Harvard Law Review* 532.

[19] Cf. Mr. Justice Douglas, concurring, in Bakery and Pastry Drivers and Helpers Local 802 of International Brotherhood of Teamsters *et al.* v .Wohl *et al.*, 315 U.S. 769 (1942) at 776–77.

[20] 310 U.S. 88 at 105.

[21] The one picketing case in which "a context of violence" led the Court to discuss at length the clear and present danger test is Milk Wagon Drivers Union of Chicago,

which are very different from that out of which it arose and for which it was originally devised.

So thoughtful and fair a critic as Professor Charles O. Gregory makes two more fundamental points. First, he quite correctly observes that even peaceful picketing is an intentional exertion of social pressure, and that many people observe a picket line not out of any coldly rational analysis of their own self-interest, but through sentimentality or other more or less nonrational reasons.[22] This kind of response, however, is hardly unique to picketing; political speeches and religious sermons may provoke emotional responses. Professor Gregory calls this response to picketing coercion, but is this not to give coercion an unduly extended connotation? Does it not "confuse coercion with motive or temptation?"

His second criticism really comes to this: that legislatures and not courts should make labor policy.[23] It is a variant of the general argument that judicial review is a limitation on democracy and a somewhat illegitimate one. But he does not make that general argument; indeed, he rejects it. If courts ought to protect speech under the First Amendment, and speech does occur on the picket line, does one really give sufficient grounds for excluding that speech from any constitutional protection whatsoever by labeling it an unconventional kind of speech? Unconventional speech is the kind most likely to need judicial protection.

Two other cases in which the Supreme Court has extended constitutional protection to labor unions under the First Amendment in order to ensure their rights of assembly and communication in situations that did not involve picketing may help to clarify the Court's doctrine in regard to picketing. One of these is *Hague* v. *Committee for Industrial Organization*,[24] the other *Thomas* v. *Collins*.[25] The first, decided in 1939, arose out of the actions of the administration of Mayor Frank Hague, who was quoted as saying, "I am the law in Jersey City," to prevent efforts to organize labor unions in that large industrial city. City ordinances prohibited distributing handbills on the streets and the holding of public assemblies without first obtaining a permit from the city Director of Public Safety. The city authorities not only used these ordinances in a discriminatory fashion to refuse any opportunity for public discussion of the rights guaranteed by the National Labor Relations Act, but also in a completely lawless manner broke up peaceful meetings and drove labor organizers and other speakers out of the city. The CIO, the American Civil Liberties Union, and individuals sued to restrain the city authorities from continuing to violate their rights under the Constitution of the United States. They brought their suit under provisions of the Civil

---

Local 753, *et al.* v. Meadowmoor Dairies, Inc., 312 U.S. 287 (1941). Contrast, e.g., the most important of the picketing cases following upon Thornhill, Carpenters and Joiners Union of America, Local No. 213, *et al.* v. Ritter's Cafe *et al.*, 315 U.S. 722 (1942) for a clear recognition of the necessity for balancing the economic interests of members of the public as well as of the disputants in these picketing cases.

[22] Gregory, *op. cit.*, pp. 346–48.   [23] *Ibid.*, pp. 334–37, 348–49.
[24] 307 U.S. 496 (1939).   [25] 323 U.S. 516 (1945).

Rights Act, enacted during Reconstruction, that forbade anyone acting under color of state law to deprive persons of rights secured by the Constitution or to deprive citizens of the privileges and immunities so guaranteed. Mayor Hague was the boss of the state and a vice-chairman of the Democratic National Committee. Without the intervention of the federal courts it appeared doubtful that there was any immediate prospect of overcoming his forcible interference with the rights of the unions.

The Supreme Court affirmed the injunction that had been granted, with some modifications. Some members of the Court thought that the decision should be rested on the statutory power to protect the privileges and immunities of citizens of the United States from abridgment; some relied on the broader and more traditional ground of protecting the rights of personal liberty guaranteed to all persons. The difference was more than a narrow technical matter, but is not a vital one in our context. In that context what is significant is the assertion of the supremacy of the national Constitution to prevent local authorities from illicit interference with the rights of association of labor.

The result, it is of some interest for our general theme to notice, was accomplished even though the Court held that the two associations could not maintain the suit, for they could not claim these rights or privileges which belong only to natural persons.[26] The suit still did not fail, for individual officers of the associations had been parties to the suit. In this left-handed way the unions' rights were protected. It seems unfortunate that in reaching a sound result in this case the Court did not take the opportunity to examine critically the shibboleth that an association can claim property rights but not liberty under the Constitution or under provisions of general remedial law like the Civil Rights Acts.

In *Thomas* v. *Collins*, decided in 1945, it is of interest that four of the five Justices who had affirmed the injunction in the Hague case were still on the bench, and that three of these four, Chief Justice Stone and Justices Roberts and Reed, dissented in the latter case, joined by Mr. Justice Frankfurter. Mr. Justice Black was the only member of the Court in the majority in both cases; in *Thomas* v. *Collins* he was joined by Justices Douglas and Murphy, by Justice Jackson, who concurred hesitantly, and by Justice Rutledge, who wrote the opinion of the Court. Although *Thomas* v. *Collins* has never been overruled, it seems unlikely that it would have been decided as it was if it had arisen either six years after 1945 or six years before, when the Hague case was decided. For *Thomas* v. *Collins* was decided upon an absolute view of the First Amendment that went further than the decision in the Thornhill case and well beyond anything needful to protect labor's rights of association.

As part of a general statute for the control of labor unions the state of Texas had required that anyone soliciting persons to become members of a labor union must register his name and that of the union for which he was acting as an organizer with the Secretary of State. That official was to furnish to the solicitor an identity card; to solicit without this card was an offense.

[26] 307 U.S. 496 at 514, 527.

The Secretary of State had no discretion to deny a card to anyone who registered; his duty was purely ministerial. There was thus no problem of the state's attempting to pass upon the character or qualifications of an organizer,[27] nor was the state exacting large fees which would raise the question of a "tax" or financial burden on speech. The Texas law contained other provisions restrictive of union rights and evidenced less than enthusiasm toward organized labor, but unless the requirement of registration and identification in itself were to be construed as an unlawful prior restraint, this provision would seem unobjectionable. Although unobjectionable it may be unnecessary, but it is scarcely customary for courts to hold that an excess of caution is unconstitutional. Besides, as our review of some of the problems connected with religious or charitable solicitation suggested, there may be good reasons for protecting the public from solicitors who make fraudulent claims to represent an organization.

R. J. Thomas, then a prominent officer of the United Automobile Workers, went to Texas for the expressed and well-publicized purpose of testing this provision. He refused to register and procure an identity card before speaking to a meeting of oil workers in an organizing drive.[28] After addressing them on the benefits of union membership, he urged them to join a union of petroleum workers and specifically solicited one man present to join the union. He was arrested and given token punishment for violation of the law. This was the case.

A bare majority of the Court held the provision unconstitutional. They insisted that the solicitation for which the act required registration might be construed to include a speech on the value of unionism, since a speech of that kind might persuade men to join a union, and that so construed it would be illegal prior censorship of speech. The trouble with this position was that the highest court of Texas, whose right and duty it is to construe the state statutes authoritatively, had denied that the law required registration from one who merely desired to speak in behalf of trade unionism.[29] Identification was required only of those who solicited individuals to join and were prepared to sign them up. Mr. Thomas had not only made a speech, but had deliberately also solicited in this narrow sense, and it was for this latter act that he had been found in violation of the law.

The majority opinion also contained intimations that when speed was of the essence in a union-organizing drive, a hostile state official might delay the issuance of the required card. Such acts sometimes happen, and when they do, it is often difficult to obtain the proof required in a court of law that the act is deliberate and willful misconduct. Even if proof is established, relief may come too late to be of practical value. In this way, the majority seemed to fear, this provision might be used in somewhat the same fashion

[27] Cf. Hill *et al.* v. State of Florida *ex rel.* Watson, Attorney General, 325 U.S. 538 (1945).

[28] Thomas' opponents did not wait for him to break the law; they secured an injunction forbidding him to solicit without a permit. It is hard to estimate how much this fact affected the majority's view of the case, but equally hard to believe that it did not have considerable influence.

[29] 323 U.S. 516 at 524–25, 549.

and to the same effect as the labor injunction in the past. But there is more than one trouble with this argument. It assumes, contrary to the general and sound rule, that public officials will act illegally. If there had been evidence of a course of conduct of this kind in delaying issue of the cards, this assumption might have been justified. But no evidence was offered of a single instance of such misconduct. Certainly Mr. Thomas could not claim that he had been so treated, for he had refused to apply for a card.

Justice Roberts for the minority based the dissent heavily on Texas' argument, and thereby did not contribute to clarification of the issue as he might have. The state stressed that its enactment was merely the regulation of a commercial or business calling. But even if this be true, is it the decisive question? This question of commercialism we have already seen beclouding the issues in some of the religious cases before the Court.[30] If the state thought that there was danger of persons fraudulently soliciting for the Red Cross and pocketing the contributions, would it be improper for the state to require the registration and identification of Red Cross solicitors, even though the proceeds went to a nonprofit association? And if there were such a danger of a fraud would not the Red Cross welcome a law protecting its interests as well as those of the public? It seems unlikely that *Thomas* v. *Collins* will have the practical impact on the control of such practices that the voluminous controversial literature on its doctrine would suggest, and there are good reasons why it should not.

With the ending of abuses of the labor injunction the rights of association against improper governmental infringement were about as well established for labor unions as they can be. There government might properly have stopped, for the other two principles beneficial to associations are not constitutional mandates but simply permit government to take additional steps toward aiding associations. Government may extend to associations public powers and privileges; it may also create new legal duties which private persons must observe toward associations. The testimony of John L. Lewis, president of the United Mine Workers, before the Senate Labor Committee in 1953 provides an illustration of the difference. He proposed that Congress repeal the Labor Management Relations Act of 1947, which represents Congressional enforcement of these two permissive principles, because it also utilizes the two principles restrictive of associational rights, and rely upon the Clayton Act and the Norris-LaGuardia Act. Unions, he contended, have grown strong enough as a result of the governmental privileges and the protection against private interference afforded them by the original Wagner Act to achieve their purposes now without this assistance so long as their rights are protected against governmental infringement.

[30] Justice Roberts had introduced this distinction in a brief opinion in the curious case of Valentine v. Chrestensen, 316 U.S. 52 (1942). The general proposition that when speech or writing is motivated by hopes of private profit it has an inferior claim to constitutional protection, which certainly seems to be the implication of that case, deserves careful examination rather than the uncritical acceptance it received there. The difficulties it has spawned can be seen in these later cases. Perhaps we should coin the maxim that trivial cases make bad law—when they are disposed of too casually.

FREEDOM FROM PRIVATE COERCION

Employers have of course placed greater obstacles in the way of union growth and activity than government. Indeed, the most serious criticism of the labor injunction has been that it put too much public power at the disposal of private persons too hastily and carelessly. Interestingly enough, the first important Congressional act to assist labor unions was not directed at governmental infringements of their rights, but sought to protect the right to be a union member from interference by private employers. This was the Erdman Act of 1898, which was the matured Congressional response to the Great Pullman Strike of 1894. Section ten of that act forbade interstate railways to exact the hated yellow-dog or iron-clad contract as a condition of employment or to discriminate against employees on account of their union membership. In *Adair* v. *United States* a divided Supreme Court invalidated this provision.[31] Of course when the state establishes a new legal right for an association or its members, conversely it imposes a new legal duty upon others or, one may say, replaces their former right or liberty to act as they choose with a legal duty. Those who must fulfill the new legal duty may ask the courts to declare it an unreasonable deprivation of their liberty or property. Writing for the majority near the close of a long judicial career often marked by sturdy respect for individual rights and sympathy for the underdog, Justice Harlan could not conceive the question as one of freedom of association from overreaching private interference. Instead the law seemed to him an unjust abridgment of the freedom of contract of the employee as well as the employer. The employee was perfectly free to accept the employer's terms or seek work elsewhere. In *Coppage* v. *Kansas* the Court reiterated this stand, but Justice Pitney betrayed a more modern recognition that the problem did involve rights of association, if only by his almost sarcastic remark that a state had no constitutional power to pass laws for the "upbuilding of unions."[32]

With their right to exact these antiunion promises from their employees assured, employers next moved to recover damages from union organizers who induced employees to breach their yellow-dog contracts by joining a union, and even to restrain them altogether from speaking to their employees in order to organize them. With scant regard for the issue of free speech presented, the Supreme Court imposed this further restraint upon the right of the unions to solicit members.[33]

In order to destroy this almost impenetrable judicial barrier to union growth some of the states and Congress in the Norris-LaGuardia Act moved more cautiously but effectively. Instead of forbidding yellow-dog contracts altogether, they simply declared them against public policy and so instructed the courts not to enforce them or penalize organizers for inducing their breach. In a changing political and legal climate of opinion courts bowed to this renewed expression of legislative will.

---

[31] 208 U.S. 161 (1908).   [32] 236 U.S. 1 at 16.
[33] Hitchman Coal and Coke Co. v. Mitchell, 245 U.S. 229 (1917).

The National Labor Relations Act of 1935 went far beyond any previous American legislation in developing the principle of protection of the rights of association against private interference. So much careful scholarship has been lavished upon this epochal statute that it would be vain here to enter into its details. But let us recall the brief words which are the heart of the act and the magistral phrases that are the heart of Chief Justice Hughes's opinion sustaining it. The act made it an unfair labor practice for employers to deny the rights of association guaranteed in the famous section 7 :

Employees shall have the right to self-organization, to form, join, or assist labor organizations, to bargain collectively through representatives of their own choosing, and to engage in concerted activities, for the purpose of collective bargaining or other mutual aid or protection.

Quoting these words the Chief Justice said :[34]

Thus, in its present application, the statute goes no further than to safeguard the right of employees to self-organization and to select representatives of their own choosing for collective bargaining or other mutual protection without restraint or coercion by their employer. *That is a fundamental right.* Employees have as clear a right to organize and select their representatives for lawful purposes as the respondent has to organize its business and select its own officers and agents. Discrimination and coercion to prevent the free exercise of the right of employees to self-organization and representation is a proper subject for condemnation by competent legislative authority.

The Chief Justice's reasoning is a landmark in the American constitutional law of association.[35] Because these rights of association are "fundamental rights," constitutional rights which the government may not unlawfully abridge, the state in turn has the constitutional right to require private persons not to abridge them either.

Far-reaching as the legal, political, and economic results of this doctrine as applied to trade unions have already revealed themselves to be, it would be shortsighted to presume that we stand today at the terminus of this development instead of in its midst. Whether or not the full potentialities of this doctrine will be consummated, or how or to what purpose, no one can yet foresee. The day may come when the protection of rights of association from private interference will be raised from the plane of legislative discretion to the level of constitutional imperatives judicially enforced. Or the rights against private interference now being defined, specified, and elaborated may some day be translated back into rights against governmental interference. These legal developments now seem unlikely. Certainly they would be fundamental changes in our constitutional theory and practice. But the law does not lead a life of its own, and if men should change their eco-

[34] National Labor Relations Board v. Jones & Laughlin Steel Corp., 301 U.S. 1 (1937) at 33.
[35] Cf. Edward S. Corwin, *Constitutional Revolution, Ltd.* (Claremont, Calif., 1941), pp. 66–67.

nomic goals and political outlook enough, they might forge new concepts of association to reach them.

The sudden thrust of the Wagner Act against private interference with union rights produced a reaction. Among the many types of employer interference that became unfair labor practices subject to restraint one may be singled out for comment, for it epitomizes the sweep of the act, the delicacy required for a fair balancing of interests, and the reasons for reaction. That is the question of "employers' free speech," as it is usually called. The National Labor Relations Act itself did not specifically or explicitly condemn an employer's communicating to his employees his opposition to organization as an unfair labor practice; what it forbade him to do was to "interfere with, restrain, or coerce employees" in the exercise of their rights.

But the National Labor Relations Board rightly considered that under some circumstances such speech might be coercive. If an employer told his workers that he would permanently close down his plant if they organized, there would likely be a coercive effect, even though, if he were stubborn enough to carry out his threat, he would have the right to go out of business. The Board also believed that it should consider the employer's words as part of the evidence when an unfair labor practice was charged to see if they helped to establish a coercive course of conduct. These enterprises were risky enough, but the attitudes of the agency and some of the formulas it conceived must have compounded the difficulty.

These difficulties may be gathered from a scholarly study by one of the most sympathetic and well-informed interpreters of the Board's work.[36] She says that in the beginning the Board adopted a theory of "neutrality" under which the employer's duty was to "keep his hands off" (a genteel euphemism for keeping his mouth shut) while his employees were organizing. In short, the Board extended the meaning of coercion to influence. The difficulty is akin to that we noticed in the released-time religious education cases and in the argument against treating picketing as free speech. This theory of "neutrality" the Supreme Court not unnaturally rejected by implication in the first case of the kind it took for review.[37]

The attitude with which many members of the agency approached their task is probably suggested more tellingly than the author intended when she says: "The function of the Board . . . was to protect the right of workers. . . . Protection of the basic right of free speech, on the other hand, was in the hands of the Courts."[38] Inasmuch as the courts considered themselves bound by the terms of the act to uphold the findings of the Board if they were supported by substantial evidence, whether or not this was the preponderant evidence, one is left to wonder where the right of free speech was given its full weight.

[36] Harry A. Millis and Emily Clark Brown, *From the Wagner Act to Taft-Hartley* (Chicago, 1950), pp. 174–89.

[37] *Ibid.*, pp. 176–78; the case is National Labor Relations Board v. Virginia Electric and Power Co., 314 U.S. 469 (1941).

[38] *Ibid.*, p. 175.

Despite widespread dissatisfaction the Board opposed any amendment as dangerous. Some of the members of the Supreme Court took occasion in the case of *Thomas* v. *Collins* to give a none too veiled warning to the Board on its treatment of this issue.[39] Nevertheless the Board proceeded to hold that an employer's assembling his employees to speak to them on his own time and at his expense, apparently without reference to the content of his communication, was an unfair labor practice.[40] Partly as a result of reversals by the federal courts of appeals and of severe criticism in Congress the Board became more reluctant to condemn employers' speech. "By 1947," we are told, "the Board was giving the benefit of the doubt to free speech, except where it found clear coercion, and this was as it should be."[41] But if the First Amendment is to be given its proper weight, this was how it should have been from the day the Board began to function in 1935, not simply when the Board got around to it more than a decade later.

By 1947 it was too late anyway. The Taft-Hartley Act expressed the reaction on this point as on many others. It provided:

The expressing of any views, argument, or opinion, or the dissemination thereof . . . shall not constitute or be evidence of an unfair labor practice under any of the provisions of this Act, if such expression contains no threat of reprisal or force or promise of benefit.

This provision, it has been urged, goes too far in disabling the Board from protecting workers against coercive private conduct. Perhaps it does, but if it does, it would appear that the Board itself was largely responsible for provoking the reaction weakening labor's protection against employer interference. The reaction in the Taft-Hartley Act may at many points in turn have gone too far. One inference from the history of employers' free speech seems clear: in this delicate, controversial, and continuing application of the rights of association to labor relations those who press a momentary advantage too hard are likely to find at the next turn of the wheel that they have lost more than they had gained.

The principle that private interference with rights of association may be restrained carries with it as a necessary corollary the power to require private persons to enter into legal relations with an association. The scheme of the National Labor Relations Act gives an important illustration of this corollary in the duty imposed upon employers to bargain in good faith collectively with the representatives of a majority of their employees. Of course there would be no sense in imposing the duty unless there was a reasonable expectation that agreement would result. Naturally enough, the courts have held that if an agreement is reached, good faith requires an overly squeamish employer to put it in writing and sign it.[42] Still, the duty is only to bargain, not to make a bargain; to negotiate, not to agree.

[39] Particularly Justice Jackson, 323 U.S. 516 at 548.
[40] Millis and Brown, *op. cit.*, p. 184.
[41] *Ibid.*, p. 188.
[42] H. J. Heinz Co. v. National Labor Relations Board, 311 U.S. 514 (1941).

If the state can require the employer to enter this far into legal relations with a union, why can it not require him to enter this much further into legal relations and make a bargain? To go this much further, one must recognize, would be to impose compulsory arbitration upon both union and employer, for if having a duty to make a bargain they failed to make one, almost inevitably the next step would be for the state to impose terms. To do this, the Supreme Court said in 1923, would violate both the employer's constitutional property rights and the worker's constitutional liberty to strike.[43] That decision has not been overruled, but the concept upon which it was based has been discarded, for it was held that at least compulsory arbitration could not be imposed on businesses not "affected with a public interest." Since then, and even before, in both world wars we have had arbitration voluntary in form but very nearly compulsory in fact.[44] It would therefore be rash to predict what extension of the requirement of union and management to enter into legal relations the future may see. But it is noteworthy that Congress in rejecting President Truman's plea to draft railway strikers into the army, and the Supreme Court in overturning his seizure of the steel mills prevented what in effect would have been compulsory arbitration. Yet in the Steel Seizure[45] case no member of the Court doubted that Congress could do what the President had attempted, as long as the public footed the bill. But then the public, as taxpayer or consumer, always does.

Even the duty to bargain has raised a question of transcendent importance for the future of our economy. Bargaining in good faith, the courts hold, means that the employer must do more than meet a union proposal with stony silence; he must offer a counterproposal. How can the subject matter of these proposals be limited? What management thinks of as the prerogatives of management have already been thrown upon the bargaining table. Distressing as that fact is to many businessmen, the Taft-Hartley Act made no effort to keep any of the "prerogatives of management" off the bargaining table. The duty to enter into legal relations with a labor union thus continues to hold the potentialities of great transformations in our economic system.[46] But if union pension funds are invested in stock of the employer corporation, the day may come when it will be hard to tell who is entering into legal relations with whom at the bargaining table.

GOVERNMENTAL AID TO UNIONS

By another principle of the law of association government may promote the opportunities of individuals to associate by appropriate means and may grant appropriate privileges and powers to associations when the public interest will be fostered by doing so. For the past forty years, and especially in the last twenty, organized labor in the United States has received incal-

---

[43] Wolff Packing Co. v. Court of Industrial Relations, 262 U.S. 522 (1923).

[44] Edward S. Corwin, *Total War and the Constitution* (New York, 1947), pp. 55–62.

[45] Youngstown Sheet and Tube Co. *et al.* v. Sawyer, 343 U.S. 579 (1952).

[46] For a recent case which is quite suggestive in regard to these problems cf. National Labor Relations Board v. American Nat. Ins. Co., 343 U.S. 395 (1952).

culable benefits from the application of this principle. Some of these benefits belong to the realm of politics rather than law, but the legal position of labor has been immensely though indirectly strengthened by them, and the student of law should not be unaware of them. A few illustrations will suffice. The national government and state governments have encouraged organization of workers through propaganda. Symbolism is a powerful kind of propaganda, and it is not without interest that Labor has one of our generally observed secular holidays along with the Declaration of Independence, the war dead, and George Washington. Abraham Lincoln barely makes this select list; Christopher Columbus and the Constitution miss it; and Labor even takes precedence over Mother and Father, who have each had to settle for a Sunday. More important was the establishment of the United States Department of Labor in 1914 as a means of investigating and publicizing labor's problems and voicing labor's interests and desires to the rest of the government and to the public.

Partly as a result of the Department's efforts many measures have become law that have been of great indirect aid in building and maintaining labor union membership. Among the most important of these laws is a large group which in various ways reduces the competitive pressure in the labor market from what labor economists call substandard labor. To illustrate, one may cite the restriction of immigration, minimum wage and child labor laws, the Walsh-Healey Act for payment of prevailing, that is, union wage scales on government contracts, bans on the commercial sale of convict-made goods, and old-age and unemployment compensation.

Our concern must be limited to the more direct encouragement and grant of privileges which the national government has offered to the unions. Of these by far the most important are, first, the privilege of resorting to the National Labor Relations Board, and second, the right of a certified union to be the exclusive representative of all the employees in a bargaining unit for the purposes of collective bargaining.

In regard to the privilege of resort to the Board, two facts so obvious that they can easily be overlooked stand out. In the first place, although individual employees can resort to the Board, if unions could not be parties before the Board the administration of a national labor relations policy would be greatly complicated if not impossible. The same result would follow if the rights and remedies provided in the act were left, as they theoretically could be, to enforcement through the ordinary judicial process without resort to an administrative agency.

Resort to the Board has been called a privilege, and so it is, in the sense that Congress was not legally obligated to provide it nor is Congress any more bound to maintain it. The restrictive regulation of labor unions in the Taft-Hartley Act is sometimes justified on the grounds that Congress may make the privilege of resort to the Board conditional upon union compliance with these regulations. I do not mean to suggest that it cannot, and should like to defer a fuller examination of the problem of conditional privileges to the chapter on subversive associations. But it is appropriate to say this much here. If Congress had provided the same rights but left unions to resort to the courts to enforce them, we would probably not so readily assume that this much more traditional privilege of access to the courts could be conditioned in any way that Congress saw fit. The argument of conditional privileges pressed to its logical extreme, as some are wont to press it, leads to startling consequences, consequences truly subversive of our theory and practice of government.

Should a union certified as the choice of a majority of the employees of a defined bargaining unit be permitted to represent exclusively not merely those who voted for it or those who are members of the union, but all the employees in the unit? This question will evoke for the student of political theory all the important and difficult problems of representation theory discussed over the centuries from Aristotle and Marsilius of Padua to John Stuart Mill. Perhaps some of the confusion and inadequacy in discussion of this problem and the resulting question of the nature of a collective bargaining contract negotiated by a union under this privilege results from a failure of specialists in labor relations to profit from available political wisdom.

It is crucial to recognize at the outset the truth of the conclusion set forth by Justice Jackson in his searching opinion in *J. I. Case Co.* v. *National Labor Relations Board* in 1944, in which the Court sustained an order of the Board declaring that the company had committed an unfair labor practice by refusing to bargain with a certified union despite the company's defense that it had individual labor contracts with some 75 percent of its employees. He said:[47]

The very purpose of providing by statute for the collective agreement is to supersede the terms of separate agreements of employees with terms which reflect the strength and bargaining power and serve the welfare of the group. . . . But it is urged that some employees may lose by the collective agreement, that an individual workman may sometimes have, or be capable of getting, better terms than those obtainable by the group and that his freedom of contract must be respected on that account . . . but we find the mere possibility that such agreements might be made no ground for holding generally that individual contracts may survive or surmount collective ones. The practice and philosophy of collective bargaining looks with suspicion on such individual advantages. Of course . . . it is possible for the collective bargain . . . to leave certain areas open to individual bargaining. But except as so provided, advantages to individuals may prove as disruptive to industrial peace as disadvantages. They are a fruitful way of interfering with organization and choice of representatives; increased compensation, if individually deserved, is often earned at the cost of breaking down some other standard thought to be for the welfare of the group and always creates the suspicion of being paid at the long-range expense of the group as a whole. . . . *The workman is free, if he values his own bargaining position more than that of the group, to vote against representation; but the majority rules, and if it collectivizes the employment bargain, individual advantages or favors will generally in practice go in as a contribution to the collective result.*

[47] J. I. Case Co. v. National Labor Relations Board, 321 U.S. 329 (1944) at 338–39. Italics mine.

The largest and certainly the loudest part of the prolonged and continuing argument over the Wagner Act and the Taft-Hartley Act has been carried on not by disinterested persons but by self-interested partisans or their advocates. On the one side are many employers whose expressed zeal to protect the rights of individual workers is justifiably suspect. On the other hand are union leaders and their friends who regard union organization and collective bargaining as a transcendent good, an end so desirable that it must be achieved by almost any means short of violence, and not always short of that. The Board has quite generally, quite heavily, quite naturally, and to some extent quite properly thrown the weight of its authority into the scales on the side of those who want to promote union membership. This emerges clearly, not from the charges of those who have opposed the Board, but from the record of its actions, and from the statements of its defenders and leaders. The policy of the act, they have often insisted, is to promote union organization and collective bargaining.[48]

There is a very important qualification to this contention, and the failure of the Board to recognize it in its interpretation and administration of the law has at times in the past made it vulnerable to criticism. The policy of the act, as Congress intended, is to promote union organization and collective bargaining *to the extent that employees genuinely desire it*, and not to the extent that union officials or the Board desire it any more than to the extent employers might be willing to permit it. Persuasion often seems more tedious than compulsion to men who deeply cherish an ideal. But are not the gains from trade unionism likely to be somewhat less than hoped for if union membership is not the result of real conviction? The faith of members of a state-established union could be as superficial and perfunctory as that of the members of a state-established church.

Several of the doctrines evolved by the Board in determining what constitutes majority choice seem open to grave challenge in the light that political theory can throw on them. The Board early decided that in representation elections the choice should be that of a majority of those voting, rather than those employed, apparently on the theory that these elections are just like political elections.[49] But plainly they are not. When we vote for United States Senator, for example, we have already decided by an extraordinary majority that someone shall represent us as senator. The question in a representation election, however, is whether or not, so to speak, there shall be any senator at all. The decision of the majority voting can be justified if it is assumed either that those who do not vote do not really care or that if they did vote they would divide in about the same way that those voting divided. The decision of the Board has been upheld by the courts and left undisturbed by the Taft-Hartley Act and is within reason.

Of course the division of the labor movement in the United States has painfully complicated the work of the Board. The Board's definitions of

48 Millis and Brown, *op. cit., passim.*
49 *Ibid.*, chap. 5, particularly p. 134.

bargaining units, the election districts, so to speak, have been bitterly criticized, particularly by craft unions in the American Federation of Labor, as gerrymandering to their disadvantage. Recalling Justice Jackson's words, it is understandable that minorities of craftsmen in large enterprises may expect to receive better terms than the majority of the workers and that they may be unwilling to take their chances on a perhaps hostile "majority" representative instead of their own union. The Board's decisions have been stoutly defended, but the defenses largely failed to satisfy those who felt most injured. Congress, which knows something about the need in a country like ours for balancing the demands of federalism with those of majority will, decided in the Taft-Hartley Act to limit sharply the Board's discretion on this issue, in favor of federalism.[50]

Another consequence of the split in American labor has been that in many representation elections two unions were competing for the suffrages of the employees, some of whom might desire no union. If neither of the unions nor the nonunion voters got a majority, the Board devised run-off elections. After experimentation the Board finally decided in 1943 that unless the vote for no union had been the largest of the three on the first ballot, the run-off ballot would simply give the voters a choice between the two unions, thus making possible the certification, as the Board itself conceded, of a union not desired by the majority.[51] The Board's insistence that it could find no better way than this to get at the real wishes of a majority must sound a little odd to anyone who has even a casual familiarity with the possibilities of a simple preferential ballot. The only possible reason for not using it would seem to be that the voters were too unintelligent to understand it when it was carefully explained to them, an assumption which certainly should not be lightly made. Congress did not order a preferential ballot in the Taft-Hartley Act, but it did require the Board to make a run-off election a choice between the two alternatives which had received the largest vote out of the three on the original ballot.[52] A knowledge of simple arithmetic is all that is required to understand that this is a better ballot in such situations if the object is to respect majority desires rather than to ensure union representation.

RESTRAINTS ON UNION ACTIONS INJURIOUS TO OTHER PERSONS

Labor unions in the United States enjoy today great although not the fullest possible benefits under all three of the principles which rationalize the exercise of rights of association. In consequence they have grown from a relatively minor and beleaguered force in the nation's economics and politics into one of the great powers that be in our society. Their power is a natural consequence of our adherence to constitutional democracy and could not be destroyed unless we broke with our own history. It is a commonplace that the exercise of this power, even for otherwise justifiable purposes, can and some-

---

[50] Section 9b (2) of the act; cf. Millis and Brown, *op. cit.*, pp. 521–26.
[51] *Ibid.*, pp. 134–35.
[52] *Ibid.*, pp. 519–20.

times does have injurious and even ruinous consequences for other persons, just as do the powers exercised by the business corporation. As long as labor unions retain the rights they have now achieved, society through the state will be engaged in deciding how it will restrict, as justly as it can, these rights when they result in too great injury to the interests of others.

We cannot survey the welter of legislation or judicial decisions attempting to define the interests of other persons entitled to protection from labor's use of its rights that have already come about in response to labor's new power.[53] Not all of the unions' power impinges on employers or on consumers. Sometimes it adversely affects the interests of workers, both union members and the unorganized. For neutrality's sake as well as brevity's, let us examine the Supreme Court's treatment of several arresting cases exhibiting the protection of workers' rights.

Even before the passage of the Taft-Hartley Act several of the states had outlawed the closed shop so far as they had jurisdiction to do so. Without repeating arguments for and against the closed shop that time has staled but not silenced, suffice it to say that too many sympathetic students of trade unionism, including British trade union leaders, have found objections to the closed shop, particularly if it is coupled with the closed union, for anyone to claim that a legislature in forbidding it is lost to reason.

That is the gist of the short answer Mr. Justice Black in 1949 gave in sustaining laws banning the closed shop in Arizona, Nebraska, and North Carolina.[54] All three states had also forbidden what is usually called the union shop, or union security contract. In this respect they had gone further than the Taft-Hartley Act does. The North Carolina statute and the Nebraska constitutional amendment also forbade discrimination by employers because workers were union members. In cases from these two states the Court was unanimous. Arizona's constitutional amendment did not, but since Arizona law also forbade yellow-dog contracts, the Court did not think that there was a denial of equal protection of the laws. In this case Justice Murphy dissented alone and without opinion.

The unions claimed that these provisions deprived them of their freedom of speech and assembly under the Fourteenth Amendment. To accept this view, declared Mr. Justice Black, the Court would have to revert from wise adherence to judicial restraint to an earlier Court's uncontrolled impulse to substitute its own economic predilections for the legislative judgment in interpretation of the due process clause, and he reminded labor of its justifiable

[53] For a thorough and careful, although unsympathetic account of the Taft-Hartley Act and ensuing National Labor Relations Board and court decisions Millis and Brown, *op. cit.*, is valuable. The mass of state legislation and state administrative and judicial decisions is ably surveyed in Charles C. Killingsworth, *State Labor Relations Acts: A Study of Public Policy* (Chicago, 1948).

[54] For the Arizona Law, American Federation of Labor *et al.* v. American Sash and Door Co. *et al.*, 335 U.S. 538; for Nebraska and North Carolina respectively, Lincoln Federal Labor Union No. 19129, American Federation of Labor *et al.* v. Northwestern Iron and Metal Co. *et al.*, and Whitaker *et al.* v. State of North Carolina, 335 U.S. 525 (1949).

protests against that habit. He rejected "the rather startling ideas" by which the unions had sought to prove an invasion of their civil liberties, saying:[55]

There cannot be wrung from a constitutional right of workers to assemble to discuss improvement of their own working standards, a further constitutional right to drive from remunerative employment all other persons who will not or cannot, participate in union assemblies. The constitutional right of workers to assemble, to discuss and formulate plans for furthering their own self interest in jobs cannot be construed as a constitutional guarantee that none shall get and hold jobs except those who will join in the assembly or will agree to abide by the assembly's plans.

Mr. Justice Frankfurter in concurring agreed that the question was one for the exercise of legislative policy, but set out some of the policy considerations against the closed shop urged by Justice Brandeis, as well as Harold Laski's later confession of the dangers that come from hypostasizing any group. "If," he said, "concern for the individual justifies incorporating in the Constitution itself devices to curb public authority, a legislative judgment that his protection requires the regulation of the private power of unions cannot be dismissed as insupportable."[56]

Justice Rutledge in concurring tried to reserve a question from the rather plain implications of the decision.[57] Suppose a union struck to enforce a closed or union shop, that is, "in defense of the right of union members not to work with non-union men." If a state made such a strike illegal or permitted it to be enjoined, he thought that that might violate the Thirteenth Amendment. Consider the consequences of this view. If a union did have a constitutional right to strike for a closed shop when a law forbidding the closed shop was valid, the employer would have the choice of economic ruin or violation of the law. The argument, which Justice Rutledge did not make but only wondered about, recalls President Buchanan's notion that the states had no constitutional right to secede but that he had no constitutional right to stop them.

Within three months the Court had a picketing case that presented almost this very question.[58] A union in Kansas City, Missouri, attempted to force ice companies in that city to refuse to sell ice to nonunion retail ice peddlers. (About 160 of some 200 peddlers were members of the union. These peddlers may be called self-employed businessmen, but if so, they were really small businessmen, doing the same work whether union members or not.) All the ice companies except one in the city agreed. The union threw a picket line around the company that did not, and because no other union members would cross the picket line (they could have been expelled if they had), 85 percent of the company's ice business melted away. But Missouri's antitrust law made it a felony for the company to restrain trade in the way that the union demanded and also made it liable for triple damages to the nonunion peddlers. It obtained an injunction against the picketing.

[55] 335 U.S. 525 at 531.   [56] 335 U.S. 525 at 545.
[57] 335 U.S. 525 at 559.
[58] Giboney et al. v. Empire Storage and Ice Co., 336 U.S. 490 (1949).

The union in this case did not rest on its rights of free speech. It argued that since its purpose was the admittedly legitimate one of improving wage and working conditions, the state could not intervene at all to protect others from its action. With a seeming forgetfulness of the constitutional right to the equal protection of the laws, it magnanimously conceded the state's right to punish businessmen for violating the antitrust law while insisting that union workers were constitutionally exempt. Unless one believes that an association's rights are absolute and cannot be regulated to protect others from severe injury, arguments like these pretty well refute themselves. This time Mr. Justice Black announced the opinion of a unanimous Court sustaining the injunction.

Some unions, unfortunately, refuse to admit Negroes to membership. Under a closed shop or union shop contract it is plain that this amounts to a complete bar to their chance of a job. Even in an open shop in which such a union is the bargaining agent, such a bar means that Negro workers can have no voice in the policies of their bargaining agent. A number of the states have enacted fair employment practice laws which forbid both employers and unions to discriminate against persons on account of their race, color, religion, or national origin. In 1945 the Court unanimously upheld the FEPC law of New York against the objection of a union of postal clerks that it deprived them of their liberty under the due process clause to select their members.[59] The Justices made short work of this antediluvian claim, saying that .

A judicial determination that such legislation violated the Fourteenth Amendment would be a distortion of the policy manifested in that amendment which was adopted to prevent state legislation designed to perpetuate discrimination on the basis of race or color.

Unfortunately also, Congress has not yet seen fit to use its powers over commerce to pass a national fair employment practices law. It should be said in passing that the sincerity of the sponsors of the Taft-Hartley Act in their desire to protect the rights of workers against injury by unions would have been a good deal more apparent if they had at least sought to forbid unions and employers to discriminate in this way. As a result of Congress' failure the Supreme Court was faced in 1944 with a perplexing case.[60]

The Brotherhood of Locomotive Firemen and Enginemen, which was established under the national Railway Labor Law as an exclusive bargaining agent, denied membership to Negroes. Although on a number of railroads in the South Negroes were not hired as locomotive engineers, by custom they had long held jobs as firemen. The union determined to drive them out of these jobs. To that end it and certain railroads made contracts, the effect of which would be finally to squeeze the Negro firemen out, in the

---

[59] Railway Mail Assn. v. Corsi, Industrial Comr. of New York, 326 U.S. 88 (1945).
[60] Steele v. Louisville and Nashville R.R. Co. *et al.*, 323 U.S. 192 (1944) ; cf. the companion case of Tunstall v. Brotherhood of Locomotive Firemen and Enginemen, Ocean Lodge No. 76, *et al.*, 323 U.S. 210 (1944).

interim forcing them into poorer jobs with lower wages than their seniority warranted. When a Negro fireman sued for damages and an injunction against this conduct, the Supreme Court unanimously sustained his complaint. Chief Justice Stone said:

We think that the Railway Labor Act imposes upon the statutory representative of a craft at least as exacting a duty to protect equally the interests of the members of the craft as the Constitution imposes upon a legislature to give equal protection to the interests of those for whom it legislates. Congress has seen fit to clothe the bargaining representative with powers comparable to those possessed by a legislative body both to create and restrict the rights of those whom it represents . . . but it has also imposed on the representative a corresponding duty . . . [T]he statutory power to represent a craft and to make contracts as to wages, hours and working conditions does not include the authority to make discriminations among members of the craft not based on . . . relevant differences. Here the discriminations based on race alone are obviously irrelevant and invidious. Congress plainly did not undertake to authorize the bargaining representative to make such discriminations.

Undoubtedly the holding of this case is applicable to any similar discrimination practiced by unions empowered to act as bargaining representatives under the national Labor Management Relations Act, and also under state labor relations acts, which cover some of the unions accused as the worst offenders. Justice Murphy in concurring suggested, however, that the protection extended by the Court, leaving the unions still free to exclude from membership on the basis of race, was likely to be inadequate protection; and close observers have agreed.[61] Our Constitution not only requires legislatures to give all persons the equal protection of the laws; it also forbids the states or the nation to prevent a citizen from sharing in the choice of his political representatives on the basis of his race or color. The statutes establishing unions as collective bargaining agents are actually delegating to them state power fully as much as the state confers power on a political party. Since the more recent holding that a political party may not bar a person from membership in the party or from voting in its primary because of his race,[62] to be consistent the Court should, whenever it has an opportunity to decide this question, hold that no union established by law as an exclusive collective bargaining agent can constitutionally bar persons from membership on the grounds of race or color.

These cases have all dealt with the protection of workers not members of a union, although one assured the right to become a union member. Congress in the Taft-Hartley Act and the states have also been much concerned with protecting union members against certain abuses. The elaborate pro-

[61] For further evidence cf. Graham et al. v. Brotherhood of Locomotive Firemen and Enginemen, 338 U.S. 232 (1949) and Brotherhood of Railroad Trainmen et al. v. Howard et al., 343 U.S. 768 (1952). In the latter case a union of Negro train porters was struggling to retain jobs its members had long held against an exclusively white union which had forced the railroad to agree to give the jobs to white "brakemen."

[62] Rice v. Elmore, 165 F. 2d 387; certiorari denied, 333 U.S. 875 (1948).

visions for filing information concerning union finances and salient provisions of the union's regulations for the conduct of its internal government are an example. Protests that this is a burdensome duty should be heard with the recognition that the maintenance of liberty is always burdensome. The protests that such requirements are unnecessary are, in respect to many unions, true. But with respect to some it has not been true, and a union which can be proud of its record for honesty and fairness toward its members might consider it an honor and an opportunity to let the public take a look at the record, rather than an irksome duty. Besides, the public is not obligated to rely on confidence in such matters, even if confidence is deserved. In fact, government has thus far properly been very circumspect in regulating the freedom of the unions in their internal government, and may have to go further rather than retreat in imposing standards of honesty and fairness where evidence of abuse warrants.

The Supreme Court has had few cases dealing with a conflict of the interest of a union and its members. The most important arose out of a situation in which a union and a railroad had been in disagreement over the interpretation of certain working rules in the collective labor agreement.[63] If the union's interpretation were accepted, a number of its members would be entitled to substantial back pay, and their claims had been filed under the Railway Labor Act. The dispute was finally settled through the complicated procedure of the National Railroad Adjustment Board. The railroad agreed in effect to follow the union's interpretation of the rules thereafter and to settle the claims filed for back pay, and the union agreed that this settlement was a final and complete settlement of all past claims made or that could be made. Some members of the union thought that they could get more money from the railroad after this settlement and filed suits in a federal court to recover pay they claimed. The court disallowed their claims, holding that the general settlement made by the union had barred any further individual claims.

The Supreme Court saw the crucial question as whether or not the union's constitution authorized it to make such a binding settlement for its members and whether or not the Railway Labor Act authorized a bargaining agent to make such a settlement. As a matter of fact, neither the union constitution and by-laws nor the statute was very clear on the point, but a majority of the Supreme Court, perhaps leaning over backward to see justice done to the individuals, said that neither authorized the union to make a binding settlement. Justice Rutledge held for the majority that the test to be applied was that of the strict common law of agency to determine if the men had authorized their union to act for them. The Court did not apparently realize how it was disrupting and confusing long-standing practice under the act.

Mr. Justice Frankfurter did. In his dissent, which includes one of the clearest recognitions in the Court's reports of the nature of a group from a sociological point of view in contrast to a narrowly technical legal view, he protested that the only proper way to test the question was not to talk of

[63] Elgin, Joliet and Eastern Ry. Co. v. Burley et al., 325 U.S. 711 (1945) and 327 U.S. 661 (1946).

common law rules of agency but to look at the long-established and widely accepted customs of the group.[64] In that light there was overwhelming evidence that the union had had the authority to make the settlement and that it was binding on the individuals. The turmoil that he had predicted followed. The settlement of all such disputes under the Railway Labor Act simply collapsed for more than a year. The Court had to grant a reargument. It clung to its common law standard but in a face-saving opinion so watered it down that Mr. Justice Frankfurter said that the result would be to uphold the union settlement. But he protested about fastening the common law test on the future. And he could note that both the government and a great many unions had come into court as *amici curiae* to show how its prior decision could demoralize all collective bargaining. But if the decision leads unions to clarify their authority to act for their members in such matters, perhaps something has been gained.

UNION POWER AND COMMUNITY RIGHTS

The other principle on which the restriction of an association's activities may be justified is that its rights may not be used to the injury of the whole society or of its political institutions. That principle as it bears on labor unions has brought to the United States Supreme Court in the last decade three cases of major importance. One of these concerned the use of union funds in political campaigns and is better reserved for our discussion of political parties.[65] A second considers the propriety of legislative efforts to hamper or prevent communist leadership of labor unions, and is better deferred until we examine the problem of control of subversive associations.[66] The third poses the question of what a free society may legitimately do when it is confronted with a strike of such magnitude that it threatens the public health, safety, and welfare. That twin case is *United States* v. *United Mineworkers* and *United States* v. *John L. Lewis*.[67]

The case is replete with technical niceties; they need concern us all the less because their resolution is rather aptly described by the saying that hard cases make bad law. The importance of the case lies almost entirely between the lines of the opinions. For those who need to be reminded of the larger facts, they were these. In the spring of 1946 a strike in the coal mines finally led the President under power conferred by the War Labor Disputes Act to seize the mines. The government speedily concluded an agreement with the union that gave it much of what it had unsuccessfully sought from the private operators. In the autumn of 1946 the president of the union demanded that the government reopen negotiations. Although denying that it was obligated to, the government did so. When no agreement was reached the union announced that it was terminating the contract and the miners went out on strike. The government sought and obtained a temporary restraining

---

[64] 325 U.S. 711 at 757–58.

[65] United States v. Congress of Industrial Organizations *et al.*, 335 U.S. 106 (1948).

[66] American Communications Assn., C.I.O. *et al.* v. Douds, 339 U.S. 382 (1950).

[67] United States v. United Mine Workers of America, 330 U.S. 258 (1947).

order and a temporary injunction. The union had opposed the injunction on the ground that the Norris-LaGuardia Act forbade a federal court to issue it. The union and its president defied the order of the court, were tried for contempt, and convicted. The union was fined $3,500,000 and its president $10,000. The strike was then ended, and the case appealed.

A bare majority of the Supreme Court held that the Norris-LaGuardia Act did not bar the United States government from obtaining an injunction in a federal court in a labor dispute between itself and its employees, as the coal miners were held to be for the purposes of the case. Among the dissenters on interpretation of the act was Mr. Justice Frankfurter, generally regarded as its "author." But he and Justice Jackson agreed that that question was debatable enough for the lower court properly to entertain it, and that while considering it the court could restrain the strike. A different majority of the Court reduced the fine upon the union to $700,000 conditional upon its purging itself of contempt. Justices Murphy and Rutledge entirely dissented.

The Taft-Hartley Act has changed the law. Under it the President is authorized to seek and the courts to grant an injunction for a period of eighty days if he finds that a strike or lock-out imperils the national health or safety and the court agrees. If this cooling-off period does not produce a settlement of the dispute, Congress has decided to face that emergency only when it comes. There are those who decry the provision as a "slave labor" law. That is exaggerated rhetoric. There are those who think the law should not be applied lest it be defied. That is either falsely pessimistic or truly a confession of legal and political insolvency. There are those who say that the provision is inadequate because it attempts to treat the symptoms rather than the causes of industrial strife. That criticism is undoubtedly true, but the criticism itself is not a solution but only an admonition to create a better one.

"The logic of history is chronologic," in Professor Corwin's epigram. This review of some of the applications of the principles of the American constitutional law of association to labor union affairs is also a brief sketch of the life history of organized labor in America. Once freed from the threat of governmental suppression, the unions as their strength grew could demand and secure from the state privileges and powers and legal protection from interference with their activities by private persons. This new legal status in turn has further enhanced their power. Now they face limitations on their activities in behalf of individuals who are damaged, and even of a whole society fearful of crises brought on by great strikes. It is this history which prompted Justice Jackson to say "the labor movement has come full circle."[68] Though the wheel has come full circle, it has also traveled a linear distance and carried society over an irreversible span of history. There is a great—and wise—difference between the way the law treats John L. Lewis and the way it treated the Luddites.

[68] Hunt et al. v. Crumboch et al., 325 U.S. 821 (1945) at 830.

5

THE POLITICAL PARTY: FROM PRIVATE CLUB
TO PUBLIC CONCERN

Since the early days of the New Deal there have been three distinct waves of writing about American government, and their sequence is suggestive. As the New Deal measures met judicial resistance culminating in the Supreme Court crisis of 1937, the role of the judiciary in the American system first received new emphasis.[1] The settlement of this crisis and the coming of the war with its vast new concentration of power in the President pushed forth next a wave of writing about the American Presidency.[2] But the end of hostilities brought us new dangers and responsibilities such as the American government had never had to struggle with before. The Supreme Court cannot settle these questions, nor can a President settle them by himself. Congressional decisions of a new order of magnitude are required, but these are heavily dependent upon the crystallization of public opinion, and in that process political parties and pressure groups have a major part. Thus we have a third new wave of writing, which shows as yet no sign of subsiding, anxiously inquiring whether our traditional pattern of party politics can save us from disaster.[3]

Many of these recent writers on American party politics declare their belief—some explicitly, some implicitly—that unless we drastically revise our traditional ideas of how parties should function and make the necessary changes in our political customs, laws, and even in the Constitution itself to assist and compel parties to act in a new way, serious trouble, if not dis-

[1] Notable were Edward S. Corwin, *The Twilight of the Supreme Court* (New Haven, 1934) ; Dean Alfange, *The Supreme Court and the National Will* (New York, 1937) ; Robert H. Jackson, *The Struggle for Judicial Supremacy* (New York, 1941) ; Edward S. Corwin, *Constitutional Revolution, Ltd.* (Claremont, Calif., 1941).

[2] Important contributions to this literature have been Edward S. Corwin, *The President: Office and Powers* (New York, 1939) ; Harold J. Laski, *The American Presidency, an Interpretation* (New York, 1940) ; George Fort Milton, *The Use of Presidential Power, 1789-1943* (Boston, 1944).

[3] Outstanding studies of Congress, the parties, and pressure groups of this period are E. P. Herring, *The Politics of Democracy* (New York, 1940) ; W. E. Binkley, *American Political Parties: Their Natural History* (New York, 1945) ; E. E. Schattschneider, *Party Government* (New York, 1942) ; Thomas K. Finletter, *Can Representative Government Do the Job?* (New York, 1945) ; George B. Galloway, *Congress at the Crossroads* (New York, 1946) ; Roland Young, *This Is Congress* (2d ed., New York, 1946) ; David Truman, *The Governmental Process* (New York, 1950) ; Arthur N. Holcombe, *Our More Perfect Union* (Cambridge, 1950) ; Ernest S. Griffith, *Congress, Its Contemporary Role* (New York, 1951).

93

aster, does await us. Other writers have questioned this conclusion. Still others, without denying the need for these changes, see little hope of achieving them.

Important as it may be to know where the truth lies in this controversy, we cannot decide that here. But a clear understanding of what our traditional view of the function of parties is and of new views that we are urged to adopt is necessary to deciding. The laws regulating political parties reflect a traditional view of the function of the parties. This traditional view is itself a changing one. Important changes have been emerging in the twentieth century, but they develop rather than negate our tradition.

The current debate seems to continue an argument that got under way more than fifty years ago between two schools of thought about the weaknesses and needed reforms of the American party system. It may be helpful to begin by sketching in the boldest strokes the outlines of these two schools even at the risk of perpetrating a caricature.

One school found an early leader in Henry Jones Ford, who came to Princeton at Woodrow Wilson's invitation.[4] It looked at the sprawling, brawling sectional coalitions led by a host of captains without a commander in chief that serve as the two major national parties in the United States and compared them unflatteringly with the theory and practice of party politics in England in the late nineteenth century. It emphasized the role of political parties in governing and in providing an opposition in the legislature rather than their role in popular elections. It concluded that the most serious defect of the American parties is their lack of unified leadership and centralized authority. On this finding it based many counts in its indictment. American parties fail when in power to carry out a tolerably consistent and broad enough program of action; under present circumstances this always discouraging and wasteful fault may prove fatal. For lack of leadership to organize a common defense the party in the legislature surrenders large sectors of the public interest before the assaults of pressure groups inferior in numbers but superior in discipline. Since the party in opposition is as leaderless and disorganized as the party in power, the issues that divide them appear so confused that the electorate can hold neither party responsible for its actions and is reduced at best to lashing out blindly when it can bear its frustrations no longer. The reform proposed follows naturally; the lack of unified central authoritative leadership must be supplied to make the parties effective and responsible.

A little later the other school gained a powerful exponent in the Russian Ostrogorski, who came to this country after completing a monumental study of English politics which suggested this early that Ford and many of his successors in the other school had drawn their moral from a somewhat "literary theory" of British politics.[5] Certainly twentieth-century developments in the English party system have strengthened rather than weakened

---

[4] Henry Jones Ford, *The Rise and Growth of American Politics* (New York, 1898).

[5] M. Ostrogorski, *Democracy and the Organization of Political Parties* (New York, 1902).

this rejoinder. As a matter of fact, Ford in *The Rise and Growth of American Politics* had employed a method which has since been thoroughly discredited. Dominated by the belief in evolutionary analogies then so common in anthropology, law, and politics, he inferred that the course of development of English and American politics is the same, with the United States a century behind England.

It was far-fetched to see in American politics of Mark Hanna's day the equivalent of England under Walpole and the Whig oligarchy. The mistake led Ford into some strange prophecies. His prediction of the withering away of the Presidency[6] was refuted by his friend Wilson as well as by both Roosevelts. His expectation that party organization on the local level would likewise disappear proved equally fallacious.[7] But his tantalizing vision of an American government that would be a parliamentary system in fact although not in form[8] still bewitches not a few of his followers.[9]

The gist of Ostrogorski's argument was based on what he saw in America. His fresh vision confirmed that of many native students. The worst trouble was not the leaderless character of American parties but their freedom from popular control. It is not, this school has insisted, that American parties lack leaders, but that they have bad leaders. And they have bad leaders because a party's rank-and-file members do not succeed in using their rightful power to exert control over their leaders. The phenomenon on which this school focused our eyes, especially in the years of the Progressive movement, was the American boss. American parties might lack commanders in chief, but there were generals among the captains, especially in the great cities. If any comparison to foreign politics should be made, these bosses resembled Chinese warlords with their unslaked thirst for squeeze, graft, boodle, and the fix.

What must be expected if such a party managed to establish a general staff? The answer seemed all too apparent. The bosses would be this general staff, and their chief of staff would be the worst because the most powerful among them. But their successful organization might well enable them to sweep the field and conduct great national depredations modeled on their local foraging raids. Unfortunately this was no nightmare of the future; from time to time the bosses did organize themselves, and when they did, they ran affairs in Washington as they were accustomed to in New York and Philadelphia and Chicago. An all-powerful leadership free from popular control would be as big a curse in a modern party as it had been in the state itself.

This analysis, our history makes plain, is much closer to what Americans have long considered the root of political evil. Time and again we have rejected or weakened or destroyed centralized party control because it has

[6] Ford, *op. cit.*, p. 369.

[7] *Ibid.*, p. 370.

[8] *Ibid.*, pp. 365–68.

[9] The criticisms above are not meant to imply that he did not write with great insight about American politics.

seemed a threat to popular control.[10] The parties had been accepted in the first place as the only known alternative to the direction of affairs by a rather well-unified but unpopular coterie of the rich, the well-born, and the able. Democracy quickly made the electoral college for their choice of the President an anachronism. Under Andrew Jackson an outraged democracy went on to smash the aristocratic Congressional caucus which had arrogated to itself the nomination of Presidential candidates, and replaced it with the national party conventions, which were to be representative of the grass roots of the parties. The agitation for a civil service merit system that grew during Reconstruction carried appeal not only because it promised more efficiency and economy in government but also because it threatened to deprive party leaders of the opportunity to build disciplined machines out of public employees.

In the last two decades of the nineteenth century public opinion throughout the country forced adoption of the Australian ballot in order to reduce the arbitrary practices of the party machines in elections. At the turn of the century Mark Hanna's bid to make the national party chairman a real leader instead of a figurehead collapsed. It has never been repeated with even as much success. Soon afterward the aggrandizement of power by which the Speaker of the House of Representatives had become the party leader of the House was abruptly smashed in the spectacular revolt against Czar Cannon. At about the same time party stalwarts in the state legislatures were forced by constitutional amendment to surrender their power to choose United States Senators to the people. These were only part of the flood of measures of the Progressive era; there were others. Many states adopted the initiative to enable the voters to force through laws over the obstruction of party machines in the legislature, and the referendum to enable them to kill measures which the party machines had attempted to push through. Even more significant was the successful drive to replace the party conventions, once regarded as the epitome of popular control, with the direct primary election as the method of selecting party candidates.

When in our own day Franklin Roosevelt broke the two-term tradition, many students thought that at last the barriers against unified central party leadership might be going down. Jefferson had set the tradition of only two terms for the Presidency as a device to prevent the entrenchment of leadership. The newest amendment to our Constitution makes it about as plain as possible that President Roosevelt succeeded not because popular support of the tradition had waned but in spite of the fact that it remained strong. The demands for extension of the direct primary to the choice of Presidential candidates following on the campaign of 1952 suggest that this long struggle to strip party leaders of uncontrolled power over candidates and policies had not yet come to an end. For although many of the advocates of these suc-

---

[10] It may be objected that these actions were urged by party leaders and adopted by party organizations for partisan advantage rather than by "we" the public. But is it not significant that, granting the full force of this argument, either major party has usually acquiesced readily and fully in those changes which were initiated by the other?

cessful efforts have confessed their disappointment at the inadequacy of the results, few have doubted that the principle on which they have proceeded is wrong.

If lack of popular control is the evil of American parties, what is the remedy for it? At this point we cannot fail to notice an ambiguity in the thinking of this school. Granting that party members do not exercise control over the party, is it because they cannot or because they will not? Is the failure due to obstacles raised against the ordinary members by a party oligarchy? Or is the vision of an oligarchical leadership itself a mirage, and the apathy of the rank and file the reality? Ostrogorski himself seemed to waver. He had been one of the first to emphasize how the English Liberal party had reached its high state of parliamentary effectiveness through a leadership that had consciously set out to stimulate the party membership into organized electoral activity. The party leadership drew its strength from popular support; it had popular support because it acknowledged its obligation to abide by the wishes of the party membership. In turn the party members willingly accepted guidance from a leadership that truly represented its wishes. Strong party leadership and discipline were reciprocal with popular control of the party. But for America Ostrogorski seemed at times to place an almost mystical faith in the improvised popular revolts that sometimes produce ephemeral reform movements in our great cities. In doing so he cast aside his own insight.

It should be clear that these two schools had the same objective. Both wanted a strong party leadership which draws its strength from the approval of an active membership. They differed in their emphasis on the two aspects of the same ideal, sometimes so much that the more zealous and less thoughtful adherents of each school appeared to believe that they were supporting two contradictory ideals.

The explanation for this confusion does not lie in any naïveté of earlier students. They were struggling as we still are to understand the significance for representative government of a new phenomenon: the political party based upon universal adult suffrage. The achievement of this longstanding liberal goal brought new problems. The shift from a restricted to a broad suffrage raised the political party from a private club to a public concern. Earlier political theory about the role of party took form before representative government had become democratic government. No amount of repetition of the elegant periods of Burke or of Madison, therefore, can supply all that is needed to fit the modern democratic party into the modern democratic state.

The committee on political parties of the American Political Science Association in its report entitled "Toward a More Responsible Two Party System" has made one of the most ambitious efforts to provide an adequate modern theory.[11] In that report one can watch the coalescence of these two schools of thought, although the report is phrased primarily in the language

[11] *The American Political Science Review*, Supplement (September 1950).

of those who stress the need for strong party leadership. Yet it insists upon the necessity of grass roots activity to secure the ideal kind of top leadership and calls for "local party leagues playing a creative role in shaping the *national* program, and with activities integrated into the national party structure." These new local groups, we are told, must not, as do existing local party committees, "look too much to patronage, nominations, and elections; their attitude, by and large, is too much one of indifference toward issues."

Then comes the most revealing sentence in the entire report: "Certainly such units would add to the vitality of the party and tend to make the individual members more enthusiastic supporters."[12] Is this a scientific conclusion or the voicing of a slender hope? Apathy about public affairs among a mass electorate is disappointing if not disconcerting to liberal hopes. Yet apathy is a massive fact, in the past and the present at least. We resort to campaigns utilizing all the techniques of a soap-selling drive just to persuade voters to go to the polls. But casting a vote is near the minimum of political participation. Many reasons help explain why American pioneers in extension of the suffrage have lagged behind in voting and in activity in the parties, but the most important may well be that at least until recently they have not felt so great a need. In this light the recent spate of writing on the role of the parties expresses a newly felt need among alert students in the face of world crisis.

It is important to understand clearly that most of the recent wave of writing about the need for reform in our party system and the call for more responsible party government has not been motivated by a desire for ideological parties expressing deep social divisions, although the language in which some of it has been cast might mislead a casual reader. The concern of most of these writers has not been that without strong and unified party leadership we shall fail to achieve economic and social justice but that we shall fail to preserve our national security in the cold war. In reality they do not want two strongly disciplined parties with sharply contrasting foreign and defense policies competing to represent the majority at all. Their real concern is that there is now too much division of opinion over these questions and too little realization as yet of the price we must all pay for national security. Public opinion, they believe, has not yet caught up with the dangers that confront us. They do not want a continual debate carried on between an internationalist and an isolationist party; they want it settled by united public opinion reflected in both parties. And they do not want such a policy in defense and foreign affairs whittled away by pressure groups seeking exemption from their share of the necessary burden. One must wonder, however, if the solution of this problem does lie in strong and disciplined parties or in a prodigious effort in adult education. If it is the latter, is it realistic to rely so much on the parties to carry out such an educational program successfully as a partisan enterprise?

[12] This quotation and those immediately preceding it are at p. 68.

Is it fair to our citizens to ask them to rely primarily on the adversary proceedings of partisan debate, on the florid language, the rhetorical tricks, and the parliamentary stratagems from which even the Lincoln-Douglas debates, perhaps our best example of a political campaign as a medium of adult education, are not entirely free? Are they to sift from this, not simply abstract truth, but the grounds for decision of questions on which their and the Republic's life may well depend? Is it fair to the parties, whose resources for carrying on adult education are limited and whose leaders in the legislature and the executive branch are often nearly exhausted in the daily struggle to make decisions that will not wait, to declare them primarily responsible for this grave undertaking too? Surely those who think our parties are now inadequate for their tasks ought to pause before laying this additional burden upon them.

Political parties are unique among the great voluntary associations in their purpose. They seek to gain and keep control of the machinery of government and thus to direct the great involuntary association, the state. They can scarcely deny that they are intimately concerned with "the things of this world" which Locke assigned as the province of the state itself. This being so, they may not reasonably expect the wide ambit of freedom from the state's regulation that churches can claim. Unless the struggle for the control of the state among the political parties is to degenerate into a contest of fraud and outright force there must be legal sanction to ensure that elections—which are the battlegrounds of the contending parties—will be free and honest. Our election laws, if they are enforced, provide this assurance. But legal limitations upon freedom of association for political parties have gone far beyond this minimum in the United States.

The introduction of the Australian ballot also required the state to provide elaborate rules for determining the grounds on which a party would be given a place on the official ballot as well as for establishing which party officials could authenticate party nominations and the procedures which they must follow to claim that authority. These regulations, like those protecting the freedom and honesty of elections, arose before the twentieth century and no longer pose novel constitutional problems.

In the last fifty years we have gone beyond these kinds of regulation of the rights of association for political purposes in seeking to require parties and other groups involved in politics to perform the functions which popular American ideas of political democracy assign to them . These new regulations fall into three main groups. First are those which attempt to make a party reflect the will of a majority of its members and, in a few instances it would seem, of the entire electorate. Second are those which move toward equalizing the resources of the major parties in manpower and money. It is almost as if government were acting as a handicapper in the race between the parties, whether they wear the silks of the "ins" and the "outs" or of the richer and the poorer. Last come the still tentative steps toward definition of a *modus vivendi* for pressure groups in modern democracy. These public responses to the questions raised by modern mass parties echo some themes in the scholarly debate we have already listened to. They also raise some perplexing issues in the constitutional law of association.

MAJORITY RULE WITHIN THE PARTIES

The first of the democratic impulses shaping the nature of American parties seeks to make the party reflect the will of a majority of its members and sometimes of a majority of the electorate. What could be more natural for a people long dedicated to the proposition that the state itself should reflect the majority will? As a nation we are steeped in majoritarian traditions, even though we also carry in our political baggage certain ideas like fundamental rights and judicial review, which we think of not as contradictions but qualifications of the faith.

How deeply rooted this desire for majority rule is can readily be seen from looking at a cherished notion of how our electoral decisions should be made. Of course we accept the fact that our elections must be decided by the majority of those voting, but we are not really satisfied with it. We tend to think that an election should reflect the will of all the citizens, of all the people eligible to vote. So strongly do we feel this that many of us strive to make the ideal come nearer actuality. We have nonpartisan campaigns to get out the vote, and lecture and editorialize on the theme that voting is a civic duty and the nonvoter is a shirker. We are proud of a big vote and ashamed of a small one.

Of course our majoritarian impulse has long since given almost all adults the right to vote. Why have we been unwilling to stop there; why have we gone on to call a right a duty? Why should anyone feel he must vote if he thinks that the outcome will make no difference as far as he is concerned, or that he does not know enough about the candidates or the issues to make an intelligent choice? We reply that he ought to be concerned and he ought to inform himself. Political scientists constantly have to remind themselves that most people are not very interested in politics, for they are so fascinated with politics that they find it hard to understand why others are not.

But even most political scientists I know do not take a very active part in partisan politics. If they are asked why, they are likely to give a number of fairly plausible but not entirely convincing answers, but if they are pressed hard enough, they are likely to admit that they do not spend much time in party affairs because they think they have something better to do.[13] And that is exactly the way most of their fellow citizens feel.

The depth and pervasiveness of this majoritarian ideal and the frustrations that result when it is confronted by the normal human desire to cultivate one's own garden is one of the profound facts in American thinking about politics and the parties, and we cannot understand very much about our party system without keeping it always in our mind's eye.

The legal aspect of the effort to make the parties reflect the will of a

---

[13] Of course quite a few political scientists do take an active part in party affairs; nor is any implication intended that they are making a poorer use of their time than those who do not.

majority of the members is of course the statutory provisions of the states for defining party membership. Outwardly the astonishing fact is that the states have deprived the parties of almost all right to determine who may become a member, and on what conditions, or to expel a member, and on what conditions. Yet these rights seem to be of the very essense of a voluntary association, and their infringement by government would be deeply resented by most other types of associations. Still more astonishing, then, is the fact that these laws were devised and passed by the party leaders in the legislatures. With only one exception, which proves the rule, have parties made any objection to the loss of these rights.

Although the details of the several states' provisions for defining party membership vary considerably, their common characteristic is that the citizen elects himself to membership in the party by registering his choice with public authorities. And he can leave one party and join the rival party in about the same way and just about as easily. The question that naturally comes to mind is, can we properly call our major parties voluntary associations at all? Some students attempt to avoid this awkward question by suggesting that we can if we will think of the party as made up of only the active core of party workers, but this solution is hardly satisfactory, for then what are we to do with all the persons who call themselves members, although their only participation in the party is to vote for some of its candidates when they feel like doing so?

The actual differences on this score between the political party and other associations like churches and labor unions and many other groups are, however, not nearly so great as the difference in their legal rights suggests. The great associations in modern American society, the associations, like churches, unions, and parties, which present the great constitutional problems, are not what the sociologist calls primary, or face-to-face groups, like the family. Within each great association many primary groups do exist, whether union locals, church parishes or congregations, or party committees, but the over-all associations are secondary groups with a life, if we must call it such, almost as disembodied and impersonal as that of the state itself (and sometimes much more so). Gierke can mislead us if we think of these great associations as organic fellowships bound by strong fraternal ties and suffused with *Gemütlichkeit*. The great associations like the churches, the parties, the unions, and the business corporations are much less fellowships than great machines for getting some part of society's urgent business done. Like the state and the family they are instruments of social control.

Their social responsibilities greatly limit their formal legal freedom. Most churches are reluctant to deny anyone admission and even more reluctant to excommunicate anyone. We joke that many of their members seldom see the inside of the church save on Easter Sundays and to be married and buried. The details of this picture must be varied for union members and corporate stockholders, but the total effect is much the same. Nor is it much different with the parties.

The part of its business which society remits to the parties is of course manning the positions and running the machinery of government. In other words, the party does the work of the state as Locke described it; it must procure, preserve, and advance our civil interests of life, liberty, health, and indolency of body, and the possession of outward things. To do that a party must be "established" by the state, just as many states establish a church to see to the salvation of souls. The similarity of the party in power to an established church is clarified by the status of the elitist parties in modern totalitarian states. Elitist parties are permanently established because they alone, so they think, know the one true way to civil salvation, and no other heretical party may be entrusted with the task of following it.

We are almost as reluctant to establish a party as we are to establish a church. But with parties we can find no way generally of escaping the necessity. Much of our local public affairs about which men do not differ significantly in the way to civil salvation is carried on by nonpartisan government sometimes explicitly and even more often implicitly, even though party labels are attached to the local officials. In national public affairs, however, men do take different roads to civil salvation and form themselves into differing political sects. One of them must be established as the party in power. Deep in American political consciousness, or even in our subconsciousness, is the wish that we did not have to, or the dream that we need not, and we bridle as our English brethren do not at the very thought of a party established in power. It would be unthinkable for the party in power in the United States to refer to itself as the "*government* of the day." Such talk would be regarded as high-toned pretentious arrogance to be humbled by the citizens at the first available chance. We are rebels still, more than we realize.

Describing the government of Switzerland Professor Dicey, with that delightful insularity of the British people, had this to say:[14]

The . . . most original Swiss conception is one which it is not easy for foreigners bred up under other constitutional systems to grasp. It is that the existence of political parties does not necessitate the adoption of party government.

No American would have the slightest difficulty in grasping this "original Swiss conception," for he would immediately recognize it as his own. As Professor Arthur Holcombe has said so well, American government is not just party government; it is also constitutional government.[15]

Since, like other modern democracies, we must establish a party, we require it to receive the approval of the majority in order to claim its title, and we provide for opportunity for the majority to disestablish it (although we have ceased to insist that where *annual* elections end, there tyranny begins). We also go much further than most other democratic states—so far that they find us hard to understand—to hedge it about while it enjoys its

<hr>

[14] Albert Venn Dicey, *Introduction to the Study of the Law of the Constitution* (8th ed., London, 1914), Appendix, Note VIII, p. 518.

[15] For a profound discussion of this thesis, cf. Arthur N. Holcombe, *Our More Perfect Union.*

momentary privileged status with constitutional devices to see that its hierarchs get no immodest ideas of their dignity or power. The necessity of obtaining majority approval under universal suffrage in order for a party to establish its right to power goes far to explain why our parties have no grievance in their loss of legal right to exercise choice of their members. They are prepared to welcome almost anyone with open arms and strive to make almost anyone feel at home in their midst.

A necessary consequence of this aim to please is the characteristic of our major parties so natural to Americans and always so astonishing to foreigners: they are like identical twins. Yet is it a *necessary* consequence? Although parties in other democratic states also have to secure the approval of a majority, it is true that many of them are not so promiscuous with their affections as are the Democrats and the Republicans. This striking difference demands an explanation, which lies also in the deep, almost inarticulate American majoritarian ideal.

A majoritarian ideal is an equalitarian ideal. Each man is to count as one, and no man for more than one. At least until now almost all Americans almost all the time have accepted as a fundamental article of their political credo the faith that there is not and ought not to be any permanent, deep, and inherent division in the political community. The momentary differences on election day are seen as transient, superficial, and accidental results of a man's location on the map[16] or in the cycle from shirt sleeves to shirt sleeves.

We may call this a myth if we like, for we all realize and always have realized that it doesn't exactly correspond to reality. But as De Tocqueville saw long ago, the ideal had a much closer correspondence to reality in America than anywhere else in the world. Since his time other democratic states have increased the correspondence of the same ideal with their own social realities. Today many Americans, and especially many American intellectuals, think that since De Tocqueville's time the correspondence of American reality with the ideal has diminished, and that it would be better to discard the myth and build ideological parties that would honestly express social divisions among us.

Despite the assurance of some of these new believers, who disregard much impressive evidence that does not fit their theory, it would require a Solomon among social scientists to judge truly whether the democratic ideal and the American reality have grown further apart or closer together in the course of the last century, and it would probably be beyond his wisdom to prophesy accurately whether ideological parties would on balance tend to unite or to separate the ideal and the reality in the future. Under these circumstances the American people will come close to the wisdom of Solomon if they refuse to allow anyone to beguile them into accepting this new belief without far

[16] And this is true whether the map is one of the United States showing the "sections" in terms of which our older rural politics has been analyzed or a ward map of one of our great cities from which much can be learned about the "class" basis of modern urban politics. Cf. Arthur N. Holcombe, *The New Party Politics* (New York, 1933), and Samuel Lubell, *The Future of American Politics* (New York, 1952).

better evidence for it than any of its advocates have yet been able to offer them.[17]

We can now perceive why it is that the American major parties do not care who their members are, and why it is that we have proceeded by law to make it possible for a majority of the members, if they choose to do so, to exercise their control by such devices as the party primary for the selection of party candidates and the popular election of party officials themselves. Some of our states, particularly those in the West distinguished for their majoritarian impulses, have attempted in this century to go even further, and submit control of the parties' affairs and candidates to the majority of the whole electorate by such devices as the open primary in which the voter need make no profession of party allegiance in order to vote in its primary, cross-filing for nomination by candidates in both parties, and even the blanket primary in which voters may vote for candidates of either party.

Some writers on American politics have devoted considerable attention to these new devices and have speculated lengthily on the probabilities that they will break down party discipline.[18] Most of this discussion is quite pointless, for it proceeds from a premise more false than true. It considers the destruction of something that hardly exists: party discipline, party unity, and party ideological uniqueness. The gross evidence before our eyes is that party politics is carried on in these states in much the same way that it is in states that have not gone so far legally. For in the states that have closed primaries, in which only attested party members may participate, it is seldom very difficult for the voter to change his party allegiance readily. Certainly the party into which he wants to come will not attempt to drive him away unless it is firmly convinced he is only helping carry on a hostile raid. And the party which he leaves will hesitate before it tries to prevent his voting in the other for fear of angering him further and losing a chance to win him back.

Of course this lack of party discipline and cohesion must not be over-emphasized, nor should it be supposed that the electoral laws of the states generally prevent parties from imposing disciplinary measures when they think it necessary or desirable. A very recent case decided by the Supreme

[17] It is only fair to say that this recommendation against encouraging ideological parties, which is similar to the position of Professor Holcombe and Ernest Griffith (see note 3 *supra*) is "conservative." Our present party system, as President A. L. Lowell pointed out many years ago, conceals issues rather than reveals them. The British development suggests, though not conclusively, that in a two-party system *with universal suffrage*, once a "left" party has developed, the "right" party must talk and even act in "me too" fashion if it hopes to be elected. Such a lesson might be drawn from an English Tory party which is now well to the left of either American party. But of course there are other circumstances which must be considered in interpreting this development; cf. Leslie Lipson, "The Two Party System in British Politics," 47 *American Political Science Review* 337 (June 1953). One may suspect that the rise of disciplined ideological parties waits upon the growth of deeply felt division among the electorate, though the existence of such parties may increase or decrease this feeling.

[18] The committee which produced "Toward a More Responsible Two Party System" endorses this view at pp. 70–72 of its report.

Court well illustrates this disciplinary power.[19] In 1948 the Dixiecrat revolt against the Democratic party in several of the Southern states resulted in two factions fighting for control of the party. In Alabama, among others, the Dixiecrats were successful in gaining control. Their Presidential electors were chosen and cast the state's vote for the Dixiecrat candidate for President. As the Presidential campaign of 1952 approached, Democratic leaders in that state were determined to prevent a successful recurrence of a Dixiecrat revolt and to ensure that the state's vote would be cast for the candidate chosen by the National Convention of the Democratic party. The state executive committee of the party, acting under statutory authority, required a pledge from candidates for Presidential elector that they would support the nominees chosen by the party in the forthcoming convention before the committee would certify their names to appear on the primary ballot. (They thus anticipated the effort in the National Convention to require the Southern states suspected of Dixiecrat sympathies to give a similar pledge before their delegations could participate in the choice of the Presidential and Vice Presidential candidates.)

A man who wished to be a candidate for the Democratic party nomination as a Presidential elector without being willing to give the required pledge sought and obtained in the state courts a writ of mandamus to compel the chairman of the state executive committee of the party to certify his name to the Secretary of State for inclusion on the party primary ballot. The state court reasoned that under the Constitution Presidential electors are free to exercise their own discretion in selecting a President and must be left so. This decision the Supreme Court reversed.

For five members of the Court Mr. Justice Reed, conceding that the original intention of the founders had been to secure a nonpartisan choice of the President through the Electoral College, observed that the rise of parties had resulted in a custom that left the electors chosen by the parties legally free but morally bound to cast their votes for the party choice. Even if these promises are legally unenforceable,[20] it does not follow that a state may not authorize a party to demand such a pledge from its candidates. A party does not have to expose itself to attempts to capture it by those not willing to abide by its rules. For those who are dissatisfied "the state does offer the opportunity for the development of other strong political organizations . . ." To put such customary discipline on a legal basis does not seem a very drastic step. For that reason the dissent of Justice Jackson, in which Mr. Justice Douglas concurred, is revealing of the traditional American fear that central authority in the party may interfere with popular control.

Justice Jackson indicated his dissatisfaction with the electoral college and his preference for a system of direct national popular election of the President. The decision, he thought, strengthened the worst features of this

[19] Ray v. Blair, 343 U.S. 214 (1952).
[20] Mr. Justice Reed is admirably cautious in leaving this question open; 343 U.S. 214 at 228–30.

antiquated and distorted method of choice, although he admitted that it did "no more than to make a legal obligation of what has been a voluntary general practice." But "A political practice which has its origin in custom must rely on custom for its sanctions." Then he expressed a traditional American view that might even have startled Ostrogorski by its sweep:[21]

This device of prepledged and oath-bound electors imposes upon the party within the State an oath-bound regularity and loyalty to the controlling element in the national party. It centralizes party control and, instead of securing for the locality a share in the central management, it secures the central management in dominance of the local vote in the Electoral College. If we desire free elections, we should not add to the leverage over local party representatives always possessed by those who enjoy the prestige and dispense the patronage of a national administration . . . party control entrenched by disfranchisement and exclusion of nonconforming party members is a means which to my mind can not be justified by any end. In the interest of free government, we should foster the power and the will to be independent even on the part of those we may think to be independently wrong.

One consequence of this long drive to subject the parties to the will of the majority whenever they wish to exert it and of our reluctance to think of a party as a government is that we tend to think of the parties primarily as electoral devices and much less as a means of carrying out majority will in the government. We assume that once we have established a party in power, the self-interest of its leaders will cause it to carry out what the majority want. The problems on which the parties will have to take some stand in the day-to-day business of government are so numerous and so complex that we citizens could not possibly inform the parties very clearly about our desires unless we were willing to take the time also to study the problems and see what desires we have, or if we have any at all. That undertaking would require us to spend all of our leisure time in continuous political caucus, a prospect at which the mind rebels. Yet political leaders in other democratic countries also have to rely on much the same hit-or-miss testing of the winds of majority will, and there is a widespread impression that they feel much more responsible to their membership and the public in their governmental capacity than do the parties in Congress.

The difference, so far as it is a difference, is readily explained. It does not stem from the willful disregard of majority opinion by American party leaders.[22] On most questions the outlook of the membership of both major parties is similar enough that the best way to proceed is for Congress to do the small amount of logrolling needed to satisfy everyone reasonably well. Members of Congress, in fact, pride themselves on the nonpartisan character of most of their work and legislative output. Even on the relatively few questions about which there are deeply felt divisions among the electorate the process of compromise goes on.

[21] 343 U.S. 214 at 234.
[22] It may stem in part from the assiduous attention given to the wishes of organized minorities.

There is, finally, one exception that proves the rule that the belief in our state as a united association in which no permanent, deep, or inherent divisions exist among the members is the foundation upon which our traditional party system rests. This exception also explains why we can conceive that our parties ought to represent not only a majority of those who wish to belong to them but even a majority of the whole people. That exception is the struggle in the South to exclude the Negro from political participation and hence from membership in the Democratic party.[23] For the full significance of the white primary is the manifestation of a feeling that the Negro is not and should not be a member of the American state. The declaration that the white primary is a violation of the fundamental law of the land is a reaffirmation of our traditional democratic faith and an inspiring example of how the judicial enforcement of a democratic constitution can, at its best, at once summon and assist a people who live under it to carry forward the never-ending struggle to make and keep their faith a living one.

The sequence of the white primary cases has become familiar to many citizens who do not ordinarily read the United States Supreme Court reports. After the agonizing effort of the Civil War to start the Negro on the road to becoming a full member of American society, our resolve faltered and for decades seemed almost exhausted. With the turn of the century the first faint stirrings of law and opinion gave promise that the struggle would be renewed and that the promise might yet be redeemed. It was then that the white primary was invented as one more weapon of resistance. Within a few years the only party of consequence in the one-party system of the South had used its freedom of association to bar Negroes from membership in the party and thus from voting in its primaries, which make the effective choice of the government of these states and of a large part of the government of the United States.

An obscure factional fight in the Democratic party in Texas persuaded the legislature of that state it must exclude Negroes from voting in the party primary by law. When a case challenging this law reached the Supreme Court in 1927, therefore, Justice Holmes, who wrote the opinion of the Court, was not called upon to consider the right of a political party itself to limit its membership.[24] He thought it would be "hard to imagine a more direct and obvious" violation of the denial of the equal protection of the laws which the Fourteenth Amendment guarantees than the Texas statute.

Texas responded by repealing its law and enacting in its place one which authorized the state executive committee of the Democratic party to make rules prescribing who could vote in the party primary. That committee promptly exercised its power to deny the vote to Negroes. When this law and the committee's action were similarly challenged in 1932, Justice Cardozo

[23] Exclusion from voting in party primaries has of course not been the only device used to restrict political participation by Negroes.

[24] Nixon v. Herndon, 273 U.S. 536 (1927). The sequence of these white primary cases has been discussed too much to warrant more than brief summary here.

proceeded cautiously for the Court.[25] He held that it was unnecessary to consider the power of the party as a voluntary association to exclude Negroes, because the party authorities had been authorized to do so by state law and had acted in pursuance of the power delegated to them by the state, since they had received no power from the party so to act. Their action was therefore state action and rested on a state law, which like its predecessor denied the equal protection of the laws.

Rebuffed again, the Democratic party of Texas in convention assembled did for itself what the state legislature had twice been forbidden to do. It proclaimed its right to exclude Negroes from its primary elections. When confronted by this action in 1935 the Supreme Court momentarily lost the courage of its convictions.[26] Justice Roberts for the Court found that the party under Texas law was a private voluntary association, and that it conducted and paid for the expenses of its primary elections, as was true in some of the other Southern states although not the general practice throughout the nation. Clearly in this case the action had been taken by the party and not by the state. Therefore the Court decided that there was no denial of equal protection of the laws by the state, although it was as evident then as later that the candidates whom the party nominated in its primary could not be elected to public office except as the state recognized the party's choices and put them on the ballot in a general election. The right of a party as a voluntary association to select its members, the Court held, included the right to practice racial discrimination and was a private concern, not a public one. Of course what the Court had done was to refuse to consider seriously if the principle that the rights of association may not be used to the injury of other persons or to subvert the political institutions of a free society demanded a limitation on this absolute freedom of political association.

The Court drew some sustenance for this decision from a confused case it had decided in 1921, when a bare majority had reversed the conviction of Truman K. Newberry for spending more money than the law permitted in a campaign against Henry Ford to win nomination in a party primary as a candidate for United States Senator.[27] Congress in early corrupt practices legislation had placed limits on the expenditures of Congressional candidates in primary as well as general elections; the law had been passed before the Seventeenth Amendment had been adopted. Four members of the Court seemed to take the antiquarian view that since there had been no party primary elections at the time the Constitution was adopted, the powers of Congress over the election of members of Congress could not extend to party primaries. This was equivalent to saying that since there were no railroads when the Constitution was adopted, Congress could not enact the Interstate Commerce Act under its power to regulate commerce among the states. But the necessary fifth member of the majority simply doubted that Congress

25 Nixon v. Condon, 286 U.S. 73 (1932).

26 Grovey v. Townsend, 295 U.S. 45 (1935).

27 Newberry v. United States, 256 U.S. 232 (1921).

had intended the law to apply to senatorial primaries, since it had been passed before direct popular election of senators became part of the Constitution. The case did reflect a view that party primaries were a private concern.

In 1941, however, the Court sustained the conviction of an election official for making a false count of votes cast in a Democratic party primary election in Louisiana in which a party candidate for the House of Representatives had been chosen.[28] The conviction had been obtained under the provisions of a law passed during Reconstruction which made it a criminal offense for anyone to conspire or to act under color of state law to deprive any person of rights secured to him by the Constitution of the United States. Justice Stone held for the majority that since the right to vote for members of Congress is a right secured by the national Constitution,[29]

. . . where the state law has made the primary an integral part of the procedure of choice, or where in fact the primary effectively controls the choice, the right of the elector to have his ballot counted in the primary is likewise included in the right protected. . . .

Thus the Court recognized that the rights exercised by parties to choose candidates for public office make the conduct of the party primary a matter of public concern. The state of Louisiana, unlike Texas, itself conducted and paid for the party primary, but in both states the "primary effectively controls the choice." The Court had opened the way to reversal of the third Texas white primary case.

Mr. Justice Douglas dissented for himself and Justices Black and Murphy. They objected mainly to applying the federal criminal statute to this offense because they thought the law too vague to meet the constitutional requirements for a criminal statute. They also relied on a more sophisticated but no more convincing version of the argument of Justice McReynolds in the Newberry case. Although they agreed that Congress had the constitutional power to regulate primaries even though primaries did not exist when the Constitution was written, they argued that the statute of Congress to protect the citizens' constitutional rights did not extend to deprivations of those rights in primary elections because primaries did not exist when the statute was written. It might seem odd if the applicable provisions of the railroad safety appliance act were held inapplicable to Diesel locomotives because there were only steam locomotives when the act was passed.

In 1944 the Court, after having the case reargued, summoned up its courage again in the fourth Texas white primary case.[30] Except for Justice Roberts, who protested the overruling of his opinion in the third case, the Court was unanimous in forbidding the Democratic party of Texas to bar Negro voters from its membership. Mr. Justice Reed pointed to the telltale laws of Texas requiring the party to hold primaries and providing for plac-

[28] United States v. Classic et al., 313 U.S. 299 (1941).
[29] 313 U.S. 299 at 318.
[30] Smith v. Allwright, Election Judge, 321 U.S. 649 (1944).

ing its candidates so chosen upon the general election ballot. These laws made the party primary in Texas "an integral part of the procedure of choice" and also made the party's action a public concern. The state of South Carolina tried one last evasion. It repealed all its laws providing for party primaries and left the Democratic party to its own private devices. Of course the state could not find a way to avoid taking account of the nominations made by the party privately. In 1948 the Federal Court of Appeals brushed aside this patent subterfuge.[31] In doing so, Chief Judge Parker said:

> The fundamental error . . . consists in the premise that a political party is a mere private aggregation of individuals, like a country club, and that the primary is a mere piece of party machinery. The party may, indeed, have been a mere private aggregation of individuals in the early days of the Republic, but with the passing of the years, political parties have become in effect state institutions, governmental agencies through which sovereign power is exercised by the people.

The Supreme Court did not think it necessary to review the case,[32] and the battle to prevent a political party from abusing its rights of association to bar citizens because of their race from participation in the state was won, to the extent that judicial action can win it.[33]

EQUALIZATION OF PARTY RESOURCES

The second way in which the majoritarian impulse of democracy has imposed itself upon the political parties in the twentieth century, it was suggested, is in the effort to equalize the resources of the parties in men and money. The effort to equalize the manpower available to the parties began in the nineteenth century. Under a spoils system governmental payrolls form a pool of money which can be drawn upon, as well as brigades of shock troops that the party in power can throw into the fray in an election campaign. The effort to equalize these resources of manpower between the parties, therefore, is designed to produce something like equality between the parties viewed as the ins and the outs, by neutralizing the civil service and forbidding financial assessments. Of course there were other important

---

[31] Rice v. Elmore, 165 Fed. 2d 387 (1947).

[32] 333 U.S. 875 (1948), certiorari denied.

[33] In Terry et al. v. Adams et al., 345 U.S. 461 (1953), the Court recently confirmed and went beyond Rice v. Elmore. It held that the Jaybird Democratic Association of Fort Bend County, Texas, which considered all white voters in the county to be members, could not exclude Negroes from a "primary" election it held before the official primary to endorse candidates in the official primary and general election. This Jaybird nomination or endorsement primary, which was run without state approval or assistance, was quite informal but equally effective. Mr. Justice Black in the opinion of the Court treated this scheme as a subterfuge which ensured white control in the first and effective step of a three-step election. The majority was badly divided, with two concurring opinions. But only one member of the Court, Mr. Justice Minton, dissented. He thought that the Jaybirds were merely a private pressure group who had a perfect constitutional right to practice racial discrimination in politics.

reasons for removing the spoils system and introducing a merit system which would at the same time remove the threat of the bureaucracy from politics and the threat of politics from the bureaucracy. These other purposes of securing efficiency and economy in government may well be more important, but the effort to prevent the party in power from using government employees to intrench itself in power has strengthened support for civil service reform in the United States.

One important difference in the bearing of this reform on the parties in the United States and Britain deserves mention. In England patronage had been a powerful engine for building a united and centrally controlled party. It should not be assumed that the effect in the United States was exactly the same. Quite aside from the fact that our federal form of government means that the party out of control of the national government is always still in control of a substantial share of state and local governments and hence has troops available at crucial local points along the front, there is the effect of the custom of Senatorial courtesy, and for that matter, what ought to be called the courtesy of the House of Representatives, by which many patronage appointees are the liegemen not of the President but of the local party leaders. It would be difficult if not impossible to reach a very clear judgment whether the virtual elimination of spoils in the federal government has weakened or strengthened the President's hand against the Congressional members of his own party, but it should not go unnoticed that Presidents have been stronger supporters of civil service reform than Congress, though doubtlessly not simply because of their calculations of relative political advantage. The hypothesis occasionally advanced by some politicians that neutralization of the bureaucracy works against the party which is poorer in monetary resources by thus depriving it of tax-supported helpers and contributions from their salaries is even less susceptible of empirical study, for financial resources not only help a party get into power but also are likely to flow more generously toward a party in power.

The Supreme Court early approved the strict federal civil service rules forbidding employees under the merit system to engage in any partisan political activity, and for many years thereafter the constitutional questions involved in thus limiting their rights of political association slumbered.[34] It is hard to believe that the great majority of government employees under a merit system have ever regarded these rules as a tyrannical deprivation instead of a welcome protection. With the great increase in the size of the federal establishment under the New Deal, much of it hastily improvised outside the merit system, as well as the increase in state employees administering programs supported by federal funds from the burgeoning federal grants-in-aid, concern arose anew. The legislative results were the Hatch Acts, which, broadly speaking, applied to both these new groups the bans against activity in partisan politics in force for federal merit system employees. In 1947 the Supreme Court sustained provisions of this legislation relat-

[34] Ex parte Curtis, 106 U.S. 371 (1882).

ing to both federal nonmerit system employees[35] and state employees administering federal funds.[36] The Court conceded that the law and regulations did restrict the employees' rights of speech and association but traced the history of the movement for neutralization of the civil service to show and justify the basis for the Congressional judgment. Justices Black and Douglas each prepared dissenting opinions. There is a distinction between this and the earlier civil service law applying only to employees exempt from removal for political reasons. The federal employee in this case, a mint worker who had served as a local party official, was not protected against removal for political reasons. But Mr. Justice Black's opinion if it had become law would have raised grave doubts about the constitutionality of restricting the political activity even of those under the merit system, so absolute was his construction of the employee's rights.[37]

Mr. Justice Douglas did not take so uncompromising a stand. He stressed the purpose of the merit system to remove from political influence those employees who, although not at the top policy-making level, which changes with a change of party, nevertheless are in subordinate but important policy-making positions. These employees he thought Congress might appropriately bar from political activity. But he called attention to the great increase of manual and mechanical and clerical workers like this mint worker who do not make policy but are thus barred from an active part in politics. He suggested that as more persons become government employees the ban would become more serious and instanced the different policy followed in Great Britain toward this class of employees.

Both dissenting Justices thought that Congress had gone further than was necessary to accomplish the purposes sought. They felt reliance could be placed on forbidding the employees' superiors to coerce them to contribute money or services for benefit of the party in power, leaving the employees free to participate or not as they chose. Mr. Justice Douglas' objection was a thoughtful one, but it is questionable if the dissenters appraised realistically and adequately the subtle and manifold possibilities for coercion to which employees left "free" to engage in politics could be subjected under their proposals.[38]

The legislation to move toward equalization of the monetary sinews of war which each party may use is a twentieth-century development. No one could seriously question the prohibition of the use of money in elections for bribery and buying of votes. From their popular title one might suppose that these are the abuses prohibited by the Federal Corrupt Practices Acts.

[35] United Public Workers of America (C.I.O.) et al. v. Mitchell et al., 330 U.S. 75 (1947).

[36] State of Oklahoma v. United States Civil Service Commission, 330 U.S. 127 (1947).

[37] 330 U.S. 75 at 110–12.

[38] It hardly seems enough, as both dissenting Justices suggested, to forbid superior officers in the government to bring pressure to bear on their subordinates. Party officials outside government employ can bring pressure to bear just as effectively—and frequently have done so.

In fact they and similar state laws encompass much more. Their reliance upon the principle of disclosure of the source of contributions to and the use of funds by parties and candidates would also seem unobjectionable, although a recent decision of the Supreme Court seems to throw doubt upon them.[39] The requirement of disclosure is a recognition of the public interest in elections and of the value of the voters' having all significant facts available in making their choice.

It is not my purpose to evaluate at length the effectiveness of all this legislation. Those who have done so uniformly testify to its limited force, partly because of the loopholes in the laws, loopholes perhaps deliberately inserted, and partly because of public indifference. Disclosure of contributions and expenditures has not been as effective as some hoped, for the latter reason. Information about the sources of contributions is by and large not newsworthy for the same reason that a dog biting a man is not; everyone expects it to happen. If members of the Du Pont family gave large sums to the Socialist party instead of the Republican party we can be sure that they would make the front page of every newspaper in the country.

The corrupt practices laws, however, also attempt to limit the amounts of money individuals may contribute and the sum that a party organization or a candidate may expend. These provisions are of course easily avoided by the creation of a number of campaign committees all directing their efforts and expenditures to the same end. The intent of some who have sponsored such legislation has been to equalize the money available to the parties by putting a ceiling on the amount that the richer party could spend. It has not had this effect because it is easily avoided. Given the effort American candidates and parties generally agree that they must make to reach and interest the electorate, the limits on expenditures were unrealistic when established and become more so with the passing of time. The new opportunities for using mass media like radio and television for campaigning also mean new expense. If our limits on expenditure are set as a fixed amount, they do not, as the English limit of a certain sum per eligible voter does, allow for the considerable increase of adult population either. Neither do they take into account the apparently secular trend in the depreciation of the value of our money. Some observers believe that the multiple organizations created to avoid these limits also weaken centralized authority and responsibility in the parties. Serious students have called for the repeal of the limits on party expenditures and individual contributions.[40] Within thirty years, and in the case of the provisions added by the Hatch Acts within fifteen, they have approached that state which President Cleveland called innocuous desuetude.

Had they been more effective, great constitutional questions would have been raised. It is indicative of our egalitarian ideals that little of the criticism of such laws has rested on this constitutional question. The First Amendment forbids interference with freedom of speech, of the press, and of the

[39] United States v. Rumely, 345 U.S. 41 (1953).
[40] Cf. "Toward a More Responsible Two Party System," p. 75.

right to petition the government for a redress of grievances. Freedom of speech and press include the right to publish one's views through all the media of communication. It is a challenging thought that private citizens or political parties may be forbidden to use their own funds or those donated to them for the purpose of publishing their views in a political campaign. Yet that is precisely what these provisions of the corrupt practices laws undertake to do. If one takes an absolute view of these rights or even the view that they can be limited only on the strictest showing of a clear and present danger, it is difficult to see how one could deny that these provisions are unconstitutional on their face. If one does not, he is still confronted with the novel question of the extent to which a purpose of limiting plutocratic influence upon politics justifies a democracy in restricting the exercise of these vital freedoms. It is not without interest, as Professor Herman Finer has shown, that this egalitarian spirit is at work elsewhere, and particularly under the aegis of the Labor government in England, which, although it has no First Amendment, has demonstrated a long and deep devotion to its principles.[41] It would be hard to find a sharper conflict of the ideals of liberty and equality.

Not until a few years ago did the Supreme Court have to face a question of this kind growing out of the provisions of the corrupt practices legislation. As early as 1907 Congress forbade business corporations to make any contributions to political campaigns for federal office. In 1947 in a section of the Taft-Hartley Act Congress amended and strengthened this law by forbidding expenditures as well as contributions. It also applied the amended provision to labor unions. Students of English law and labor will recognize the similarity of the issue thus raised to one which agitated British politics for forty years, and still does.[42]

Philip Murray, president of the Congress of Industrial Organizations, promptly challenged the act by ordering the insertion in a paper published by his organization and supported out of the labor association's funds of an "advertisement" calling on its readers to vote in a Democratic party primary election in Maryland for a certain candidate for the House of Representatives. He and the CIO were indicted (the law in this case made it possible for an unincorporated association to be a criminal) and pleaded the unconstitutionality of the provision as a defense. The trial judge held it invalid and dismissed the indictment. The government appealed the point of law to the Supreme Court.

[41] Herman Finer, *Theory and Practice of Modern Government* (rev. ed., New York, 1949), pp. 294–98.
[42] In 1910 trade unions were forbidden to make compulsory levies for political use in Amalgamated Society of Railway Servants v. Osborne (1910) A.C. 87. In 1913 Parliament permitted the unions to make political assessments provided that a majority of the members approved and that any member unwilling to pay could "contract out." After the General Strike of 1926 Parliament in the Trade Disputes Act of the following year made it more difficult for the unions to raise political funds by requiring that such political levies could be made only on each member who explicitly consented, instead of on all who did not explicitly object. One of the first actions of the Labor government in 1946 was to repeal this 1927 act.

In *United States* v. *CIO* a bare majority of the Court sustained dismissal of the indictment, but refused to pass upon the constitutionality of the law.[43] Mr. Justice Reed for four members of the Court construed, or as many have persuasively claimed, misconstrued the statute as not forbidding the kind of expenditure made here, although it is the one kind of expenditure that Senator Taft and President Truman seemed to agree the broad and sweeping terms of the law did prohibit.[44] Mr. Justice Frankfurter concurred in the result because he thought that the government had argued the case so poorly and carelessly below that otherwise the Court could do little more than pass on the issue of constitutionality abstractly.

Justice Rutledge wrote a powerful concurrence—perhaps his best constitutional opinion—declaring that the Court should have held the provision unconstitutional. In this he was joined by Justices Black, Douglas, and Murphy. Summarizing Congress' conception of the objectives of the law he said :[45]

These were : (1) To reduce what had come to be regarded in the light of recent experience as the undue and disproportionate influence of labor unions upon federal elections; (2) to preserve the purity of such elections and of official conduct ensuing from the choices made in them against the use of aggregated wealth by union as well as corporate entities; and (3) to protect union members holding political views contrary to those supported by the union from use of funds contributed by them to promote acceptance of those opposing views.

In regard to the first two of these purposes he observed :[46]

If the evil is taken to be the corruption of national elections and federal officials by the expenditure of large masses of aggregated wealth in their behalf, the statute is neither so phrased nor so limited, even in its legislative construction. . . . The Government stresses the "undue influence" of unions in making expenditures by way of publication in support of or against candidates and political issues involved in the campaign rather than corruption in the gross sense. It maintains that large expenditures by unions in publicizing their official political views bring about an undue, that is supposedly a disproportionate sway, of electoral sentiment and official attitudes. In short, the "bloc" power of unions has become too great, in influencing both the electorate and public officials, to permit further expenditure of their funds in directly and openly publicizing their political views.

This assumption Justice Rutledge sharply questioned.

The expression of bloc sentiment is and always has been an integral part of our democratic electoral and legislative processes. They could hardly go on without it.

The opportunities for a bloc, in other words, a pressure group, to express its views is, he urged,

essential to the full, fair and untrammeled operation of the electoral process. To the extent they are curtailed the electorate is deprived of information, knowledge

---

[43] United States v. Congress of Industrial Organizations *et al.*, 335 U.S. 106 (1948).
[44] 335 U.S. 106 at 135–39.   [45] 335 U.S. 106 at 134.   [46] 335 U.S. 106 at 142–43.

and opinion vital to its function. To say that labor unions as such have nothing of value to contribute to that process and no vital or legitimate interest in it is to ignore the obvious facts of political and economic life and of increasing inter-relationship in modern society.

The Achilles' heel of this argument is, of course, that the law does not prevent unions from using in political campaigns money raised expressly for that purpose. Senator Taft had agreed that the act did not prevent unions from acting in political campaigns through special committees, like the CIO Political Action Committee, but insisted that funds for such activity must be contributed only by those individual union members who were willing to do so specifically for political purposes; the unions could not use funds obtained from ordinary dues or assessments. This left unions some and perhaps quite enough freedom, but Justice Rutledge doubted that the last purpose of protection of the rights of indivdual union members justified the severe restrictions of the laws.

In its political activities should the union be seen as a group, and should the principle of majority rule applied to the collective bargaining agreement in the economic sphere be applied to a union's decision to enter into the political arena? The minority suggested that this might be the proper position for the law to take. Since this issue has disturbed thoughtful statesmen and scholars for so long a time in Great Britain, and is the crucial issue in the case, extensive quotation of Justice Rutledge's argument, which must have impressed the majority, is called for.

Under the section as construed, the accepted principle of majority rule which has become a bulwark, indeed perhaps the leading characteristic, of collective activities is rejected in favor of atomized individual rule and action in matters of political advocacy . . . Union activities in political publicity are confined to the use of funds received from members with their explicit designation given in advance for the purpose. . . .

It is true that the union could ask and in many instances secure the required explicit assents. It seems to be suggested that this might be done by expressly designating a specific portion of the dues for political uses, possibly though not at all clearly by by-law or constitutional provision, possibly by earmarking upon statements of dues payable. But it is not made clear whether the member could refuse to pay the earmarked portion and retain membership or would have to pay it to remain in that status. If the latter is true, the section affords little real "minority protection"; if the former, the dissentient is given all the benefit derived from the union's political publicity without having to pay any part of its cost. . . .

The section does not merely deprive the union of majority rule in political expression. . . . It rests upon the presumption that the majority are out of accord with their elected officials in political viewpoint and its expression and, where that presumption is not applicable, it casts the burden of ascertaining minority or individual dissent not upon the dissenters but upon the union and its officials. . . . Unions too must often operate under the electoral process and the principle of majority rule. Nor does it seem reasonable to presume dissent from mere absence of explicit assent, especially in view of long-established union practice.

If merely "minority or dissenter protection" were intended, it would be sufficient for securing this to permit the dissenting members to carry the burden of making known their position and to relieve them of any duty to pay dues or portions of them to be applied to the forbidden uses without jeopardy to their rights as members.[47]

The decision of the Court left these questions for another day, but also left the bearing of the law in great doubt. It is not likely that we are done with the matter; Senator Taft, among others, agreed to the need for clarification of policy. Hovering over the future is the fundamental question: will organized labor in the United States go through a metamorphosis from a pressure group in politics to a political party?

That question leads us on to contemporary efforts to define the place of pressure groups in our party system, but before turning to it, we should recall the principle that Sir Ernest Barker propounded :[48]

The State will demand from an association that it shall have a definite basis of action, and that such a basis shall be unitary, in the sense of not combining different kinds of action. If the State does not exact a definite basis, members of the association will not know to what they are pledged; if it does not demand a unitary basis, members who join the association for one kind of action of which they approve will have a just complaint, if they are forced to join in another kind of action of which they disapprove.

If the pressure of circumstances and the weight of the state's own law do not force men into an association—in other words, if the association is a voluntary one in fact as well as in theory—one may question whether the state is justified in so restricting the group. But if it is not, and labor union membership is no longer wholly voluntary in this country, Professor Barker's thesis should command earnest attention.

REGULATION OF PRESSURE GROUPS

The third evidence of the majoritarian spirit at work in shaping the law relating to rights of political association in twentieth-century American democracy is the search for a *modus vivendi* among the state, the parties, and the pressure groups. Under the constitutional right of the people "to petition the Government for a redress of grievances" the interest groups have developed that right from which the House of Commons in medieval England slowly moved toward the supremacy of Parliament into the big business of lobbying—a business so big and so impressive in its products that many Americans sometimes wonder if these associated petitioners have evolved from the supplicants into the masters of legislatures.

From fragmentary beginnings the Congress as recently as 1946 in the Legislative Reorganization Act enacted a rather elaborate but somewhat

47 335 U.S. 106 at 147–49.
48 *Political Thought in England, 1848–1914*, p. 156.

vague code for the registration of lobbyists and the pressure groups whom they serve.[49] The law proceeds on the principle of regulating them and their activities no further than exposing them to public knowledge and the force of public opinion, so far as their activities can be reconstructed from a disclosure of the money that they get and spend. The act would seem to be constitutionally unexceptionable, if practically modest in achievements, if it were not for a recent Supreme Court decision rebuking a Congressional investigating committee for making similar inquiries.

That case is *United States* v. *Rumely*, decided in 1953.[50] Disturbed by rumored evasions of the Regulation of Lobbying Act of 1946, the House of Representatives in 1949 created a Select Committee on Lobbying Activities, commonly called the Buchanan Committee after its chairman. The House Resolution provided that: "The Committee is authorized and directed to conduct a study and investigation of (1) all lobbying activities intended to influence, encourage, promote, or retard legislation. . . ." The committee called as one of the witnesses in its extensive hearings one Edward A. Rumely, secretary of the Committee for Constitutional Government, an ultraconservative organization registered under the lobbying act. When the witness refused to answer some of the committee's questions or to produce some of the organization's records of its financial transactions, the committee recommended that the House cite him for contempt. After debate, the House did so. (Although each house of Congress retains the ancient power to punish for contempts committed against it, Congress long ago provided for an alternative of trial of a contempt citation before a judge and jury in a federal court, and in this case, as is customary, this alternative was used.) The defendant Rumely was convicted of contempt and sentenced to a fine of one thousand dollars and imprisonment for six months.

On appeal of the case to the Supreme Court Mr. Justice Frankfurter wrote the opinion of the Court, reversing the conviction on the ground that the committee had exceeded its powers under the authorizing resolution in the questions it addressed to the defendant. His opinion was brief and rather abstract, giving little attention to legislative history, which he has so often used to place questions in a realistic context. He emphasized that the Court put its decision on the narrow ground that the committee had misinterpreted its powers under the resolution (which had been sponsored by its chairman) in order to avoid grave constitutional questions, which would result if the resolution were interpreted to give the committee "power to inquire into all efforts of private individuals to influence public opinion through books and periodicals, however remote the radiations of influence which they may exert upon the ultimate legislative process. . . ." Instead, the Court adopted a narrower interpretation of lobbying, said to be "its com-

<hr>

[49] For a succinct account cf. George B. Galloway, *Congress at the Crossroads* (New York, 1946), pp. 302–8, 341.

[50] 345 U.S. 71 (1953).

monly accepted" sense.[51] Lobbying was defined as "representations made directly to the Congress, its members, or its committees" as distinguished from "attempts 'to saturate the thinking of the community.'"

It is only in the concurring opinion of Mr. Justice Douglas, in which Mr. Justice Black joined, that the issues become clear. The Committee for Constitutional Government had spent about two million dollars from October 1946 to August 1950. The federal lobbying act requires disclosure of contributions or expenditures of five hundred dollars or more by registered organizations. The Buchanan Committee had found that the Committee for Constitutional Government had

adopted a policy of accepting payments of over $490 only if the contributor specified that the funds be used for the distribution of one or more of its books or pamphlets. It then applied the term "sale" to the "contribution" and did not report them under the Regulation of Lobbying Act.

Other practices which the organization used to circumvent or violate the law, the committee suspected, included

Dividing large contributions into installments of $490 or less, and causing the records . . . to reflect receipts of each installment on a different date, and/or causing the records . . . to give credit, for the several installments, to various relatives and associates of the actual contributor.

Mr. Justice Douglas also thought, and his demonstration is an impressive one, that the House had clearly intended to authorize its committee to investigate the "bookselling" activities of the Committee for Constitutional Government, which had been mentioned by name in debate on the resolution. This position had been reaffirmed in debate on the contempt citation. The lobbying act itself applies to efforts to "influence, directly or *indirectly*, the passage or defeat of legislation by the Congress." The committee was to study the effectiveness of this act.[52]

Under these circumstances Mr. Justice Douglas thought the question of the power of Congress to require disclosure of such transactions could not be avoided. He insisted that the First Amendment forbids compulsion to reveal sources of financial support for such propaganda efforts. "We have here," he wrote, "a publisher who through books and pamphlets seeks to reach the minds and hearts of the American people. He is different in some respects from other publishers. But the differences are minor." In this last statement Knopf or Macmillan, Harper's or the Stanford University Press might understandably think a printer had erroneously read *major* as *minor* and the proofreader had failed to catch the error. It is true that in law this distribution of literature is publication. But this lobbying organization is hardly a publisher as the trade conceives the term.

[51] In doing so Mr. Justice Frankfurter was moved to say, "To give such meaning is not barred by intellectual honesty." 345 U.S. 41 at 47.
[52] 345 U.S. 41 at 52–56.

The concurrence then turns to that demand to "resist beginnings" which not so long ago served a conservative majority so well in striking down New Deal legislation, and to a "parade of horribles" :[53]

If the present inquiry were sanctioned the press would [not even might] be subjected to harassment that in practical effect might be as serious as censorship. . . . A requirement that a publisher disclose the identity of those who buy his books, pamphlets, or papers is indeed the beginning of surveillance of the press. . . . Once the government can demand of a publisher the names of the purchasers of his publications, the free press as we know it disappears. Then the spectre of a government agent will look over the shoulder of everyone who reads.

Since one of the "readers" in this case had "purchased" over fifteen thousand copies of the same book and had the "publisher" send each one to a different library, the spectral government agent assigned to look over his shoulders would have had to journey as long as the Flying Dutchman following his reader around to all those libraries to read the copy of his book in each. Aside from all his wearisome travel, what a dreary task he would have to read the same book fifteen thousand times, especially over someone else's shoulder! One is tempted to retort to this kind of argument that the Supreme Court should not lose its hold on common sense in the course of imagining that Congress might.

This argument of *obstat principiis* deserves more than that retort, for, along with the accompanying judicial technique of testing the validity of an asserted power by posing the logical extremes to which it could hypothetically be carried, it has been responsible for some of the most questionable decisions which we have explored. Both the doctrine and the technique have a long history in American constitutional law, reaching back to *Marbury* v. *Madison*.[54] Whatever merits either the doctrine or the technique has are lost, however, when judges forget that they will still have power to resist the bad developments from a good beginning, or that hypothetical logical extremes as seldom recommend themselves to the good sense of legislatures as they do to courts. There would be time enough for courts to act if Congress subpoenaed Scribner's invoices or *Life's* subscription lists.

Had the minority view been adopted by the Court in this case, the search for a *modus vivendi* with pressure groups would have been badly hampered. More than that, the corrupt practices laws requiring disclosure of party contributions and expenditures could hardly stand, for does not a party committee spending millions in an election campaign also fall under Mr. Justice Douglas' definition of "a publisher who through books and pamphlets [and radio and television] seeks to reach the minds and hearts of the American people?" The majority opinion lends too much weight to the minority view by regarding the constitutional question raised as so grave that it must be avoided, or evaded. But at least Mr. Justice Frankfurter's opinion has the

[53] 345 U.S. 41 at 57.
[54] 1 Cranch 137 (1803).

negative merit of saving the Court from committing itself rashly to a position from which further reflection may still warn it away. For the effort to prevent the pressure groups from playing a gigantic confidence game on the public is an important item of unfinished business on the agenda of democracy. The court should be careful not to cross it off the list by too bold a sweep of its pen.[55]

[55] Since these words were written the Court has had more realistic second thoughts. In 1954 it handed down a decision in a case testing the validity of the Federal Regulation of Lobbying Act. United States v. Harriss et al., 347 U.S. 612 (1954). Under the leadership of Mr. Chief Justice Warren a bare majority of the Court upheld the constitutionality of vital sections of the act requiring reports of contributions and expenditures and registration of paid lobbyists. In doing so the Court limited the meaning of lobbying to that of "direct communication with members of Congress" adopted by Mr. Justice Frankfurter in the Rumely case; although it included an "artificially stimulated letter campaign" within this narrower definition. The Chief Justice held that, so construed, the act was not void because of vagueness and did not violate the First Amendment. He added, "Otherwise the voice of the people may all too easily be drowned out by the voice of special interest groups seeking favored treatment while masquerading as proponents of the public weal." This time Justices Douglas and Black dissented. They thought the act too vague, although they "did not mean to intimate that Congress is without power to require disclosure" by a statute that would be narrowly drawn. Justice Jackson dissented separately, making similar objections. Mr. Justice Clark did not participate.

6

SUBVERSIVE ASSOCIATIONS: WORMS IN THE ENTRAILS OF LEVIATHAN

In the preceding chapters we have examined the contemporary development of the American constitutional law of freedom of association and the application of emerging legal principles to three of the most important types of the great associations in American society. In this chapter, however, we shall not be examining a particular type of association. We shall look at one of these principles and ask how it is to be related properly to another of these principles as both are applied to one of the most perplexing problems in contemporary American life. That principle holds that the rights of association shall not be used to do serious injury to society as a whole or to the organized political institutions of that society. It must be considered *in pari materia*, as the lawyers say, with the principle which affirms that the rights of individuals to associate shall be protected against unlawful governmental infringement. But conceiving the problem of dealing with subversive associations primarily as a question of constitutional rights and powers is quite inadequate.

It is inadequate because the constitutional question is the last of three questions which must be asked, and the two that precede it must be answered before it can be sensibly considered. First we must determine if there is a danger of subversion of our society and its political institutions, and if there is, what the threat is and how and why it is dangerous. We must remember, moreover, that an answer requires us not only to interpret past data but to predict future events.

We must next decide, if a danger of subversion has been established, how that danger can best be overcome, or to put it another way, what the probable effects of measures that may be taken to overcome it are likely to be. This question like the first is a question of opinion and of prediction. Yet we know little of the effects of what has already been done. Extensive empirical research would be required to make even a rough estimate of the number of persons in the United States who since 1945 have been adversely affected in any measurable fashion by the entire range of antisubversive controls. Those subjected to criminal punishment would certainly be a far smaller number than those removed or barred from public employment, or those who have felt in any measurable way, such as financial loss, social disapproval. As one recollects the period impressionistically, one is likely to conclude that it is not the measures which may seem abstractly sterner, that have produced the most or the most serious instances of possible miscarriages of justice, although the secret nature of some of them defeats an accurate appraisal. On the whole, however, it seems likely that the public has been a harsher and less careful judge than the executive and judicial officers who administer the legal controls. The most disturbing characteristics of the social pressure exerted by the public have been, as always, carelessness in weighing the evidence disclosed and a spirit of retribution that too often puts those who have of their own volition repudiated groups to which they once belonged in an almost hopeless position.

Another possible consequence is even less susceptible to empirical study. That is the belief Professor Zechariah Chafee has stressed, that the most dangerous result of such measures is to silence those who are innocent but timid, or as is sometimes said in rather vivid rhetoric, to create a reign of terror. Undoubtedly there is much insight in Professor Chafee's comment, but as one observes the steady volume of open adverse cricitism of these measures one ought to hesitate to push this hypothesis too far.

Only after he has carefully formed his opinions in regard to these two questions should a Supreme Court Justice, a legislator, a social scientist, or a citizen venture a judgment on the constitutionality of any law regarding subversion, for otherwise he is making uninformed generalizations in a vacuum. The question of constitutionality is also a question of opinion, not of absolute truth.

Another perspective can be gained from recalling that we are not discussing a particular type of association, but the purposes which give a group a reputation. Every type of the great associations has at one time or another been considered subversive. In the sixteenth and seventeenth centuries religious wars reflect this belief about churches. Common law doctrines of conspiracy applied to labor unions in the eighteenth and nineteenth centuries manifest the same conviction. Even fraternal groups have not been free from suspicion, as the history of freemasonry shows. Today in the United States it is a political party that excites concern. Let us then for a moment consider the subversiveness of associations *sub specie aeternitatis* for what perspective it can provide.

The subversive character of a group is a matter of opinion. History reveals that opinion about the subversive nature of these groups has differed among different societies at the same time and has also changed in the same society over a period of time. Why should this be? There are several reasons. Circumstances may differ among some societies or change in the same society. The purposes or the tactics of the suspect group may also change. Even without much change in circumstances or in the group itself society may conclude that it had misinterpreted the facts and may revise its opinion.

Needless to say, none of these associations ever has regarded itself as subversive. Locke said pithily that "every church is orthodox to itself." Even if a group openly proclaims a purpose to destroy the political institutions of a society, it will do so in the name of benefiting that society as distinguished from its government.

An association may hold as its objective the overthrow of the existing government and, as men later come to believe, in the light of events, the harm of the society, without creating a dominant opinion that it is subversive. The growth of the Nazi party in Germany seems to be an example of the price society pays for making such an error. An association may also be widely regarded as subversive and yet go largely unrestrained by the government unless those who believe it to be so are numerous enough or powerful enough or disturbed enough to secure legal action against it. The fading of the revived Ku Klux Klan in the United States in the 1920's makes an instructive case study.

Several stages occur in the treatment of a group charged with subversion. First, those who consider an association subversive seek to convince others that their view is correct, while the accused group strives to disprove the charge. This might be called the propaganda stage, and while it lasts the disputants may exert strong and frequently ugly social pressure against one another. Eventually, a large part of the public may be convinced and throw the weight of its disapproval against members of the distrusted group. Denunciation, ostracism, deprivation of livelihood may all be inflicted. These acts are a natural consequence of the wide liberty allowed to individuals and, within some limitations like the laws of libel, are entirely lawful. They may be enough to destroy or disable a group without any governmental action.

METHODS OF LEGAL CONTROL

The next stage, if it occurs, consists in the application of the specific social controls of law. If the state is democratic this action comes in response to widespread popular opinion. At this stage a choice must be made among a great variety of possible measures. In the past as well as at the present time in the United States so many types of restraint have been imposed that one is almost bewildered by legal inventiveness. But three general types of restriction can be discovered; they are publicity, security, and outlawry.

The government may rely on publicizing facts about the association and reasons for regarding it as subversive. By this method government essentially supports and reinforces social pressure against the group. In order to obtain information about the association the government may conduct investigations by various methods available to it. In these investigations, whether legislative, executive, or judicial, witnesses can be compelled to testify under penalties of contempt and of perjury.

Under the Constitution witnesses in federal investigations may invoke their privilege against self-incrimination unless the law guarantees them complete immunity against any criminal prosecution which could be brought on the basis of their testimony. There are, however, three more important qualifications besides that of compulsion to testify only under immunity. First, this right against self-incrimination, so far as the Constitution of the United States is concerned, can be invoked only against the national government. It was recently held by a sharply divided Court not to be so fundamental a liberty that the states are forbidden to deny it by the due process clause of the Fourteenth Amendment.[1] Second, it has long been held that since a corporation cannot claim this right, which is limited to natural persons, officers of a corporation must give testimony regarding corporate affairs, even though such evidence also incriminates them personally. Recently the Supreme Court has extended this precedent to the officers of unincorporated voluntary associations.[2] Third, the Supreme Court also held recently that if the government requires an individual or organization to keep records of a prescribed kind, these must be produced by and may be used against the person legally responsible for keeping them, even though they are incriminating.[3] This result was reached because such records are "official," that is, they are considered the property of the government, which may demand their possession at will. None of these recent precedents, it should be added, was laid down in cases involving Communists.

Additionally or alternatively government may place the association and its officers under legal obligation to make periodic disclosures of its purposes, regulations, activities, officers, members, and financial receipts and expenditures, either confidentially or for general public inspection. Incorporated associations quite free from any taint of subversion have long been under similar obligations of "visitation." A kind of routinized continual investigation is thus established.

The second type of regulation presupposes that something more than exposure of the association to the force of public opinion is necessary. Government may seek to prevent injury to itself and to society by anticipating and forestalling or prohibiting under penal sanction certain acts of the association and its members. It may also undertake to reduce the financial resources of the association in ways that go beyond unfavorable publicity. These precautionary or security measures differ from the third method in that they do leave some lawful sphere for the group and its members.

Security measures may also be carried out by the executive, legislature, or the courts. Their wide range may be illustrated by methods currently in use: administrative techniques and legislative penalties to prevent espionage and sabotage, police surveillance, prevention of infiltration of government agencies or of other groups by members or followers of the suspected group through investigation and test oaths, denial of admission or naturalization to aliens connected with the group, restriction of travel abroad by members of the group, prevention of assemblies of the group which threaten physical violence, prohibition of the use of paramilitary uniforms and drills, denial of a place on the ballot in elections for the candidates of the group, and denial of tax exemption privileges on financial contributions to the association.

Last, there is the type of regulation loosely and popularly called outlawry, which I shall use for want of a better single word. It is based on the assumption that it is not enough either to expose the group to social pressure or to limit by law some of the activities and the resources of the

---

[1] Adamson v. People of State of California, 332 U.S. 46 (1947).
[2] United States v. White, 322 U.S. 649 (1944).
[3] Shapiro v. United States, 335 U.S. 1 (1948).

group, but that it is necessary to prohibit the very existence of a group found to have subversive purposes. Even in the category of outlawry a range of proscriptions is available. Not only may attempted revolution be punished, but planning or training for it, or even teaching or advocating it. Forming or leading a subversive association may be a crime, or mere rank-and-file membership may be forbidden, or even affiliation with or substantial support of the group may be prohibited. At some point, if such criminal punishments can be effectively enforced, it is clear that the association must cease to exist. This is what is meant by outlawing an association. As a matter of fact, the statutes of the United States, as they have been construed by the Supreme Court, to say nothing of the laws of many of the states, do forbid an individual to do every one of the acts just mentioned if the association concerned is one which purposes the overthrow of the government by force and violence.

These three categories of publicity, security, and outlawry may appear to be arranged in an ascending order of severity. But the rigor with which any measures in these categories are executed may be more important than their appearance on the statute book. Nor can the effectiveness of any of these provisions be measured simply by its severity. It is not even true that these three types of legal action are adopted in any chronological order.

PROBLEMS OF JUDICIAL REVIEW

Although many of the illustrations of efforts to control subversive groups have been drawn from American practice, they have their counterparts in the experience of other nations. But in the United States there is still a third stage in the treatment of subversion that is almost if not quite unique. That stage develops, of course, when the courts are called to pass upon the constitutionality of the regulatory measures taken. It is this stage in the treatment of subversive groups and this question of constitutionality to which we must now devote our attention. In doing so the considerable number of judicial decisions that have already accumulated makes it advisable to limit our consideration to the opinions of the United States Supreme Court and to only the most fundamental questions on which the Court has passed.

In considering the constitutionality of antisubversion laws, is the Supreme Court concerned either with the soundness of the legislature's view of the danger or with balancing the likely good and evil effects to be expected from the law? The answer must be that it is and it isn't. It does not necessarily follow that a statute is unconstitutional because the danger at which it is aimed seems imaginary or because it will do harm and probably more harm than any possible good. It does not necessarily follow, either, that an act aimed at a real danger and effective in meeting it is therefore constitutional. Yet it would be a miracle if judges entirely excluded from their minds considerations of the wisdom and effects of these statutes, considerations which now-familiar learning tells us enter in some degree into all other constitutional adjudication.

If the rights of free speech, press, assembly, and others involved in association were regarded as absolute, subject to no qualifications or limitations, no legal control of subversive groups would be possible, except conceivably that which remitted them to the arbitrament of social pressure. No Justice of the Supreme Court when faced with the concrete social problems created by associations has been willing, despite his dicta, to construe the constitutional guaranties as giving absolute immunity.

Is American constitutional law contrary to the political theory of liberalism in this respect? Since intimations that it is are heard from time to time, the question deserves an answer. The answer is clear in any liberal theorist who has discussed the problem, from Milton to Hobhouse. Liberal theory has held as a basic tenet the legal right of men to criticize and to limit one association, the state itself, and in extreme cases the moral right even to destroy it, if those in control of the state use their power to subvert the good of society. A theory that goes so far must and does acknowledge that the ethical right of the people, acting through their common association, the state, to prevent other associations from doing injury to them all is founded on the same principle. The political theory of liberalism is a sword that has in the past humbled absolute monarchs and checked the haughty pretensions of ecclesiastics. It cannot now be twisted into armor for any group trying to conquer a society.

From the beginning one of the Court's difficulties has been how to take account in the judicial process of the fact that communism is an organized movement, and an international one, and what weight to give this fact; in short, to visualize the problem of communism as one of association rather than merely one of individual rights of freedom of speech and press and assembly. Our theory of the rights of associations, as we have seen, is based on an eighteenth-century view of the rights of individuals. Communism is a twentieth-century phenomenon. In recent years Justice Jackson stressed more than any other member of the Court the nature of the Communist party as an association; it would be interesting to know how much of his insight came from his experience as the chief prosecutor in the Nürnberg war crimes trials.

This difficulty has been compounded by lack of judicial precedent for the task. During the Civil War organized, secret, conspiratorial societies of disaffected persons existed in both the North and the South. The threats which they posed were fearfully exaggerated but were nonetheless real. Both governments took drastic actions against some of their members but did not go so far as they understandably might have gone. Yet in our constitutional law only the names of two individuals, Clement Vallandigham and Lambdin P. Milligan, remind us of the Order of American Knights, the Knights of the Golden Circle, and the Sons of Liberty.[4]

The first modern subversive movement (now an old-fashioned one) to plague the country was anarchism, but as Justice Jackson observed in the Dennis case, "extreme individualism was not conducive to cohesive and disciplined organization." During the First World War, under the leadership

---

[4] *Ex parte* Vallandigham, 1 Wallace 243 (1864), and *Ex parte* Milligan, 4 Wallace 2 (1866).

of Eugene Debs, some members and some local units of the Socialist party undertook to oppose the draft act. It was Justice Holmes, let us remember, who ultimately sent both Debs and Schenck to jail.[5] Late in that war there occurred the momentous event which was to provide the setting of our present problem. The old Socialist party was torn asunder by the Bolshevik Revolution. Under moderate leadership the right wing remained the Socialist party. As the years passed, only the most obstinately credulous could believe that Norman Thomas was subversive; long before many non-Socialist liberals he described the true nature of the home of the Communists. And as the years passed, the Socialist party membership dwindled.

In the murkiest shadows of the national scene in Calvin Coolidge's day the left-wingers from the old Socialist party splintered and resplintered into groups that were as obscure as they were odious to most of their fellow citizens. To these days belong Anita Whitney and Benjamin Gitlow. They are proper symbols of the period, for both were or were to become dissenters in the midst of dissentient groups. The gently bred niece of Justice Field went to prison, but was pardoned and returned to her former ways.[6] Gitlow came out of prison to expose old comrades-in-arms, if we may call them such.[7]

Far stronger than any of these puny leftist groups in the 1920's was the revived Ku Klux Klan. Its resort to violence, its religious bigotry, and its preachments of racial hatred were all subversive of the law of the land. Only in the state of New York, however, was a vigorous attempt made to proceed by law against the Klan as an association. A few days after the Presidential election of 1928, in which prejudices stirred and reflected by the Klan had been turned against Governor Al Smith of New York, a conservative and Republican Supreme Court sustained the New York legislation.[8] Its action must have been some consolation to the defeated Democratic Presidential candidate, who had been governor when this act was passed in 1923.

New York had relied on the principle of disclosure. Its law figuratively unhooded the Klan. The law provided that every organization requiring an oath of its members, except labor unions and benevolent orders recognized under state law, must file with the Secretary of State and thus open to public inspection "a sworn copy of its constitution, by-laws, regulations, and oath of membership, together with a roster of its membership and a list of its officers for the current year." The statute had a sting for individual members:

Any person who becomes a member of any such . . . association, or remains a member thereof, or attends a meeting thereof, with knowledge that such. . . association has failed to comply . . . shall be guilty of a misdemeanor.

[5] Debs v. United States, 249 U.S. 211 (1919), and Schenck v. United States, 249 U.S. 47 (1919).
[6] Whitney v. California, 274 U.S. 357 (1927) ; cf. the account of the case in Zechariah Chafee, Jr., *Free Speech in the United States* (Cambridge, 1941), pp. 343–51.
[7] Gitlow v. New York, 268 U.S. 652 (1925) ; cf. Chafee, *op. cit.*, chap. 9.
[8] People of State of New York *ex rel.* Bryant v. Zimmerman, 278 U.S. 73 (1928).

The Klan did not comply, and when one of its members was arrested and held for trial under the statute, he sought habeas corpus on the ground that the law violated his rights under the Fourteenth Amendment. Justice Van Devanter denied that the law abridged any privilege or immunity of federal citizenship and devoted most of his attention to the charges that it deprived the accused of his liberty without due process of law and that it denied him the equal protection of the laws by singling out, in effect, the Klan for registration. The law was "not arbitrary or oppressive, but reasonable and likely to be of real effect." It was justified

on the two-fold theory that the state within whose territory and under whose protection the association exists is entitled to be informed of its nature and purpose, of whom it is composed and by whom its activities are conducted, and that requiring this information to be supplied for the public files will operate as an effective or substantial deterrent from the violations of public and private right to which the association might be tempted if such a disclosure were not required.

Nor did the statute deny the equal protection of the laws by singling out the Ku Klux Klan. The Court was prepared to go far in accepting legislative opinion of the subversive nature of the Klan.[9] No elaborate investigation of the Klan had apparently been made by the legislature and certainly not by the courts. But enough of the Klan's creed and behavior was a matter of public knowledge to justify its regulation. Among these the Court took notice of "a manifest tendency . . . to make the secrecy surrounding its purposes and membership a cloak for acts and conduct inimical to personal rights and public welfare" as "shown by experience!" The Court would "assume" that the New York legislature knew that the Klan

was conducting a crusade against Catholics, Jews, and Negroes, and stimulating hurtful religious and race prejudices; that it was striving for political power, and assuming a sort of guardianship over the administration of local, state, and national affairs; and that at times it was taking into its own hands the punishment of what some of its members conceived to be crimes.

No more was needed to justify the special regulation of this association. It would be difficult to criticize the Court if it had demanded stricter standards of proof in regard to the subversive character of the Ku Klux Klan. It could reasonably be criticized for not doing so, even though no intelligent, informed, and honest person, then or now, could deny that every one of these allegations against the Klan, of which the Court took official notice, was true.

Slowly in this same decade there was growing the Communist party of the United States, an association dedicated to follow unswervingly the Stalinist line as far and as soon as it was permitted to discern it. When the United States recognized the Russian government in 1933 it exacted a promise that

[9] How far is indicated by the Court's suggestion that it *assumed* the New York legislature was familiar with the "readily available" information, including the report of a Congressional investigation and two books, 278 U.S. 73 at 76.

Russia would not aid the American party. To all but the most guileless it soon became apparent that this pledge received a Russian interpretation of the sort with which we have become painfully and repeatedly familiar.

Judicial difficulties in recognizing communism as a problem of association rather than of simple individual rights were heightened by a theory that, so far as it regarded communists as a group, considered it to be one possessing a special immunity from restriction because it is a political party. The major premise underlying this notion is sound enough: free political parties are essential to the maintenance of a modern democracy. But our study of the political party as an association has already shown the fallacy of the inarticulate minor premise—to paraphrase Justice Holmes—in this syllogism. No more than a church, indeed even less, can any political party be allowed to hold itself or its members above the law on the grounds of "conscience." Yet exactly this notion is implicit in the argument that anti-Communist measures are somehow unlawful because many of the states have "recognized" the Communist party, that is, allowed it a place on the ballot. The logical absurdity of this idea may be readily tested by asking if their recognized status would afford the Republicans legal warrant for putting a plank in their platform calling for the assassination of the leaders of the Democratic party or even one advocating disobedience of the income tax laws.

This argument is strengthened by two others. Even if recognition of the Communist party by a state had any legal significance for that state's regulation of the association, it would have none for national legislation, for the national laws and Constitution are supreme over the law of any state. In addition, to regard membership in an elitist Communist party, in this or any other country, as having the same significance as membership in our major parties, although Justice Murphy and a bare majority of the Supreme Court did so as late as 1943, is inexcusable naïveté.[10]

Nor should liberals suppose that they are surrendering an important constitutional defense of rights of association by discarding this fallacious doctrine—even though it has had distinguished sponsors—of pitting governmental "recognition" of a political party against governmental power to regulate it. For if the constitutional rights of an association are thus rested on some form of legal action which government is not obligated to take, and which therefore it can hardly be denied the right to repeal, the constitutional rights of association vanish. In truth, such arguments express the concession theory of the rights of an association, under which it may have no rights except those which the government grants.

FUNDAMENTAL CONSTITUTIONAL QUESTIONS

From this review of some of the Supreme Court's difficulties let us pass to some of its solutions. The solutions we shall examine are responses to the following questions. First, what constitutes adequate legal proof of the

[10] Schneiderman v. United States, 320 U.S. 118 (1943) at 154–55; cf. Chief Justice Stone, dissenting, at 183–87.

subversive character of an association, and how is the proof to be established in consonance with due process of law? Second, can verbal advocacy of a group's purpose of violent revolution be validly punished, or is that kind of speech protected by the First Amendment? Third, can punishments or other legal disabilities validly be imposed for membership in an association held to be subversive? Are such measures a lawful sanction against overt criminal acts or a violation of the legal principle that there shall be no guilt by association?

These are the great and controlling questions on which the constitutional validity of the regulation of the Communist party of the United States, and of other groups legally found to be sponsored and controlled by it, depend. A summary classification of the cases dealing with the activities of the Communist party or of its members that the Supreme Court has decided or has declined to review will help to demonstrate why these are the fundamental constitutional issues involved.

The Court has not reviewed the small number of cases in which Communists or suspected sympathizers have been tried for espionage in the lower federal courts.[11] Nor do these cases raise important constitutional questions concerning communism, although several of them, like the Coplon case and the Rosenberg case, have attracted much public attention.

The Supreme Court has taken few of the cases of contempt or of perjury arising out of Congressional and federal grand jury investigations of persons and groups charged with subversive activity. Some of the perjury cases have been even more spectacular than the espionage cases; among them are the Hiss case, the Remington case, and the Lattimore case, all of which arose on indictments for perjury. None has been reviewed by the Supreme Court. In the less well-known Christoffel case, arising out of Congressional investigation of an allegedly Communist-inspired strike in an important defense plant, the Court reversed the conviction on the questionable technical ground that the record did not show a quorum of the committee present at the moment the perjured answer was made.[12]

Several of the contempt trials have also attracted much notoriety, notably the Eisler case, the Dennis case, and the Lawson and Trumbo cases, upon which depended those of the other "Hollywood ten" in the investigation of subversion in the movie industry by the House Committee on Un-American Activities. The results of these cases, in the order mentioned, can be briefly summarized. Eisler "jumped bail" and fled the country after the Supreme Court had agreed to hear his appeal; it thereupon removed his case from its docket.[13] The Supreme Court sustained the conviction of Eugene Dennis, secretary of the Communist party, for willful refusal to appear before a Congressional committee; this it did over his protest that the presence of federal

---

[11] The dramatic special term of the Supreme Court held to review and vacate the stay of execution granted in the Rosenberg case by Mr. Justice Douglas was not concerned with any of the substantial questions of the trial. 346 U.S. 273 (1953).

[12] Christoffel v. United States, 338 U.S. 84 (1949).

[13] Eisler v. United States, 338 U.S. 189 (1949).

employees on the jury denied him a fair trial.[14] This raised a disturbing
question like that which the Supreme Court refused to review in the more
famous Dennis case, that there was a biased member of the jury.[15] The
Supreme Court declined to review the convictions of Lawson and Trumbo,
who had refused to answer a question about their membership in the Communist party without making any claim of their right to refuse on the ground
that an answer might incriminate them.[16]

Still other cases are those arising out of investigations of the Joint Anti-
Fascist Refugee Committee, and of the National Council of Soviet-American
Friendship, and the Blau cases. Officers of the Joint Anti-Fascist Refugee
Committee were convicted and the conviction was upheld by the Supreme
Court because they had refused to produce pertinent records of the associa-
tion, and the Court declined to review a case raising similar issues in con-
nection with the National Council of Soviet-American Friendship.[17] In the
Blau cases the Court upheld the right of alleged officers of the Communist
party to refuse to answer questions asked by a federal grand jury on the
ground that they might incriminate themselves.[18]

The constitutional questions growing out of these investigations, this
brief review indicates, are not questions concerning the legal rights of associations charged with subversion, or of the rights of their members. All of
these questions concerning the rights and duties of witnesses may be and
have been raised also in the course of investigations of quite different matters. Once it is admitted that government has a right to investigate the
activities of these groups and of their members to some extent (and this
right few critics of the actual conduct of some of these investigations deny),
such questions are bound to arise.[19]

Two earlier decisions of the Supreme Court, in each of which the opinion was prepared by Chief Justice Hughes, involve aspects of the right of
assembly of groups regarded as subversive. In 1931 the Court decided
Stromberg v. California, a flag salute case in which the flag was a red flag

[14] Dennis v. United States, 339 U.S. 162 (1950).

[15] Cf. Mr. Justice Black dissenting in Dennis *et al.* v. United States, 341 U.S. 494
(1951) at 580–81.

[16] 339 U.S. 934, 972 (1950).

[17] The two Supreme Court decisions arising out of the investigation of the Joint
Anti-Fascist Refugee Committee are United States v. Bryan, 339 U.S. 323 (1950), and
United States v. Fleischman, 339 U.S. 349 (1950). In the litigation arising out of investigation of the National Council of Soviet-American Friendship the Supreme Court
merely affirmed the right of the accused to try to show bias on the part of prospective
jurors who were federal employees, Morford v. United States, 339 U.S. 258 (1950). Cf.
notes 14 and 15 *supra.*

[18] Blau v. United States, 340 U.S. 159 (1950). For a generous interpretation of the
privilege, cf. Bart v. United States, 349 U.S. 219 (1955), Quinn v. United States, 349
U.S. 155 (1955), and Emspak v. United States, 349 U.S. 190 (1955).

[19] For a careful review of cases involving the investigative powers of Congress in
connection with subversive activities cf. Robert K. Carr, *The House Committee on Un-
American Activities, 1945–1950* (Ithaca, N.Y., 1952), chap. 11.

rather than the stars and stripes.[20] In an appalling imitation of the bourgeois ceremony they detested, the leaders of a Young Communist League summer camp in California ran up the hammer and sickle on the camp flagpole every morning and had their charges salute it (presumably with clenched fists) and recite: "I pledge allegiance to the workers' red flag and to the cause for which it stands, one aim throughout our lives, freedom for the working class." Perhaps the most appropriate legal action would have been a suit for plagiarism by the author of the pledge to the American flag. Instead, a camp leader was convicted under California law for displaying a red flag in a public assembly "as a sign, symbol or emblem of opposition to organized government," among other things. The Court thought that this provision of the statute was too vague to sustain a valid conviction. The Court also emphasized the importance of free discussion, although it is difficult in the light of the later cases on compulsory salute of a conventional flag to see how this revolutionary ritual made any more of a contribution to rational understanding of arguments for disloyalty than the patriotic ritual contributes to a reasoned understanding of the grounds for loyalty.

In 1937 a unanimous Court decided the case of *De Jonge* v. *Oregon*.[21] It reversed the conviction of the Communist De Jonge under a state criminal syndicalism statute for participating in and speaking at a peaceable open mass meeting called by the Communist party to protest against police brutality in a strike. He had not advocated violence at the meeting. The Court held that "peaceable assembly for lawful discussion cannot be made a crime" and that the state could not "seize upon mere participation in a peaceable assembly and a lawful public discussion as the basis for a criminal charge." The decision of the precise question at issue is doubtless still authoritative, but the Court expressly left open the question of the Communist party's advocacy of violence,[22] so that later holdings that it does advocate violent overthrow of the government must surely be understood to limit this case to what it did actually decide.

Another group of cases concerns the national government's efforts to deport alien members of the Communist party and to denaturalize citizens who at the time of taking the oath of allegiance were members of the party. In still another group of cases the Court has passed upon the validity of some of the test oaths devised to keep Communists or members of other subversive associations out of public employment or labor union leadership. These two groups of cases concern the third of the fundamental questions in the regulation of subversive groups and may profitably be deferred for consideration under that head.

In two other important cases the Court has spoken on how the proof of the subversive character of an association is to be established in accordance with due process of law. They provide a meaningful introduction to the most important of all the cases, that in which the Supreme Court sustained

20 283 U.S. 359 (1931) ; cf. Chafee, *op. cit.*, pp. 362–66.
21 299 U.S. 353 (1937) ; cf. Chafee, *op. cit.*, pp. 384–88.
22 299 U.S. 353 at 365.

the conviction under the Smith Act of eleven leaders of the Communist party. In this, the more important Dennis case, the Supreme Court had to consider both the question of what constitutes requisite legal proof of the subversiveness of an association, and of whether verbal advocacy of violent overthrow of government by a group and its members may be punished.

LEGAL PROOF OF AN ASSOCIATION'S SUBVERSIVE CHARACTER

One who believes in government under law will never find a proof of the subversive nature of a group more impressive than the legal process which established the proof, nor respect such a finding as a just one unless it has been reached by a procedure which is fair. For this reason the case of *United States v. Lovett*, in which a divided Court declared invalid a provision of an appropriation act removing from the federal payroll certain named employees the House regarded as subversive, is significant.[23] There are several issues in this case, one of only two since 1937 in which the Court has made important use of its power to declare an act of Congress unconstitutional, that lie outside the purview of this discussion. The dissent of Mr. Justice Frankfurter is persuasive in its denial that the legislation was a bill of attainder in the historic sense. The long-run value of the decision will lie in its rebuke to the casual condemnation of individuals largely because of their membership in associations.

Recently the Court was confronted with a similar problem resulting from President Truman's creation in 1947 by executive order of a program for examination of the loyalty of federal employees. Under that order the Loyalty Review Board was instructed to consider as evidence of an employee's loyalty, but not as conclusive evidence, the employee's membership in any one of a large number of organizations declared by the Attorney General of the United States after investigation to be Nazi, Communist, totalitarian, or subversive. Under these circumstances two questions must be faced. The first is whether the procedure followed by the Attorney General in finding these organizations subversive is fair. The second is whether the procedure of the Loyalty Review Board, and the subordinate boards, in weighing the evidence of an employee's membership in them is fair. Deferring the latter question, let us examine the Supreme Court's response to the former.

The action it took in 1951 in the case of *Joint Anti-Fascist Refugee Committee v. McGrath* is reassuring, even though the reasons given by the Justices are confusing.[24] This organization and the National Council of American-Soviet Friendship and the International Workers Order, Inc., had been declared Communist groups by Attorney General Clark before he was appointed to the Supreme Court. They sought an injunction to forbid the Attorney General from keeping them on his list and a judicial declaration against the use of his findings by the government in loyalty proceedings. Although they questioned the truth of his findings, their chief objection lay

[23] 328 U.S. 303 (1946).
[24] Joint Anti-Fascist Refugee Committee v. McGrath, Atty. Gen. of United States *et al.*, 341 U.S. 123 (1951).

against the method by which he had reached them. The Attorney General had published the lists of subversive organizations without affording any hearing at which a suspected organization could deny the allegations against it or offer evidence to refute the charges. In the courts below, the government had successfully moved to dismiss these complaints without defending the Attorney General's methods, on the ground that the organizations did not state a case entitling them to judicial relief. These decisions the Supreme Court reversed. Each of the five Justices who concurred in the result wrote a separate opinion; three Justices dissented in an opinion; Mr. Justice Clark properly withdrew from participation in the case.

The dissent, written by Mr. Justice Reed, in which the Chief Justice and Mr. Justice Minton joined, may be shortly summarized. The dissenters proceeded on the theory that the Attorney General's designation had no legal effect; as Justice Jackson said, they seemed to regard the listing as "a mere press release without legal consequences." Since, on this theory, the organizations had not been injured, they were entitled to no relief. The tragedy was that this beautiful theory was killed by an ugly fact. In no less than three places in his opinion Mr. Justice Reed confessed that the Attorney General's action did have legal effect, but he and his brother dissenters preferred to avert their gaze from any injustice that might result.[25]

The opposite extreme was taken by Mr. Justice Black. He said:[26]

. . . in my judgment the executive has no constitutional authority, with or without a hearing, officially to prepare and publish the lists challenged by petitioners. In the first place, the system adopted effectively punishes many organizations and their members merely because of their political beliefs and utterances, and to this extent smacks of a most evil type of censorship. . . . Moreover, officially prepared and proclaimed governmental blacklists possess almost every quality of bills of attainder . . .

The bearing of his view on the government's loyalty program is not clear. His implication seems to be that not even Congress could direct an executive agency to make such designations after full notice and hearing, any more than the President and the Attorney General could do so without legislative authority and without notice and hearing. If that is correct, how could the government effectively ensure itself of the loyalty of its employees at all? There is a less clear implication, however, that if in some fashion the program were committed to the courts, it might be permissible.[27]

Mr. Justice Burton, who announced the judgment of the Court, took the position that[28]

if the allegations of the complaints are taken as true (as they must be on the motions to dismiss), the Executive Order does not authorize the Attorney General to furnish the Loyalty Review Board with a list . . . without other justification.

[25] For Mr. Justice Reed's admissions of legal consequences cf. 341 U.S. 123 at 202, conceding the listing might be tortious if not privileged; at 203, analogizing it to an indictment by grand jury; and at 207, admitting that an employee may lose his job because of membership in the listed organization.
[26] 341 U.S. 123 at 143–44.   [27] 341 U.S. 123 at 144–45.   [28] 341 U.S. 123 at 126.

This position commended itself to no other member of the Court except Mr. Justice Douglas, who agreed that it might dispose of the case. Mr. Justice Burton, however, indicated no more than that on new trials the Attorney General would have to show to the satisfaction of the courts that he had had good reason to designate these organizations as communistic. He said nothing about the necessity of giving the organizations an opportunity at an administrative hearing to rebut the Attorney General's charges against them. His implication is that the Constitution does not require this legal process as due the organizations.

With that implication Justices Douglas, Frankfurter, Jackson, and Black disagreed. All stressed that due process demanded some form of notice and hearing for these groups before the Attorney General could take action so injurious to them and to their members in government employment. They observed that Congress in the Internal Security Act of 1950 had provided a careful administrative procedure, with notice and hearing and judicial review, in the making of similar designations, and asked why the Attorney General could not do so.[29] Of course it would be unjust to presume that the Attorney General and the Department of Justice had not prepared the lists with scrupulous care. The department undoubtedly had a mass of information of genuine probative value, much of it incontrovertible, about the groups listed. Many organizations denounced as subversive by less careful persons have never been placed on the lists by any Attorney General. But if one believeś in a government of laws in the Anglo-American tradition, one must agree with these four members of the Court that these organizations were not accorded due process of law, even though one doubts that on a fair hearing any one of them could show that the Attorney General was wrong.

In the criminal prosecution of the eleven leaders of the Communist party, the proof of the subversive character of that association was made by judicial process quite in contrast to the secret and *ex parte* methods under the Loyalty Review Program.[30] That case raises the first of our controlling questions. What constitutes adequate legal proof of the subversive character of an association? The Smith Act offers this definition of a subversive association: "any society, group, or assembly of persons who teach, advocate, or encourage the overthrow or destruction of any government in the United States by force or violence." This definition indicates the two essential elements which must be proved. First, the association must have an intent, purpose, or objective—the overthrow of government by concededly unlawful means: force and violence. Second, it must commit some act—it must teach, advocate, or encourage that which it intends.

Does the Communist party have this intent and has it committed any of the acts described? In the Dennis case 16,000 pages of evidence were taken on these points; in other judicial cases and administrative hearings many

[29] After two years of hearings the Subversive Activities Control Board established by the Internal Security (McCarran) Act of 1950 did find the Communist party to be Soviet-controlled and to have the purpose of violent overthrow of the government.

[30] Dennis *et al.* v. United States, 341 U.S. 494 (1951).

thousands more have accumulated. What kind of evidence establishes the intent and the overt acts? In the cases in which the Supreme Court has summarized its view of much of this evidence can be found at least six fairly distinct kinds that have been considered to show intent. First are the statements of the party's leaders about the purpose of the association. As in any other case courts have not been inclined to assign as high a probative value to the testimony of an interested witness as to other evidence.

Second are the writings regarded by the party as authoritative expositions of communism, particularly those of Marx, Engels, Lenin, and Stalin. In the Schneidermann case Justice Murphy had canvassed these for the majority and Chief Justice Stone for the minority. Justice Murphy thought that their meaning was ambiguous, that a reader might interpret them as advocating violence only for protection against the bourgeoisie if it first used violence to prevent the proletariat from coming to power peacefully.[31] Chief Justice Stone read them as advocating violent overthrow of government.[32] In the Dennis case Judge Learned Hand thought so too, and the Supreme Court accepted his findings without review.

Third, what inference may be drawn from evidence in regard to the secret and conspiratorial character of the party's modes of action? In the Dennis case the Court cited as significant the evidence that the party is "a highly disciplined organization, adept at infiltration into strategic positions, use of aliases, and double-meaning language."

A fourth kind of evidence always influential in determining intent is the overt acts of the accused, on the theory that a person intends what a reasonable man would expect to be the probable consequences of his acts. Thus the course of conduct of the party becomes a basis for inferring its intent. A fifth kind of evidence of intent is closely related. It is the evidence of the overt acts, the course of conduct of Communist parties and governments throughout the world. Much of this kind of evidence is really a matter of judicial notice. How far should courts go in taking notice of public facts like the Communist coup in Czechoslovakia, for example, and drawing inferences from them? Is it proper to take into account the acts of Communist parties and governments outside the United States in order to infer the intent of the party in this country? Any justification for doing so must be found in action of the party in the United States. If it receives and accepts direction and support from communism outside our borders and in turn gives assistance and support to foreign Communist parties and governments, an inference may arise that its intent is the same intent that they manifest by their overt acts.

This connection of communism in the United States with communism in the rest of the world, directed by Soviet Russia, may have been the most important evidence of intent to the Court, as it is to many others. It is worth recalling that one type of religious association which Locke declared was not entitled to toleration was one so constituted that "all those who enter into it

---

[31] 320 U.S. 118 at 157.   [32] 320 U.S. 118 at 190.

do thereby *ipso facto* deliver themselves up to the protection and service of another prince." No magistrate was obliged "to suffer his own people to be listed, as it were, for soldiers against his own government."

It is apparent that the burden upon judges and juries of reaching a judgment on the intent of the Communist party to overthrow government by force and violence is complex, even when the kinds of relevant evidence and some of the problems of inference are set forth in so abstract and skeletal a form. Is the party's intent capable of proof at all? Some have been inclined to say that it is not. On examination, however, much of this criticism of efforts to determine the objectives of the Communist party will be found to reduce to dissatisfaction with the use of circumstantial evidence and the inferences drawn from it to establish these facts. But the use of circumstantial evidence is not a denial of due process, nor is there any reason why circumstantial evidence should be rejected in these proceedings but should continue to be used in all other judicial and administrative fact-finding. The probative value of circumstantial evidence is not inherently inferior to that of direct evidence; sometimes it is superior, and sometimes it is from the nature of the case the only kind that can be obtained. In such cases to deny the legitimacy of its use is in effect to deny that law can function at all.

In the Dennis case, however, it appears that there was no disagreement that the intent of the Communist party is to overthrow the government by force and violence. In his brief dissent Mr. Justice Black did not even mention intent, and Mr. Justice Douglas dissenting used language suggesting that he agreed that this is the party's intent. In fact, he objected that the party leaders stood convicted for their intent alone, without proof of the overt acts the statute requires.[33]

Had the association committed the act of teaching, advocating, or encouraging violent overthrow of government? Here again there appears to be agreement among the Justices in the Dennis case that the evidence showed that the party had done so.[34] The Court in fact was not reviewing the jury's findings, either of the intent of the party or of its commission of the act the statute required. The Supreme Court's review was limited to the question whether this provision violated the Constitution.

The apparent agreement of the minority with the Court that the Communist party had the revolutionary intent which the statute forbids and also that it had committed the act of teaching, advocating, or encouraging violent revolution helps clarify the issue. For all agreed that the Communist party fits the description of a subversive association laid down by Congress in the Smith Act. Another agreement between the majority and the minority also brings us closer to the heart of the matter. Justices Black and Douglas agreed with the Court that Congress has constitutional power to legislate against a subversive association. They dissented because they did not agree that Congress could validly declare a group to be subversive merely because it used the rights of freedom of speech, press, and assembly to advocate revo-

[33] 341 U.S. 494 at 583.
[34] Cf. Mr. Justice Douglas at 341 U.S. 494 at 582 and Mr. Justice Black at 341 U.S. 494 at 579–80.

lution.[35] They insisted that if an association's advocacy of violent revolution falls short of incitement to immediate action which creates a clear and present danger as they interpreted it its leaders or members cannot be punished.

ADVOCACY OF SUBVERSION

In other words, their position in regard to the definition of a subversive association carries us on to the second issue : can verbal advocacy of a group's purpose of violent revolution be validly punished, or is that kind of speech protected by the First Amendment? At this point the Dennis case becomes really complicated. For Chief Justice Vinson in the opinion of the Court said, only if this verbal advocacy creates a clear and present danger. He then proceeded to adopt the rephrasing of Holmes's famous test that Chief Judge Learned Hand had formulated :[36] "In each case courts must ask whether the gravity of the 'evil,' discounted by its improbability, justifies such invasion of free speech as is necessary to avoid the danger."

Now how had this venerable, liberal, and brilliant judge arrived at his restatement of Justice Holmes's words? In his opinion for the federal court of appeals he had told the world. The Supreme Court had provided so many pages of interpretation and reinterpretation of the clear and present danger test in recent years that it had become almost impossible to know what it meant. If he were a Supreme Court Justice he could just say it meant what he thought it meant. But being only a lower court judge, he was bound to say it meant what the Supreme Court said it meant. So, after long and conscientious study of all the cases, he had concluded that this was what the Supreme Court now meant it meant by the clear and present danger test, even though it had not said it. And the Chief Justice agreed with him. Not only that, but applying Judge Hand's formula, he and the Court arrived at the same result : the advocacy charged against the defendants did constitute a clear and present danger, and they had been rightly convicted.

But Mr. Justice Douglas also agreed that verbal advocacy could be punished only if it presented a clear and present danger. Applying that test according to what he said it meant, instead of what Judge Hand had said he meant it meant, he arrived at the opposite conclusion : the defendants had been wrongly convicted.

Mr. Justice Black also thought that the clear and present danger test could be applied, but said "the other opinions in this case show that the only way to affirm these convictions is to repudiate directly or indirectly the established clear and present danger rule." By the established rule one must presume he meant the rule that was established until Chief Justice Vinson had established as the new one what Judge Hand had thought was the established one. At any rate, added Mr. Justice Black, "I believe that the 'clear and present danger test' does not 'mark the furthermost constitutional boundaries of protected expression' but does 'no more than recognize a minimum compulsion of the Bill of Rights.' "

The mystery was deepened, however, when Justice Jackson said that he agreed that the clear and present danger test had a precise enough mean-

[35] 341 U.S. 494 at 580 and 584–86.   [36] 341 U.S. 494 at 510.

ing to be quite useful in the decision of certain kinds of free speech cases, but that it was not suitable to one of this kind. Refusing to apply anyone's clear and present danger test, including his own, Justice Jackson arrived at the same result the Chief Justice had reached with one.

As if this were not enough, Mr. Justice Frankfurter repeated what he had said several times before. The phrase clear and present danger was only "attractive but imprecise words." The phrase could not be "an absolute dogma and definitive measuring rod." But the Court had talked as if it were, and[37]

In all fairness, the argument can not be met by reinterpreting the Court's frequent use of "clear" and "present" to mean an entertainable "probability." In giving this meaning to the phrase "clear and present danger" the Court of Appeals was fastidiously confining the rhetoric of opinions to the exact scope of what was decided by them. We have greater responsibility for having given constitutional support, over repeated protests, to uncritical libertarian generalities.

Having explained rather convincingly what was wrong with the Court's use of the clear and present danger test, he went on in a long and in many places an eloquent opinion to consider the case and agree that the statute was validly applied to the Communist leaders.

Justice Jackson's argument, however, may have been the most significant, for he insisted that the real danger was not from the verbal advocacy of the defendants but from their leadership of a group as highly organized, tightly disciplined, and conspiratorial as a Communist party. He intimated that the words of both the Smith Act and of the clear and present danger test had a kind of outdated unrealistic approach to a new problem: the Communist group. Justice Jackson was much too pithy, forceful, and suggestive a writer to need anyone to put words in his mouth, but since his opinion does not lend itself to brief quotation perhaps I shall be pardoned for explaining what I understand to be its central teaching.

Although the Communist party does advocate the overthrow of government by force and violence, the real threat posed by the party to the security of the United States is not these preachments, which fortunately persuade few people in this country, and which the party itself does not intend its own members to interpret as a call for "premature or uncoordinated outbursts of violence."[38] Government may legitimately punish a group for carrying on this kind of verbal advocacy, but the prosecution is somewhat like sending the leaders of a notorious criminal gang to jail for evasion of income taxes on their ill-gotten gains in default of being able to obtain the well-concealed evidence of their more deadly crimes. The few individual members of the group who are caught red-handed in crimes like espionage may be a good deal like the lesser punks in a mob, with their own code of honor which often seals their lips against betrayal of their bosses, even if their leaders leave them largely to their own fate when caught. Those who know the frustrations of the residents of our great cities when confronted with

[37] 341 U.S. 494 at 527.   [38] 341 U.S. 494 at 564.

conspiratorial gangster tactics like these will not lightly dismiss the forceful-ness of this statement of the problem of protection of the community. The worst danger with which the Communist party confronts us is not the tortuous dialectics which make up the lyrics of its would-be siren song. It is the very existence of a "permanently organized, well-financed, semi-secret and highly disciplined" group as a going concern, a going concern ready to teach and to use open violence if expedient, but relying much more on spreading confusion and hate, and using infiltration to reach positions of power from which it can spy upon and coerce the community, yet be almost beyond detection that will stand up in court.[89]

The threat presented by this subversive association does not come from isolated individual radicals. The threat presented by this subversive asso-ciation does not take the form of speeches by its present leaders or books by its canonized founders. If this is true, it is worse than futile to test the government's constitutional rights to meet the threat by asking if the *words* of *individuals* create either a clear and present or an extremely imminent and extremely grave danger of violent revolution. To insist on that is too much like demanding that a doctor call a case of chronic pulmonary tuber-culosis a case of acute pulmonary pneumonia before we will allow him to treat it, and our self-deception about the disease may confuse the treatment.

LIABILITY FOR SUBVERSIVE ASSOCIATION

The last of the three basic questions in the law of subversive groups is whether criminal punishments or other legal disabilities can validly be imposed on an individual for membership in a subversive group, or whether such action constitutes guilt by association. Those convicted in the Dennis case were leaders of the party, but the Smith Act makes membership equally criminal with leadership. The legal disability imposed most often on mem-bers of the Communist party or its front organizations is refusal of govern-mental employment. Another legal disability concerns a much smaller num-ber of people but can affect them much more harshly. This is the denial of citizenship to and deportation of resident aliens who are or have been mem-bers of such groups.

The courts have steadfastly refused to call these last two legal disabili-ties criminal punishment. In doing so they have merely insisted on holding to the traditional and limited definition of criminal punishment. Justices Black and Douglas and some distinguished legal scholars have pressed in recent years for a revision of legal thinking which would treat these other legal disabilities as criminal punishment in the older and stricter sense. It is doubtful if the advocates of this expansion have taken into account enough the ramified consequences it would produce. The underlying reasons for urging it seem to be two: first, that the principle of no guilt by association applies only to criminal punishment in the strict sense, and, second, that punishment for membership in a subversive group does amount to uncon-stitutional disregard of the principle that guilt must be personal.

[89] *Ibid.*

It is of course true that under our law guilt is personal and there can be no guilt by association. But the problems of subversive associations cannot be solved or even turned aside by using these principles as slogans. Daily experience gave rise to the adages that "birds of a feather flock together" and that "one can tell a man by the company he keeps." Surely voters who defeat a candidate for sheriff who is a known associate of gangsters, or a school board which refuses to employ as a teacher a person who is a known habitué of disreputable places is not acting irrationally or violating the principle of "no guilt by association." The right to be free from criminal prosecution and punishment for one's bad associations cannot be expanded into a right to be free from an unfavorable reputation resulting from such associations or to escape from all the unpleasant consequences of such a reputation. Losing a job or leaving this country or going to jail may all be unpleasant, but it does not follow that losing a job or leaving the country is therefore a punishment. Yet something like that *non sequitur* lies behind the argument that consideration of a man's associations in deciding on his fitness as a public employee or as a future citizen or as an alien denizen violates the principle of no guilt by association.

When this is said, it must still be admitted that these legal disabilities can work severe injury upon men, as can the obligation to appear before an investigating committee. If we should conclude, however, that even criminal punishment in the strict sense for membership in a subversive organization does not violate the individual's constitutional rights, the argument that these other legal disabilities do so would be fairly disposed of. Let us, therefore, examine that question.

Subversive purposes or activities, to be dangerous to the modern state, must be those of an organized group of individuals. Although it is conceivable that purposes held by isolated individuals or acts committed by individuals independently might be a threat to the society or the state, as the classical Anglo-American conception of treason reminds, that is a minor and peripheral problem today. Any threat posed by a subversive association results from actions carried out by individual members. The legal sanctions which can be imposed on the organization as an entity are limited and likely to be inadequate to overcome the threat. Aside from the desire, long recognized in the criminal law, to visit retribution on those guilty, the state must therefore be able to punish individual members for some of their acts if it is to deal effectively with the threat of a subversive group. Can it punish, as one of those individual acts, the act of joining or adhering to such an association? If it cannot, *precisely what in our constitutional system forbids it?*[40] Despite libertarian protests that it cannot, the argument that it cannot has never given a very clear answer to that question.

[40] Professor Chafee in *Free Speech in the United States*, pp. 470–85, makes one of the most powerful arguments against section 2a (3) of the Smith Act, which punishes membership, and says the provision creates guilt by association. But if I understand his argument correctly, he does not claim that it necessarily violates any constitutional provision; he asserts its application might not be consonant with the clear and present danger test.

One argument that it cannot rests largely on a conception urged by Justices Black and Douglas in the Dennis case and elsewhere, namely, that punishment can be imposed only for an "overt act."[41] But how can it be said that joining an association, paying dues, attending group meetings, voicing the group's purposes, and engaging in similar conduct are not performance of physical, *i.e.*, overt acts? Is not the proper contrast between physical acts, including speech, which certainly is a physical act, and unspoken belief, which cannot be reached effectively anyway? It is certainly strange to hear at one moment that speech can have such important consequences that free speech is essential to the development of our society and is therefore protected by the First Amendment, and at the next moment to catch the implication that speech is so insignificant in its consequences that it should not be regarded as an overt act at all, and that any danger from it must be almost completely ignored.

The argument against punishment of the individual for his membership can be stated more powerfully than this. It is a two-pronged argument which asserts, first, that the individual cannot be punished for doing *no more* than being a member even though joining is an overt act, and second, that even if membership were punishable, it could be so only when it was proved that the individual had a criminal intent in being a member. As for the first, it is perhaps enough to say that the individual by his membership helps make possible the existence of the organized group, that if there were no members there would be no group, and that it is precisely the fact of his membership, along with that of others, that makes possible the threat of organized subversive activity. Of course, to the extent that he contributes further to the maintenance of the group by his money or his services, as he is likely to do, his individual responsibility becomes clearer. The question of his intent in being a member quickly appears to be the more important one.

It may be urged that an individual may properly be punished for an act even though he had no criminal intent in doing it. This is certainly not uncommon in the criminal law, and it is even more common for the law to impose other than criminal disabilities regardless of intent, as the doctrine of liability without fault makes plain. If, as some libertarians are tempted to argue, mere membership in a subversive organization is not a serious offense, it is doubtful that the state should be required to prove that it is accompanied by an individual evil intent in order to punish it. Minor transgressions and trivial misdemeanors are often punishable regardless of intent. In truth, the view that individual criminal intent should be an essential element of the legal offense stems from a recognition that the crime is almost universally regarded as one of peculiar enormity and odiousness. The severity of punishment reflects popular revulsion against the offense, but the severity of punishment is itself a strong argument for requiring proof of criminal intent.

It is noteworthy that the Smith Act makes membership punishable only when the member knows the purposes of the association, and that the Su-

---

[41] 341 U.S. 494 at 584.

144   GROUPS AND THE CONSTITUTION

preme Court in the Dennis case held that even those who organize a subversive group must be shown to have a criminal intent, even though the
statute did not expressly require it.[42] The provision of the President's
Loyalty Review order directing the loyalty review boards to consider membership in subversive organizations as evidence but not conclusive evidence
of unfitness has the effect also of allowing if not requiring the boards to
consider the individual's intent in joining. Only in the legislation providing
for the deportation of aliens is the fact of membership conclusive, without
reference to intent.

How is the intent of one who is or has been a member of a subversive
association to be judged? Let us eschew the somewhat tautological phrases
about intent, willfulness, *scienter*, *mens rea*, and the like. In the simpler
language of the layman, a person's intent in adhering to a subversive group
raises this question: what did the person think he was doing in joining the
organization? Unless the individual did not think at all about what he was
doing (which sometimes, unfortunately for him, may be the case) or thought
the organization was subversive and joined it because he thought so, there
would seem to be three possible answers to this question.

First, a person may have believed that the association which he joined
was one which the law does condemn, but that the law itself was invalid
because the Constitution forbids punishment for membership in it or even
forbids any interference with the group. If this was the joiner's state of mind,
by any familiar standard of the law, he has manifested the requisite criminal
intent. Justice Holmes's "bad man" theory of the law supplies the full
answer. One who deliberately disobeys the law in the belief that it is contrary to the Constitution must expect to pay the law's penalty if his guess
proves to be wrong. He may esteem himself a hero if the Supreme Court
agrees with his view of the law, and a martyr if it does not, but he cannot
truthfully claim to have violated the law unintentionally in either event.

Second, a person may have believed that even if the group he joined
was one which the law condemns, his membership in it would not aid it in
carrying out any subversive purposes or activities. This attitude has probably been most common among members of front organizations; in the
Bridges deportation case Mr. Justice Douglas gave it considerable attention.[43] It describes a state of mind that is not merely hypothetical, but has
apparently characterized many thousands of persons. It is an unrealistic
view of the meaning of group membership; a group's purposes and activities
cannot be segmented by a member to suit his own convenience. Regardless
of his own purposes, his support of the group is support of all that it purposes
and does, even if, remaining a member, he disavows it.[44] One cannot partly

42 341 U.S. 494 at 499.
43 Bridges v. Wixon, 326 U.S. 135 (1945) at 141–44.
44 This proposition, I am well aware, will be denied by many. Suppose, it will be
urged, that a member remains in a group in order to accomplish a reversal of some policy
adopted by its majority with which he disagrees. There is force in this objection, admittedly. Mrs. Franklin D. Roosevelt adopted the position set forth above when she

dissociate oneself from a group of which one is a member. But mistaken as this attitude may be, it might under some circumstances be considered as mitigating the offense.

Third, a person may believe that an organization which he joins does not have any purposes or conduct itself in any way condemned by law. His attitude may even be so strong that he would not have joined if he believed the contrary. It would be a miscarriage of justice to hold that this state of mind amounts to a criminal intent. Of course the most difficult problem is to assess whether or not the assertion of such a belief is bona fide. Those who must weigh the question of intent in any official capacity are not obligated to believe a self-serving declaration of such a state of mind in the presence of preponderant evidence to the contrary. The problem, again, is most likely to arise in examining the meaning of membership in a front organization.

When the criminal sanctions of the Smith Act against membership in an organization advocating the violent overthrow of the government are invoked, all the guaranties provided in the Bill of Rights for accused persons in a federal trial come into play: the prohibition on *ex post facto* laws, judicial standards of proof, and protection against self-incrimination. Although the members of subversive groups do not and constitutionally need not enjoy all these safeguards when disabilities in regard to public employment or residence in the country if they are aliens are imposed, it seems very doubtful that extending to them the same constitutional standards of protection or equivalent ones would hamper efforts to protect the public. Certainly we can lessen the possibility of miscarriages of justice by extending them as far as prudence allows.

The position of aliens is particularly severe. When the Supreme Court in a series of cases in 1952 upheld the right of the government to deport aliens who at any time in the past have been members of the Communist party, it was merely adhering to a long-established principle of international as well as American constitutional law, that a government may expel alien residents for any reason or no reason.[45] In the face of the statutes that have been on the books for thirty-five years, claims that all these aliens have been surprised or entrapped are rather overdrawn. But there may well be some

---

resigned from the Daughters of the American Revolution because the organization denied Miss Marian Anderson the use of Constitution Hall in Washington because of her race. Mrs. Roosevelt's perception of the problem seems to me sounder than Miss Whitney's when all is said and done.

[45] Harisiades v. Shaughnessy, 342 U.S. 580 (1952). Without overruling such earlier cases as Bridges v. Wixon, this case leaves them standing on very narrow ground for all practical purposes. For a related issue cf. Carlson *et al.* v. Landon, 342 U.S. 524 (1952). In accord is the most recent case sustaining the stringent provisions of the Internal Security Act of 1950 for deportation of alien members of the Communist party. The Court through Mr. Justice Frankfurter held that there might be instances in which membership was so lacking in intent that the act was not intended to cover them, but that the act applied to aliens who had joined the party without being "fully conscious of its advocacy of violence." Galvan v. Press, 347 U.S. 542 (1954).

aliens now subject to deportation who joined a subversive group without any criminal intent, who corrected their error, and who have lived blameless lives since. One can scarcely believe that, if Congress offered them an opportunity to establish these facts and to stay if they could, the national safety would thereby be endangered.

Membership in subversive associations as a bar to public employment has loomed as an even larger question.[46] It should be clear from the experience of the last fifteen years that this issue of the fitness of public employees is one which deeply disturbs many citizens. It is unfortunate that the issue was at first posed in the United States so largely in terms of *loyalty*. In Great Britain the question has been expressed in terms of *security*; that phraseology is better in many cases, but it can be improved upon. The real issue, in the great majority of cases, is simply the *good judgment* of the employee. One need not and should not impugn a man's loyalty in order to question the soundness of his judgment.

At the same time, to put the question in this setting does bring a man's associations squarely within the type of evidence which is relevant to an answer. If a person who is well educated, informed about public affairs, and active in public life is shown to have joined an association at a time when it was a Communist front organization or to have remained a member after it became so dominated, whether he did so carelessly, or deliberately in the belief that it is possible "to work with Communists," it is not unreasonable to doubt the soundness of his judgment or the wisdom of entrusting him with political power. The precise facts about such associations in each particular case should be considered. The reason why it is important to do so can be briefly stated. It lies in the danger of abuse from carrying to extremes the idea that government can place conditions on a privilege like public employment.

One of the main arguments used to justify the denial of public employment to members of subversive associations is that such employment is a privilege, not a right. (It was Justice Holmes who said that a man might have a constitutional right to free speech but he did not have a constitutional right to be a police chief.) But in the sense that public employment is a privilege, so are many other things that make life worth living. In this sense public education is a privilege, social security benefits are privileges, even the "right" to vote is a privilege. No one has a right to any of them by the mere fact of his existence or even of his citizenship. Government extends these opportunities (to use a neutral word) and must necessarily define who is qualified to take advantage of them.

But it does not follow that the government can establish qualifications for the exercise of these privileges which have no reasonable relation to the purposes for which the privileges are established, or that in addition to all reasonable qualifications the government may practice discriminations which

---

[46] Among the extensive literature on this subject a study outstanding for thoroughness, although sharply differing from some of the opinions expressed below, is Eleanor Bontecue, *The Federal Loyalty-Security Program* (Ithaca, 1953).

violate constitutional rights of those who meet all the reasonable qualifications. Thus we may require that the applicants for some public position have
a certain amount of formal education and be in good health and within certain
age limits. We may in some cases even restrict the position to men rather
than women, or to residents of a particular state. These may be more doubtful, but some leeway must be allowed. But if in addition to all these qualifications, the applicant were required to be white or Protestant, constitutional bounds would clearly be passed.

. The question, then, is whether the requirement of freedom from membership in subversive groups by a public employee bears a reasonable relation to his qualifications to carry on the duties for the accomplishment of
which the position has been created. The time has passed, if ever there
were such a time, when thoughtful men would deny that for many public
positions, civil and military, such a requirement is not only reasonable but
essential. But is it as necessary a requirement for every public position (say,
for a street sweeper)?

The burden of proof is on one who feels himself aggrieved by such a
qualification to prove its unfairness, not on the government to sustain its
rationality, for in this as in all other matters there is a presumption that
government acts lawfully. And in deciding this question the importance of
public confidence in the loyalty and rectitude of the public service cannot be
ignored; in a sense every public employee, not just those in sensitive positions, must be like Caesar's wife. Given the intensity of feeling on the subject in the United States, it is likely that this consideration will continue to
be used to justify a complete ban upon members of subversive groups in
public employment, and that courts will continue to hold, as I think they
should, that the policy is a permissible one.

Only after canvassing the right of government to bar members of subversive groups from public employment can one see the frequently discussed
test oath cases in meaningful perspective. The validity of such oaths then
appears clearly secondary to and dependent upon the right to deny public
employment. If government can validly exclude Communists from the payroll, it should be plain that the test oath for public employment (oaths applicable to private persons raise different questions) amounts to no more
than a method of securing disclosure of the employee's membership if he is a
member. It is hard to understand why, if government has a right to find out
about his membership at all, it cannot take his own oath in the matter but
can investigate his entire life. No judgment about the practicability of these
oaths is intended. They must be less effective than their supporters imagine,
but they also appear to be more effective than their critics admit.[47]

[47] A brief comment must suffice. The possibilities of uncovering perjury by investigation and the severe penalties for perjury under test oath laws should make us wary of
assuming that they are ineffective, even though, as is so often said, a true Communist
will not have any scruple against taking such an oath falsely. It is not scruples that may
deter such a person but the possibility of detection and punishment. It has been rightly
remarked that the total number of federal employees of doubtful loyalty discovered
under the loyalty review program has been gratifyingly small. What we do not know is

This assumption underlies the brevity with which the test oath cases are discussed here. With the exception of the case challenging the anti-Communist oath provisions of the Taft-Hartley Act,[48] the test oath cases have come from the states. The considerable investigative and legislative activity in the states has thus far brought few other cases from the states. Almost all the other cases involving subversive associations which the Supreme Court has reviewed have arisen from Congressional investigations or Congressional legislation or from actions of the executive branch of the national government.

These cases have been raised by those who object to taking the oaths, and not as prosecutions for perjury after taking the oaths. In all but one case the oaths, differing in form, have been upheld.[49] This recent decision may mean a change in the previous unfortunate tendency of the Court to ignore the demonstrations by some of the dissenting Justices of the excessive vagueness of some of the oaths.

In upholding the anti-Communist oath of the Taft-Hartley Act, a majority had upheld, over impressive protest, the power to exact an oath regarding unspoken belief.[50] In a case raised by Los Angeles' municipal oath, a majority assumed that an employee must swear that he had not *knowingly* been a member of a subversive group, although the law did not expressly include this indication of intent.[51] The Court upheld the Feinberg law of the state of New York in a suit for declaratory judgment against it, although Mr. Justice Frankfurter urged that there was no need to do so and that there were enough ambiguities in the law that the Court should wait to see how its administrators actually applied it before sustaining it in the abstract.[52] In the Bailey case[53] an evenly divided Supreme Court had let stand a lower court's decision that a federal employee could not contest the procedure of the loy-

---

how many persons of doubtful loyalty in preceding years failed even to seek federal employment because of the requirements of a loyalty oath under the Hatch Act and the investigations they would have to face for clearance.

[48] American Communications Assn., C.I.O. *et al.* v. Douds, 339 U.S. 382 (1950). For a limitation on those labor officials who must take the oath, cf. National Labor Relations Board v. Highland Park Mfg. Co., 341 U.S. 322 (1951).

[49] The Taft-Hartley oath was upheld in the Douds case although only three Justices voted to sustain it in its entirety. The state cases in which oaths were upheld are Gerende v. Board of Suprs. of Elections of Baltimore City, 341 U.S. 56 (1951) ; Garner *et al.* v. Board of Public Works of City of Los Angeles *et al.*, 341 U.S. 716 (1951) ; Adler *et al.* v. Board of Education of City of New York, 342 U.S. 485 (1952).

[50] For the Court's position on the question of swearing in regard to belief see 339 U.S. 382 at 407–12; cf. the dissenting views on this question of Mr. Justice Frankfurter at 419–22, of Justice Jackson at 435–44, of Mr. Justice Black at 445–46.

[51] 341 U.S. 716 at 723–24; cf. Mr. Justice Frankfurter's criticism of this omission in the law and its general vagueness at 726–27.

[52] 342 U.S. 485 (1952).

[53] Bailey v. Richardson *et al.*, 341 U.S. 918 (1951). As usual in such cases, the division among members of the Court was not announced, but from evidence in Joint Anti-Fascist Refugee Committee v. McGrath, *supra*, decided the same day, one may guess that the three dissenters in that case were joined by Mr. Justice Burton in opposing the employee's contentions.

alty review boards, which admittedly falls far below judicial standards; the Court thus foreclosed an opportunity for the employee to be assured, as a matter of fundamental right, that past membership in a subversive group would not be held against her unless her knowledge of its character had been established.[54] Now, however, in *Wieman* v. *Updegraff* the Court has made clear that discharge for the mere fact of membership in a suspected group, without regard to an employee's intent, is a denial of due process of law, and that the fact that public employment is a privilege does not entitle the government to deny this due process to the employee.[55]

The constitutional power of government to impose any of these disabilities does not prove that their use to the extreme limits of that power is wise. Especially when disabilities are imposed in that spirit of retribution which has animated public opinion, rather than as a means of safeguarding the public, they are open to criticism. President Lincoln, when danger must have been as great as it is today, and when passions were as high, could see the wisdom of a purgative oath for those who had truly and freely repented of past misconduct or mistakes, and could think an oath of loyalty in the present and for the future a redemption of the past.[56] If we now did as much, we would do more than offer a humane alternative to those too honest to attempt to lie about a past they are not proud of. We would at the same time take a step in the public interest in decreasing the strength of subversive groups by offering a way out of their subversive associations to those who want to find a way out, rather than trapping them in their past.

We cannot believe that flying saucers exist, for if they did, the Kremlin would long ago have announced that they were invented by Russians. But let us indulge our fantasy and suppose that they do, and further that a flight of them is now soaring out of Moscow loaded with the precise number of dedicated members (fluent in English) of the Russian Communist party needed to replace the present membership of the American Communist party, to carry on their activities. Imagine next that these flying saucers will land secretly on American soil tonight, debark their Russian passengers, and take on board all the American Communists for the return trip. Who would doubt that the only proper thing for us to do would be to round up these

---

[54] From personal conversation with members of loyalty review boards I believe we can be sure, however, that the boards have held to the position, just as have the courts, that an unlawful *intent* on the part of the employee must be shown where membership in a subversive association is presented against him.

[55] Wieman *et al.* v. Updegraff *et al.*, 344 U.S. 183 at 189–91 (1952).

[56] Lincoln first took this position in elections in border states during the Civil War. Approving the use of federal troops in these states to prevent supporters of the Confederacy from voting, he also approved the requirement from prospective voters of an oath pledging future support to the government. Later he matured this decision into the basis for his plan of reconstructing the former Confederate states. In doing so he met opposition both from those who insisted no test oath whatsoever was permissible and from those who wanted to bar all who had previously supported the Confederacy from political participation. For the Civil War development cf. the author's unpublished "National Control of Congressional Elections" (Princeton, 1942), pp. 123–32.

substitutes as quickly as possible and put them where they could do us no harm? Why is it that we do not proceed to do the same thing with all members of the American Communist party? With a few we do. Alien members of that party are by law to be deported. A handful of the leaders of the party have been jailed under the Smith Act. And under the provisions of the Internal Security Act of 1950 (provisions proposed and supported by liberals) in a serious emergency we could round up all party members. The places for their safekeeping are even now maintained in readiness to receive them. We do not do so now, first, because we take their membership in the "one club to which we all belong" more seriously than they do, and second, because we take their capacity for doing present mischief less seriously than they do. Nor can it be said that they are held here against their will because the state is an involuntary association. For all that appears, if they wished to emigrate and expatriate themselves, we would be pleased to accommodate them. (We would certainly not have demanded that those who left on the flying saucers return.) But they like our clubhouse and apparently insist upon their right to use it. In some inverted way some of them may even like our club. They just hate the way we run the club and intend to take over its direction by hook or by crook. Since we cannot put them out, we must put up with them. But that does not mean that we must let them ruin the club for all the rest of us, nor that we cannot write and enforce the house rules to see that they don't.

After a generation of doubt and controversy it does appear that a broad coalescence of American public opinion on the treatment of this subversive group along these lines has come about. This consensus, shared by most Americans whether they call themselves liberals or conservatives, is still somewhat obscured by controversy between those who, insisting at one extreme it is inadequate and at the other that it is unfair or unnecessary, do not yet accept it. But in retrospect the achievement of the consensus will probably appear more important than the survival of the controversy.

American citizenship and Communist party membership are intellectually incompatible but physically possible.[57] This is the shape of our dilemma. Our response was for a long time to leave the question whether the combination is legally permissible in doubt. We wish that we could make the two physically incompatible. This is the meaning of President Eisenhower's proposal to strip those convicted of certain subversive crimes of their American citizenship.[58] But practically we can only make the combination legally punishable. This the Smith Act did inferentially. Professor Thomas I. Cook has argued persuasively that the law should be made explicit.[59] The legislation

[57] Cf. Chief Justice Stone's discussion in his dissenting opinion in Schneiderman v. United States, 320 U.S. 118 (1943), especially at pp. 195–96.

[58] State of the Union Message, January 7, 1954. *New York Times,* January 8, 1954, p. 1, col. 3.

[59] Thomas I. Cook, *Democratic Rights versus Communist Activity* (Garden City, New York, 1954).

proposed by Senator Humphrey and adopted in 1954 to strip the Communist party as a group of the legal rights of association, although of dubious effectiveness, goes another step in this direction.[60]

Today, therefore, the legal question of greatest practical importance is simply this: how can we protect the genuinely innocent from unnecessary injury? And it is precisely this question which legal rules and the judicial process can answer most satisfactorily. Unless one insists that knowingly taking part in the organized Communist movement in the United States is, without some further act, rather vaguely described as overt, an innocent action, it is frivolous to assert that innocent persons have been punished in the accepted legal sense by judicial process in the United States. But it is true that innocent persons have been gravely injured, particularly by some legislative investigations conducted irresponsibly in defiance of some existing legal rules and in the absence of others which the parent legislative bodies have a responsibility to adopt and to enforce in their own process. Here is a dangerous abuse which all who believe in justice should work to correct.

[60] Communist Control Act of 1954, Section 3. Public Law 637, 83d Cong., chap. 886, 2d Sess., approved Aug. 24, 1954.

THE EMERGING CONSTITUTIONAL LAW
OF ASSOCIATION

A discerning student of contemporary problems of association has written recently:[1]

Modern liberalism unfortunately has tended on the whole to step from the cherished individual of the nineteenth century to the myth of the all-benign State in the twentieth. While it seldom has been intolerant of intermediate associations, it has made little effort to formulate a theory of liberal democracy that includes them, that makes them indispensable to free, representative government.

My thesis is that what political theorists may have neglected to do the Supreme Court of the United States has been undertaking, and that in the constitutional law of association which it is creating case by case lies a set of principles which provide at the least the beginnings of "a theory of liberal democracy that includes . . . [voluntary associations], that makes them indispensable to free, representative government."

In assuming a responsibility growing out of practical necessities the Supreme Court has had to work without the benefit of altogether clear or consistent help from political or social theorists. In the first chapter a historical sketch of some of the earlier theorists who have discussed voluntary association opened our discussion. It may contribute to an understanding of the perplexities facing the Supreme Court, and therefore of the substance of its achievement, to preface this concluding chapter with a brief analysis of the present state of theory of voluntary association.

In large part discord among the major theoretical themes is more apparent than real. Social and political philosophers in discussing voluntary associations have begun by stressing as important different functions which they perform—or should perform. These functions are not contradictory, although some of the discussion suggests that they are.

One function of associations is to give individuals a sense of belonging, of feeling that they are a part of the society in which they exist, of having something larger than themselves to which they can devote their loyalties and "in whose service is perfect freedom." A group can cast its spell over men as much as an individual leader can; it seems proper to call this function charismatic. Few deny that this human need has been felt in every society of which we know. At least since Plato wrote, however, some thinkers

---

[1] Robert A. Nisbet: *The Quest for Community* (New York, 1953), p. 267.

have insisted that men cannot successfully divide their loyalties among more than one group. And since Hobbes, writers of this persuasion insist that the one association adequate to receive this loyalty is the state. In their view consequently there can be little or no place for free and vigorous voluntary associations in a healthy society.

Other political philosophers, agreeing that associations must provide men with a sense of belonging, deny the assumption that individuals have a fixed fund of loyalty. Sharing loyalty, they insist, is not the same as dividing it, for as groups satisfy this need, they create new loyalty in the individual instead of forcing him to transfer his existing loyalties from other groups. To insist that because the state has a monopoly of force it ought to have a monopoly of loyalty as well, they warn, leads straight to totalitarianism. Clearly these thinkers have the better of the argument.

Yet there is a core of truth in the opposed view. Sometimes different associations do make demands which create confusion and even agonizing conflict in the minds of those who are loyal to them. (Sometimes, it should not be forgotten, one association alone can make contradictory demands on the individual.) Reacting against the claims for a state monopoly of loyalty, the pluralists in their more extreme arguments attempted to make a virtue out of this difficulty and to see in the strenuous life of men torn between conflicting loyalties the very essence of liberty. Ordinary mortals who demur to having their character built up by constant subjection to this associational *Sturm und Drang* may perhaps be forgiven by all who are not inveterately schoolmasterish.

Modern sociologists are equally agreed on the function of groups in enabling men to escape from a feeling of isolation and nothingness. Taking their clue from an insight of Durkheim their conclusions are somewhat different from the political theorists'. They arrive at them partly through a classification of groups. (Here it may be noted that all such typologies are related to concepts of the function of groups.) Not only the modern state but many of the great voluntary associations have become far too big and impersonal for most men to comprehend or to feel that they are a significant part of them. Modern man for all the variety these secondary groups offer him often feels alienated from his society and is the victim of *anomie*. Only the primary or face-to-face group (which may be a unit of a larger association) can offer men what they need. If the state were still, like Plato's *polis*, a face-to-face group, it might satisfy his needs, but neither the modern state nor any of the secondary associations can do so. The implications of this analysis for practical policy have not yet been well developed.

Democratic theorists since Locke have emphasized the additional function of voluntary associations in increasing and strengthening the freedom of individuals. They have seen voluntary associations as a means by which men can unite not only to accomplish objects which they are too weak to achieve alone, but also to resist unjust coercion which a government might be tempted to impose in the absence of potential effective resistance. Its advocates could support their theory of the function of voluntary associations with empirical evidence. But anarchists who thought that a truly free society must be based on voluntary association only and that the state was an unnecessary evil had outrun experience and wandered into utopia.

Libertarians like Mill and De Tocqueville did not venture so far, for they realized that voluntary associations could not only be shields against governmental tyranny but could themselves coerce their members. The tyranny of the majority against which De Tocqueville inveighed would have been better described as the tyranny of organized minorities; the chief sources of the social pressure which Mill saw as a greater threat to freedom than the democratic state itself are groups. In asserting this corrective insight they of course did not deny the value of associations as barriers to overreaching governments. There is no logical inconsistency in a group's being at the same time a shield against and a source of coercion.

The third function of groups has received more attention from statesmen and jurists who must operate in the workaday world than from philosophers. Voluntary associations are also a means of getting some of society's urgent business done: they serve as agencies of social control, making possible an economy of effort for an otherwise overburdened state. The whole community has an interest, however, in how these associations conduct society's business; it has ideas of the ends to which they should exert social control. Since the community is concerned with the way in which this function is performed, it is inevitable that government as the representative of the entire community will undertake to intervene in their affairs.

The great associations are precisely those which carry the heavy burdens in the performance of this function. Aside from the family, which cannot really be regarded as a voluntary association, in the modern world these great associations are the political parties and the economic groups typified but not exhausted by the labor unions and the business corporations. Do not the churches also exercise a great amount of social control? Hobbes and other Erastians understood so well that they do that they insisted the state must control them. At this point Locke's typology of associations becomes significant. Recognizing the sense of belonging and of freedom which religious faith confers—in other words, the importance of the other two functions performed by churches—Locke sought by his antinomy between this-worldly and other-worldly associations to ensure churches the ability to fulfill these other functions by freeing them from a deadening hand laid on by governments which saw them only as agencies of social control. Churches which were treated simply as agencies of social control, Locke perceived, might not remain effective as agencies of social control. Nevertheless Locke conceded that as agencies of social control even churches are not beyond the state's supervision, for "a good life, in which consists not the least part of religion and true piety, concerns also the civil government . . ."

Locke's successors in the liberal tradition have argued that if this-worldly associations are made into departments of state they certainly cannot function as limitations on an all-powerful state; totalitarian governments agree and act accordingly. But can once-free voluntary associations which become government bureaus retain the power to perform their charismatic function of giving men a sense of belonging? No totalitarian system has yet endured long enough to prove that they can. Democracy's response to the power of groups as agencies of social control remains regulation of the manner in which they perform this function and not absorption of the function itself.

Democratic states begin with a commitment to sufficient freedom to permit associations to perform the first two of these functions. They may by positive action remove some obstacles public and private to the fullest freedom of group life and activity. Nevertheless they help most by doing nothing—nothing to weaken the basic commitment. But supervision of the manner in which associations perform the third function, carrying on society's business, does require government to play an active role. In fashioning these regulations government officials may understandably fail to consider adequately how they will affect the ability of groups to perform their other functions. In the United States the institution of judicial review enables the judges and especially the Supreme Court to require that our law of associations shall take account of all the functions which groups perform.

Can we discern principles emerging to provide a unified and coherent constitutional law of association in twentieth-century America? We have looked at enough evidence to suggest an answer. What remains to be done is to sum up that evidence under the five principles to which the cases and controversies arising out of group activity in the United States can be meaningfully related.

FREEDOM FROM GOVERNMENTAL INTERFERENCE

Of these principles the first insists that the right of individuals to associate must be protected from unlawful governmental infringement. Its ultimate vindication, in our constitutional system, is peculiarly the duty of the courts. Groups and their members have seldom, all things considered, had to call upon the judiciary to protect this right against encroachments either of the Congress or the President. Congress early followed Madison's advice, rather than Washington's, and refused to censure the precursors of our modern parties, the Democratic-Republican societies. The Abolitionist societies might well have called upon the courts to restrain Andrew Jackson's Postmaster General, Amos Kendall, when in high-handed fashion he barred their communications from the mails going to the South, but they apparently did not do so.

In the relatively few cases in which litigants have charged that Congress was overriding their rights of association the Supreme Court has rejected their claims. Congressional action against the Ku Klux Klan of Reconstruction may not have been very effective, but it survived court tests, rather surprisingly, where other civil rights legislation foundered. Mormon claims were rebuffed in the nineteenth century as have been those of various "subversive" organizations in the twentieth. Although the Supreme Court has recently found executive action in listing subversive groups to be lacking in due process and has sometimes strained to avoid constitutional questions, as in its construction of Taft-Hartley Act provisions against political expenditures by unions and of the House's recent inquiry into lobbying, the Supreme Court has never yet found a statute of Congress to be an unlawful infringement on the rights of individuals to associate. The one possible exception to this statement may be the case of *United States* v. *Lovett*,[2] for no doubt one of the reasons for the insistence of the House of Representatives that these men should be forced out of government employment was dislike of some of their associations. Significantly, the Senate had agreed reluctantly and President Roosevelt, who signed the act out of necessity, denounced the provision as unconstitutional. If this case is considered the one instance in which the Court has found a Congressional encroachment upon the right of individuals to associate, it is even more significant that it is also one of only two important occasions since 1937 in which the Court has invalidated an act of Congress.

It is far otherwise with the legislation of the states and the ordinances of their local governments. There is no more impressive piece of evidence of the Supreme Court's growing concern with the law of association than its decision in 1925 to reverse its precedents of a century, powerfully reiterated only a few years before by Justice Holmes, and give itself jurisdiction to review acts of the states trenching upon the rights of association. That decision was, of course, the reading of the First Amendment into the liberty guaranteed by the Fourteenth against improper state interference, initiated in the Gitlow case. The Court boldly made an unargued assumption of this power, and to this day the reasons for its action remain unexplained either by itself or by constitutional scholars. Had the action been taken later by a bench of libertarian and activist judges appointed by President Franklin Roosevelt, it might still have seemed a bold one, but hardly as startling as it should have seemed coming from a Harding Court during the conservative euphoria that, historians tell us, enveloped the United States in the nineteen-twenties. Yet it does not appear to have startled men at the time. For one reason, no one appreciated then the subsequent use to which the precedent would be put. In the very same year that the Court decided the Gitlow case it also successfully sponsored a major amendment to the federal judicial code by which it was relieved of the necessity of taking jurisdiction of a variety of cases which had come to overburden it. In the sequel it appears that the Supreme Court thus cleared its decks for a new engagement with the group forces that were beginning to dominate American society and politics. But even the perspicacious historians of *The Business of the Supreme Court*, writing immediately after these dual events, could not foresee such a consequence.[3]

There were two other reasons why the action might not seem out of character for a conservative and a Republican Court. *Boni judicis est ampliare jurisdictionem.* The conservative bench over which Chief Justice Taft presided did not feel the qualms so often expressed in Justice Holmes's dis-

[2] 328 U.S. 303 (1946).
[3] Felix Frankfurter and James M. Landis, *The Business of the Supreme Court* (New York, 1927).

sents about a wholesale exercise of judicial review. It had been Justice Brandeis who suggested that if the Court was determined to preserve the goose of property with a sauce of substantive due process, it might well use the same sauce for the gander of liberty. And why should his conservative brethren, who were much fonder of the basic recipe than was Justice Brandeis, be unduly reluctant to carry out this culinary experiment? Moreover, these Republican Justices had grown into political maturity in the years when the Republican party expressed the nationalizing forces that followed the Civil War. That spirit was weakening even then in the Republican party, but the Gitlow decision was consonant with the older tenets of the party. And who is to say that this late manifestation of the spirit of Republican nationalism has not been as wise a one as the spirit ever produced?

Those of us who have been spending our adult lives against the tides and storms which began to buffet us after 1929 are tempted to look back upon the decade of the nineteen-twenties as a calm and placid eddy in the stream of history in which the United States kept cool with Coolidge. But to the men whose maturity had been cleaved by the First World War, that decade presented a different countenance. They called it the "turbulent 'twenties." If the flappers and the gangsters were living symbols of that turbulence, so were the Marxists and the Ku Kluxers. In that decade Americans ceased to talk of their politics in the simple linear terms of standing pat or going forward (or "upward and onward" as Justice Holmes sarcastically put it). Of a sudden we apprehended that politics has a second dimension, and we grasped that fact because men could hear off to the left and to the right organized groups, sometimes substantial and always vociferous, calling on them to abandon the straight and narrow path of classical Liberalism, as it had long been understood in America.

By the same token we are also tempted to look back upon the Supreme Court of that decade as a conservative Court, but although the adjective tells us much that is true, it does not tell us all. For these conservatives were also liberals in the classical sense of the term. It was not simply that a conservative like Justice Butler, who was a devout Catholic, could understand the menace of the Ku Klux Klan as well as a liberal like Justice Brandeis, who was a sensitive Jew. A conservative like Chief Justice Taft could find the ideas of the Klan as repulsive as could a liberal like Justice Holmes, though neither belonged to one of the minorities which the Klan threatened. If we must call this Court conservative, we should remember that it was more united in turning back the claims of the Ku Klux Klan to utilize rights of association for its hateful purposes (in the Pierce case and the Zimmerman case) than it was in refusing to recognize rights of Benjamin Gitlow and Anita Whitney to lead the thunder-makers on the left. It is also worthy of note that those conservative members of the Court who helped read the First Amendment into the Fourteenth and who lingered on the Court in the next decade never recanted nor regretted that step in their later opinions, although they sometimes dissented from the decisions which their bold precedent had helped make possible.

As Professor Zechariah Chafee has emphasized, it was not Chief Justice Taft's Court but Chief Justice Hughes's which solidified the new principle.[4] Both on and off the bench Chief Justice Hughes had evidenced a keen perception of the importance of the right of men to associate. He and his Court not only gave hearing to these claims against state interference with increasing frequency; they also upheld these claims in regard to unpopular groups in such cases as those of Stromberg, De Jonge, Herndon, and Jehovah's Witnesses. Chief Justice Hughes himself protested the labels of conservatism and liberalism as shallow; it is no wonder when one reflects that he simultaneously softened the Court's adamant defense of the rights of property and strengthened its support of the rights of association.

The statesmanship of the Chief Justice might be summed up as *autres temps, autres droits*. In a profound and penetrating analysis Professor Edward S. Corwin has epitomized the course of American constitutional law as it has since moved along the path on which Chief Justice Hughes started it.[5] The outcome of these developments has been a decline in judicial intervention in the affairs of government and the replacement of an eighteenth-century constitution of rights of individuals with a twentieth-century constitution of powers of government. Yet this insight needs to be supplemented by recognition of one great step the Court has taken in the twentieth century contrary to this trend. The increased concern of the Supreme Court of the United States for civil liberties and its assertion of its power to shield these rights from the interference of the states is a significant counterbalance to these other trends of our constitutional law.

For it must be emphasized again that the principal result of reading the First Amendment into the Fourteenth has been the protection of the rights of individuals to associate—to assemble, speak, write, and act as members of groups. Of the scores of cases which the Court has considered under this doctrine only a handful have concerned the rights of isolated individuals. Because these twentieth-century cases are ordinarily discussed in terms of an eighteenth-century Bill of Rights, it is often overlooked that almost all of them concern groups and their members. It is scarcely too much to say that since 1925 the Supreme Court has been protecting the rights of groups against the powers of the states.

It might appear, from what has been said, that the Court has done so because it has sensed an increasing hostility toward groups in the laws of the states. Those who feel that the pressure for conformity in American life has been increasing in the last few decades are likely to accept that explanation. But it may very well be (we have no adequate studies to reveal the facts) that in the past there was less tolerance for the exercise of free communication and assembly at the grass roots than there is today, and that the spate of recent cases is more an evidence of the growing strength of groups and of greater resources and courage on their part to challenge local interfer-

[4] Zechariah Chafee, Jr., *Free Speech in the United States* (Cambridge, 1941), chap. 11.
[5] Edward S. Corwin, *Total War and the Constitution* (New York, 1947), p. 179.

ence than in the past. Thus the recent judicial concern with the rights of groups may reflect more the groups' own ability to assert and demand their rights than growing encroachments on these rights by states and local communities.

One thing is clear: the Supreme Court has recognized this first principle as a principle. It has in many subsequent cases adopted as its own the description Chief Justice Hughes gave of rights of association in the Jones-Laughlin case. These rights are "fundamental." Today, when we hear less about natural rights than our ancestors did, the Chief Justice's choice of an adjective is interesting. A right of association which does not find mention in the Constitution can scarcely be called a fundamental right because it is a constitutional right. It has become a constitutional right because it is considered a fundamental right.

The principle of freedom from unwarranted governmental interference has been used by the Court to protect many groups and many types of group activity. Churches have been among the groups protected; although most of the cases have concerned Jehovah's Witnesses, two leading cases have vindicated rights of the Roman Catholic and the Russian Orthodox churches.[6] Labor unions have been beneficiaries of the principle; locals of unions affiliated with the American Federation of Labor and with the Congress of Industrial Organizations have been involved in the picketing cases; *Thomas* v. *Collins*[7] vindicated a high official of one of the leading national unions, and *Hague* v. *CIO* one of the two parent labor organizations of the country. Even associations accused of subversion have won limited victories, as the Stromberg[8] and De Jonge[9] cases indicate, as well as the recent holding that the Attorney General of the United States had not accorded due process to organizations which he had listed as subversive.[10] There are few cases protecting political parties against governmental interference, for few cases have arisen; party members in the legislature are not likely to trample on the rights of the organizations which have helped send them there. Minor parties do not receive such favorable legislative treatment, but their complaint is not that they are denied the basic right of free association but that they are not given the special powers and privileges of the major parties, or that rules designed for the major parties work hardship on them. *MacDougall* v. *Green*,[11] in which the Court refused to relieve a candidate of the Progressive party from difficult petition requirements for getting on the ballot, stands as an example of the Court's unwillingness to intervene in what it regards as political questions. In the white primary cases the Court first held that the Democratic party in some of the Southern states had freedom to do what the Constitution forbade governments to do, but within a short time reversed

[6] Pierce *et al.* v. Society of Sisters *et al.*, 268 U.S. 510 (1925), and Kedroff *et al.* v. St. Nicholas Cathedral of Russian Orthodox Church in North America, 344 U.S. 94 (1952).

[7] 323 U.S. 516 (1945).   [8] 283 U.S. 359 (1931).   [9] 299 U.S. 353 (1937).

[10] Joint Anti-Fascist Refugee Committee v. McGrath, *et al.*, 341 U.S. 123 (1951).

[11] MacDougall v. Green, 335 U.S. 281 (1948).

itself. More recently the Court held that nothing in the Constitution forbids a party to bind persons who seek to be its candidates for Presidential electors to vote for the Presidential candidate of the party.[12]

The range of group activities protected is also wide. State interference with freedom to assemble has been struck down in a number of the Witness cases,[13] in the De Jonge case,[14] and in the Hague case.[15] Freedom of communication among members of the association and with the outside world has been upheld in other Witness cases,[16] in picketing cases,[17] in *Thomas v. Collins*,[18] and in *United States* v. *CIO*,[19] among others. Several of the Witness cases as well as *Thomas* v. *Collins* make clear that this freedom of communication includes proselyting efforts, and *Pierce* v. *Society of Sisters* gives impressive support to the right of a group to inculcate its doctrines in the young—as do the flag salute cases in another context. The Kedroff case,[20] the ultimate outcome of the Burley cases,[21] and the J. I. Case decision[22] acknowledge important autonomies of associations in self-government, even in the face of grave doubts about the fairness of their rules for individual members.

Of course many other cases can be cited in which governmental limitations upon associations have been upheld over the claims of the groups that the laws were unjust infringements on their freedom. Anyone who contends that freedom of association does not exist unless there is little or no governmental regulation can argue that these cases demonstrate that the principle of freedom from governmental interference is not honored in America. But it should be clear that that premise is untenable.

GOVERNMENTAL AID TO ASSOCIATIONS

The second principle allows government to promote opportunities for individuals to associate by appropriate means and to grant appropriate privileges and powers to associations when the public interest will be fostered by doing so. Is this principle valid as part of the general public law for all types of associations? It must be admitted that the provision against an establishment of religion in the First Amendment sharply limits its application to churches. But if there is to be religious liberty, we have seen that this provision of the First Amendment cannot be interpreted to exclude all governmental assistance to churches. The New Jersey bus case,[23] the released

---

[12] Ray v. Blair, 343 U.S. 214 (1952).

[13] E.g., Niemotko v. Maryland, 340 U.S. 268 (1951), and Fowler v. Rhode Island, 345 U.S. 67 (1953).

[14] 299 U.S. 353 (1937).

[15] 307 U.S. 496 (1939).

[16] E.g., Schneider v. New Jersey, 308 U.S. 147 (1939); Cantwell *et al.* v. Connecticut, 310 U.S. 291 (1940); and Murdock v. Pennsylvania, 319 U.S. 105 (1943).

[17] The leading case is Thornhill v. Alabama, 310 U.S. 88 (1940).

[18] 323 U.S. 516 (1945).   [19] 335 U.S. 106 (1948).   [20] 344 U.S. 94 (1952).

[21] 325 U.S. 711 (1945) and 327 U.S. 661 (1946).

[22] 321 U.S. 329 (1944).   [23] 330 U.S. 1 (1947).

time cases,[24] and the cases of peddlers' taxes imposed on the Witnesses[25] illustrate the dangers of attempting to apply the nonestablishment clause absolutely. The differences in application of this principle on the one hand to churches and on the other to groups pursuing their economic interests in this world are therefore differences only of degree, but the differences are significantly great. The nonestablishment clause is the mark of a polity dedicated to religious neutrality. The modern state does not assume a posture of economic neutrality.

Experience of religious strife convinced the Founding Fathers that the only way to avoid religious favoritism and thereby political schism was to adopt religious neutrality. Why are the arguments for religious neutrality any less persuasive for economic neutrality as the way to political peace? Can government aid one economic interest group without injuring another, or perhaps more often without hurting those who are not organized to pursue their interests? The antitheses of the market place are multitudinous, familiar, and real: producer and consumer, buyer and seller, employee and employer, landlord and tenant, professional and client, debtor and creditor, and among and against them all middlemen in endless variety. The desire to eat one's cake and have someone else's too is common enough. How far should government play the caterer to this taste?

The modern trend to extend the use of this principle on behalf of economic interest groups inevitably leads to the politicizing of these groups. For if an economic group can strengthen its bargaining position by obtaining powers and privileges from government, or weaken its competitor group's position by preventing it from getting legal powers or privileges, it must learn to be as active in the forum as in the market place. The metaphor is meant to be suggestive, for in earlier times the same ground served as both forum and market place. The philosophy of laissez faire sought to prevent this conjunction. A large part of its success was illusory, for every economy is a political economy, although some economies may be less political than others. And a large part of its success, although real enough, seemed unbearable to those who paid the price.

The politicizing of the economic interest groups has reached a stage beyond their seeking legal powers and privileges. Political parties anxious to gain or keep power learn to do so by taking the initiative in promising and giving legal aid to these groups and stimulating them to demand more in return for their support. The highest political strategy of the New Deal was the organization of labor and the farmer. The strategy was not wholly novel. Indeed, it is said with much truth that a counterbalance was needed against the political influence of organized business. In that light the strategy was hardly culpable either, for if one economic group is free to seek legal power for its own advantage and to ally itself with a political party for the

[24] People of State of Illinois *ex rel.* McCollum v. Board of Education, 333 U.S. 203 (1948), and Zorach *et al.* v. Clauson, 343 U.S. 306 (1952).
[25] The most important set of opinions is in Murdock v. Pennsylvania, 319 U.S. 105 (1943).

purpose, freedom of association demands that other economic groups have the same right. In this sense the principle we are examining grows out of the first; freedom to associate carries with it the right to associate for the purpose of augmenting the legal powers and privileges of the group. This new party politics and new politicized economy are novel by comparison with an earlier age, however, because the interests with which the parties of the nineteenth century connected themselves were much more the interests of individuals and of limited numbers of individuals. So Hamilton mobilized state and federal bondholders, and politicians from Clay to Mc-Kinley wooed individual manufacturers with the tariff. Through much of that century suffrage was limited, and even in the latter part of the century critics saw the political influence of increasingly organized business as a struggle of money against votes and of private interest against public interest, of wealth against commonwealth. Politics seemed like a morality play in which Everyman struggled against Mr. Moneybags. But the plot becomes more complicated and the ethical symbolism more obscure when we have dozens of Amalgamated Associations of Everyman struggling with one another. The true nineteenth-century forerunner of the modern mass-based politicized interest groups is not so much "the interests" of that day as the Grand Army of the Republic, which—as cynics said—having saved the country wanted it, and were taught how to get some of it by "Corporal" Tanner, the Commissioner of Pensions. Must we now speak also of labor against commonwealth, of farmer against commonwealth, of senior citizen against commonwealth? Who will be left to stand for commonwealth?

The question thus raised is what the public interest is. The principle as formulated allows the state to assist groups and give them legal powers and privileges only if it is in the public interest to do so. Among students of politics the concept of public interest in recent years has provoked sharp controversy. The public interest is a norm of extreme generality. Is it so general as to be practically meaningless? Is it a ghost that does not exist even though some scholars talk learnedly about it? Even those who say as much take for granted that private groups have interests which can be defined. But the public interest is also the interest of a group, the people organized in a state. In principle then it seems no more improper to conceive of the state's having an interest than of any other association's interest.

The argument then turns to the undeniable difficulty of formulating an authoritative and comprehensive statement of the public interest. At best it is claimed the search for the public interest is a kind of vector analysis. If we can take comfort from labeling as the public interest the sum of public policy which at any given moment has evolved from the pressures of private interest groups, we may. But we should recognize that such a generalization is descriptive rather than normative.

Despairing of the discovery or creation of a substantive definition of the public interest, some scholars have suggested that the only meaning that can be ascribed to the concept is a formal one. The public interest is satisfied when the state makes such disposition of the demands pressed by private interests that it can survive—to meet similar demands in a similar fashion in the future. So he who fights and runs away may live to fight another day. This solution hardly answers the questions of survival for what or what kind of survival. Those who propose it have been influenced by the controversy over the place of values in the social sciences, for it attempts to use the one value of survival as Occam's razor to pare away the necessity for reliance on any others.

The insistence that social science can say nothing scientific about values leads to an even more fundamental attack upon the concept of public interest. For if nothing can be said rationally for the superiority of one value over another, why should it be presumed that the public interest, whether defined formally as survival or more substantially, is entitled to prevail over any private interest? Of course most of those who take this position will agree that one may assign priority to the public interest as an article of faith, and that their position is one of theory as distinct from practice. But theories often have a way of influencing practice, and the theory that there is no rational basis for the superiority of public over private interest may be one of those which does so.

The controversy over a viable theory of the public interest is too difficult and important for anyone to pretend that it can be disposed of in a few sentences. Nevertheless the question cannot be avoided in building any theory of the law of association. It is tempting to dispose of it by saying that our constitutional system provides a method whereby legislative and executive officials define the public interest authoritatively, with power in the judges to revise these definitions, for it is true. In practice it goes a long way toward settling the most difficult problems too, for it does deny that any private interest group can set up its definition of the public interest authoritatively, and clearly implies the responsibility of public officials not to accept without examination the claims of any private group that its interests are the public interest. This answer, however, still represents a special form of positivism—juridical positivism. In plain language it means that the public interest is whatever the authorized officials say it is, and it is not an answer to the sequential question of why it is in the public interest that the public interest shall be whatever these officials say it is.

The norm of public interest is one of those ideas, like freedom of the will, without which we seem unable to carry on in the real world no matter how intellectually disreputable theorists may make them appear. When we criticize the decisions of public officials (and no democratic state can treat them as beyond criticism) we are appealing to this norm. For the consistency of these decisions is often at the very least not immediately apparent, and we suppress the query, "But are they in the public interest?" which springs inevitably to mind only at the cost of stultifying ourselves. A few examples of the public interest involved in extending legal powers and privileges to associations make the point.

If it is in the public interest to allow persons to deduct on their federal income tax returns gifts to religious organizations in the face of the nonestablishment clause, why is it not in the public interest to permit them also to deduct contributions to political parties in view of the generally conceded need for strong parties in a democracy? If it is not in the public interest to construe the power granted to a railroad brotherhood to represent all the workers in the craft to include power to discriminate against some of them because they are Negroes,[26] why is it in the public interest to interpret the power granted a bar association to control admission to the profession as including power to discriminate against applicants because they are pacifists?[27] If the public interest absolutely requires that religious groups be given the privilege of meeting on public property that does not have a roof over it,[28] why does the public interest make questionable if not absolutely improper extension to religious groups of the privilege of holding released-time education classes on public property that does have a roof over it?[29] These questions are not asked rhetorically to intimate that the decisions are stupid, careless, or unconscionable, but to suggest that it would be stupid, careless, or unconscionable to refuse to examine them simply because they were made by men who had to make some decision "by virtue of their commissions."

Extensive application of the principle that legal powers and privileges may be granted in aid of economic interest groups thus poses serious intellectual difficulties of discerning what aid is in the public interest. But when these groups are both massive and politically oriented, a further serious difficulty arises. How can elective officials, even if they are convinced that group demands are inconsistent with public interest, resist them? The judicial restraint practiced by the Supreme Court since 1937 has now continued long enough to suggest that it is very likely not a temporary aberration. One thing the courts can do, and to some extent are doing and should do, is to weigh this principle against the fourth suggested, and to limit grants of legal power and privilege to groups when the advantages seem fairly outweighed by the injuries which other persons, whether or not members of the group, suffer as a result. For this is an adjudication of rights among private parties, in which courts have long experience. But it is doubtful that courts should attempt to supplant wholesale the legislative definitions of public right or interest with their own, assuming that they could do so successfully for long.

If the determination of the public interest is left to the legislature largely free from judicial control, can the public interest survive the attempt to satisfy all potent groups by granting all demands? Madison in discussing the voracious appetite of interests thought that the necessity of their combining to achieve a majority would force each to moderate its demands.[30] A dis-

[26] Steele v. Louisville and Nashville R.R. Co. et al., 323 U.S. 192 (1944).
[27] In re Summers, 325 U.S. 561 (1945).
[28] Cf. especially Saia v. New York, 334 U.S. 558 (1948), and cases cited at note 13 above.
[29] People of State of Illinois ex rel. McCollum v. Board of Education, 333 U.S. 203 (1948), and Zorach v. Clauson, 343 U.S. 306 (1952).
[30] The Federalist, No. 10.

tinguished economist has recently reaffirmed essentially the same hypothesis in the context of contemporary politics.[81] The optimism and common sense in Professor Galbraith's concept of countervailing power are attractive, but there remains the gnawing doubt expressed succinctly by one of the sharpest political satirists of our generation:

We don't need to be concerned about pressure groups, according to one pleasant theory, because they tend to balance each other. That would be comforting if it were true. But too often the only balance that's achieved is the lightening of John Public's pockets on both sides at the same time.[82]

As long as national wealth increases it may be possible to meet more and more demands. But if they are met only by increasing the supply of money rather than wealth, the resulting inflationary economy may give the illusion of living in that utopia where all prosper by taking in one another's washing. There are remoter dangers. The necessity for closer organization of groups on a national scale in order to win governmental assistance must lead to a concentration of authority at the top. This concentration of authority in a small number of group leaders may simplify the seizure of the group by a regime bent on totalitarian control. At least the hierarchy and bureaucratization of these associations is likely to sap the vitality and spontaneity of their primary units, which sociologists tell us can best satisfy men's need for a sense of belonging. But all these difficulties with the use of the principle do not justify extirpating it from the law of association, for it is accepted and acted upon, as the statutes and the cases show.

FREEDOM FROM PRIVATE INFRINGEMENT

The third principle protecting rights of association permits government when the public interest requires it to forbid private persons to interfere with rights of individuals to associate, and to require them to enter into legal relations with an association. Of the five principles, it has been the least utilized, particularly in litigation, to the present time. There are several reasons why this principle has received less application. The first lies in the rather easygoing if not homogeneous character of American society. In a culture free from embittered partisan, religious, or economic divisions there is a spirit of accommodation and a willingness to live and let live. An interesting and significant illustration of this attitude occurs in the arrangements made by labor unions which have a closed or union shop agreement with businesses which employ members of religious sects that forbid union membership. Unions have agreed that if these employees pay the equivalent of union dues they need not become union members or participate in union meetings. There is, in short, not so much need to enforce the principle as a legal one because it has a high degree of respect as a custom; private individuals (and groups of course) do not infringe on the rights of association

---

[81] John K. Galbraith, *American Capitalism: The Concept of Countervailing Power* (Boston, 1952).

[82] Herbert Block, *The Herblock Book* (Boston, 1952).

very much. By contrast discrimination against the members of racial or ethnic groups is severe. For all of our concern with guilt by association, men suffer in the United States far more because they are stereotyped by others according to certain characteristics beyond their control than because of their voluntary membership in a group.

Very often if not always the effectiveness of private interference with rights of association depends upon the support which the state gives to the private person carrying out the discrimination. The yellow-dog contract statutes and cases are a striking illustration. The Supreme Court began by denying that the state could forbid the exaction of such a contract and thus ensured that the power of the government to enforce these contracts would be available to the employer.[33] Then it went on to assist the employer by injunction in interfering with efforts to organize employees under such contracts.[34] But later, when the courts acquiesced in legislation declaring the yellow-dog contracts against public policy and therefore unenforceable at law, employers decided that the contracts were worthless although still "legal."

The history of the yellow-dog contract suggests a third, and undoubtedly the most important, reason why the principle is applied sparingly. In the Adair and Coppage cases the Court thought that the authority of an employer to hire and fire as he saw fit was a vital part of his right to conduct his business. Eventually it admitted that the public interest demanded a curtailment of this right. But a state which respects private rights must consider carefully if these rights often do not include the right to act in ways which hamper an association. Freedom of opinion is nothing without some right to put opinions—even prejudices—into effect. There are undoubtedly avid partisans who have said that they would never hire a Democrat or that they would never receive a Republican in their home. Such exhibitions of prejudice certainly do not encourage the freest exercise of rights of association, but should they be forbidden by law? So long as we agree that a man's house is his castle, one of them should not. Yet suppose householders had to be required to take in évacués from war disaster areas, could government then be tender of their partisanship? And if partisan limitations on employment were common instead of confined to an occasional eccentric employer, would there be grounds for adding a clause forbidding them to the fair employment practices acts?

The final reason why the principle has been applied so little is simply that it is not easy for private persons to infringe on rights of association. The use of violence to do so is of course forbidden by the ordinary criminal law. Opportunities for subtler coercion are not so common. A bartender might post a sign above his bar announcing that he refused to serve any member of the Anti-Saloon League, the W.C.T.U., the Prohibition Party, or the Moslem faith—but what of it? In order to restrict rights of asso-

[33] Adair v. United States, 208 U.S. (1908), and Coppage v. Kansas, 236 U.S. 1 (1915).
[34] Hitchman Coal and Coke Co. v. Mitchell, 245 U.S. 229 (1917).

ciation, a private person must be able to withhold from a group or its members something that they value or need. Of course it does not follow that he will always exert his power, or that if he does, he is not justified in doing so. The types of private action which have been forbidden as unjustified infringements or that have raised serious questions of their propriety are mainly of two kinds.

The most common form of private interference with the right of individuals to associate is discrimination of some sort against individual members of a group. The most serious form of discrimination has been denial of employment, but undoubtedly instances of denial of housing facilities and even of opportunity for higher education can be found. Housing is denied to members of the Jewish faith, although the discrimination is not really based on their membership in a church but on ethnic origin. The same discrimination exists in higher education, and in addition there may be similar (though less) discrimination against Roman Catholic students. This discrimination has not yet produced litigation reaching the Supreme Court, but it seems clear that if and when it does, in view of the holding in the restrictive covenant cases,[35] and of the fact that the Fourteenth Amendment now is held to forbid a state's supporting religious preferences, restrictive covenants based on religious affiliation will also be held unenforceable. Since most private institutions of higher learning are beneficiaries of state support in various ways, particularly through tax exemption, it may well be argued that similar discrimination in college admissions based on religious affiliation (as well as on race) should be held unconstitutional. Of course a surer way of accomplishing the elimination of discrimination in private higher education is for the states (and the federal government) to make any assistance to these institutions conditional upon nondiscriminatory policies. In fairness it should be said that private universities and colleges (at least those which a wise student would wish to attend) have been cleaning their own houses.

Discrimination in employment has, however, brought about considerable legislation and litigation, as indicated in chapter five. From the Erdman Act to the Wagner Act Congress has steadily moved to forbid employers' discriminating against union members in employment. So have many of the states, particularly those in which there is substantial industrial employment and union membership. The Court has of course upheld these laws.[36] More recently in the Taft-Hartley Act and in many state statutes there has also been a ban on employment discrimination because men are not union members. As we have seen, these laws have also been upheld.[37] But labor unions are not the only associations which have secured state aid against discrimina-

---

[35] Shelley v. Kraemer, 334 U.S. 1 (1948).

[36] The leading case is of course National Labor Relations Board v. Jones and Laughlin Corp., 301 U.S. 1 (1937).

[37] American Federation of Labor v. American Sash and Door Co., 335 U.S. 538 (1949); Lincoln Federal Labor Union No. 19129, AFL v. Northwestern Iron and Metal Co., 335 U.S. 525 (1949); and Whitaker v. North Carolina, 335 U.S. 525 (1949).

tion in private employment. State fair employment practices acts, notably that of New York, forbid discrimination because of religious affiliation. The breadth of the Court's opinion in the Corsi case,[38] although this was not the particular issue involved, assures that if these provisions should be challenged, they will be upheld.

Quite different is the second major type of private obstacle to (for it would be prejudging the issue to call it infringement on) the rights of association. This is the denial to associations of access to the media of mass communication. It may be said that this is a question of freedom of the press. It is. But it is also and just as importantly a question of freedom of association. That it is a serious problem of freedom of association we can judge from the accusation made (and hardly to be denied) by the Democratic nominee for the Presidency in 1952 that we have in the United States a "one-party press." The problem is both extremely complex and quite delicate. Although Mr. Stevenson properly called attention to the handicap thus imposed on his party, he is much too intelligent a student of law and policy to demand hasty and ill-considered legal action.

Political parties are not the only associations which have difficulty in communicating their views to the public through the media of mass communication. Labor unions have long believed, and with good reason, that quite aside from the editorial positions which many newspapers take and admittedly have a right to take, their reporting of the unions' position in the news column is often meager or slanted. Unpopular religious sects and other voluntary associations have frequently raised similar complaints.

One difficulty stems from lack of money with which to buy space and time. Can private groups expect someone else to subsidize their communication? As long as the mass media are privately owned, the whole burden cannot be thrown on them under the euphemism of free space and time. Are the taxpayers to subsidize it, whether they like it or not? Even treating the media as common carriers would not solve this cost problem. Nor would it solve another difficulty, bias in the media. Honest reporting cannot be bought, and airwaves and newspaper columns filled with nothing but the propaganda of interested groups would be a poor substitute for it. Under these circumstances a large part of the responsibility for fair presentation of the views of these associations must rest upon the media themselves, and be reconciled with their rights to take their own point of view. The specific questions also vary markedly from one medium to another. They are beyond the scope of this book.

Thus far the Supreme Court has stayed on the periphery of these important and delicate issues. The case in which the Court held that the owners of a company town could not properly exclude Jehovah's Witnesses is not only almost a sport, but more importantly it does not deal with access to mass media, which has become vital to the success of communication. The decision giving a union the right to meet on company property under special

---

[38] 326 U.S. 88 (1945).

circumstances similarly skirts the big issues.[39] Nor can it be said that decisions of the Court opening public places to group meetings are an adequate substitute for access to the private mass media. The Commission on Freedom of the Press by entitling its report *A Free and Responsible Press* suggested that the press's responsibility is the other side of the coin of the freedom of association.[40] The whole issue is so important not only to the press and to associations but to the public that future developments of the principle that improper private infringement of associational rights may be prohibited will have to take further account of it.

LIMITATIONS ON GROUP ACTIONS INJURIOUS TO OTHER PERSONS

An association must not without adequate reason infringe upon the rights of other persons; and government must define the interests entitled to legal protection of these other individuals and groups, whether they are members or nonmembers of the association. Thus the fourth principle has been stated generally. It is protean in its particular applications, for in almost every case involving the rights of groups coming before the Supreme Court it must be weighed against the first three principles which assert the rights of groups.

The rights guaranteed groups make for power. Under what circumstances is the otherwise legitimate exercise of these powers so harmful to the interests of other persons that fairness calls for their limitation? An association contends that a governmental limitation infringes on its freedom; the government replies that it has exercised its police power to protect the rights of others who are injured by the group's action. Or a private party claims that some special power or privilege conferred on an association by government injures him; the group and the government respond by asserting that the public interest is served by the grant. Or a person whom government has forbidden to interfere with some right of some group insists that this deprivation of his freedom of action hobbles his lawful pursuit of profit or perhaps of privacy; the rejoinder is that the public interest in the group's ability to pursue its legitimate objectives outweighs the other person's loss of freedom to play dog in the manger. Thus in these cases each of the first three principles is ranged against the fourth.

In adjudicating these conflicts of interest the Court must begin with two parallel assumptions. *Prima facie* the association is acting within its rights. *Prima facie* the party injured by the action also has interests which are entitled to legal protection. One assumption must ultimately be discarded in favor of the other. The process of deciding which it must be calls for exercise of the spirit of equity. It is not easy for the judges or anyone else to articu-

[39] The two cases are respectively Marsh v. Alabama, 326 U.S. 501 (1946) and National Labor Relations Board v. Stowe Spinning Co., 336 U.S. 226 (1949).

[40] See the Commission on Freedom of the Press, *A Free and Responsible Press*, and the supporting studies published under its auspices, particularly Zechariah Chafee, Jr., *Government and Mass Communications* (Chicago, 1947).

late all of the standards which influence them in the process of deciding. Several common ones can be illustrated by referring to some of the cases involving religious sects, political parties, and labor unions examined in previous chapters.

At the outset there is an ancient equitable standard which permits the Court to dispose of a few cases rather summarily. He who demands equity must do equity. Is the object of an association in the exercise of a challenged power primarily its own benefit or principally the injury of someone else? Is it acting in good faith in its own interest or with malice toward others? The concept of malicious intent, as the history of labor law shows, is a slippery concept which ought to be used cautiously if at all. Just the same, some actions convey an ineradicable impression that they have been motivated by malice.

Violent action is particularly likely to suggest malice, but even here there is room for uncertainty. Thus in one of the picketing cases Mr. Justice Frankfurter spoke for a bare majority of the Court in sustaining a quite sweeping injunction because there had been such extensive violence in earlier phases of this labor dispute that the majority felt there remained an overhanging threat of violence.[41] The minority believed that the case should be governed by another standard, mentioned below.

The most clear-cut illustrations of the influence of this standard appear in cases involving the Negro. When they were faced with the question of malicious intent, what else could counsel do—counsel for the Democratic party in Texas and in South Carolina in the white primary cases,[42] and counsel for one union which proposed to drive Negro firemen out of their jobs and for another union which denied New York's right to require it to admit Negroes to membership—except shuffle their briefs in embarrassment?[43] Of course they had answers of a sort, but although lawyers are seldom tongue-tied they cannot always be convincing.

In his dissent to several of the Jehovah's Witness cases Justice Jackson voiced a suspicion that malice might have ruled some of their actions.[44] When vociferous droves of the sect had descended on a small town on Palm Sunday, he wondered if they were as interested in converting Catholics as they were in irritating them. But even he did not rely on this impression, and the majority did not entertain it.

The most common and most general standard calls for a balancing of the equities, for the use of the concept that is the heart of so much of the judicial process. How can equities be balanced? Mathematical precision is unavailable. Undoubtedly it is better that one party should suffer some inconvenience than the other complete ruin. And if deprivation would seem

---

[41] Milk Wagon Drivers Union of Chicago, Local 753 v. Meadowmoor Dairies, Inc., 312 U.S. 287 (1941).

[42] Smith v. Allwright, 321 U.S. 649 (1944), and Rice v. Elmore, 165 F. 2d 387 respectively.

[43] Steele v. Louisville and Nashville R.R. Co. et al., 323 U.S. 192 (1944), and Railway Mail Assn. v. Corsi, 326 U.S. 88 (1945).

[44] Cf. his comments on the record in Douglas v. City of Jeanette at 319 U.S. 167-73.

to bear about equally on whichever party is the loser, then it is preferable that the interests of many rather than a few should prevail. But all that any of these maxims can do is to guard against egregiously bad judgments. They decide only the easy cases. A court of ultimate appeal deals with hard cases. There are cases, however, that approach the outer limits indicated by these two maxims.

In *Martin* v. *Struthers*[45] the majority invalidated an ordinance prohibiting the ringing of householders' doorbells because it almost completely frustrated the Witnesses in communicating with the people of the town. The gravity of this deprivation outweighed whatever inconvenience householders might feel on being summoned by unwelcome visitors (especially since it was not clear how many would feel put upon).

In the J. I. Case decision[46] the Court held that a union chosen by the majority of employees could be empowered and the employer required to conclude a wage agreement for all employees even if it should deprive a minority of employees of somewhat better wages or working conditions which they enjoyed under individual contracts. In doing so its main line of reasoning was based squarely on the idea of the greatest good for the greatest number. The same concept underlies the opinion in *Cox* v. *New Hampshire*,[47] which denied, in the interest of all who use the streets for normal traffic purposes, that a group may parade on them whenever it desires without permission.

In trying to balance the equities the Court can often help itself to reach an answer by asking if there are alternatives open to the parties. Can the association achieve its objectives by some apparent and reasonable alternative that does not harm others? Or do those who complain of undue group pressure have available an alternative to avoid it? Thus in the Meadowmoor case, which the majority settled on the issue of violence, the dissenters protested the sweeping injunction because they considered that the alternative of an injunction and police action to prohibit violence was available and, considering the equities, the only proper one to take. In *Martin* v. *Struthers* the case against the ordinance forbidding all doorbell ringing was strengthened by the obvious alternative that an ordinance could have been adopted to protect from such intrusion only those householders who signified that they did not wish to be bothered.

The Justices who have denied the validity of the released-time programs have pointed to the alternative of holding religious education classes outside school hours, even though fewer students might attend them. The Justices who have upheld the program seem more impressed by numbers. Is it better that a few should suffer social pressure than that many should be denied the benefits of an existing program?

Another of the picketing cases provides a further illustration. The majority upheld an injunction against the picketing of a restaurant by a construction union because its owner had contracted to have a building some

45 319 U.S. 141 (1943).
46 321 U.S. 329 (1944).
47 312 U.S. 569 (1941).

distance away constructed with nonunion labor.[48] Among other reasons, it was noted that the union could picket the construction site. But the minority dissented, in part, because this apparent alternative seemed to hold far less possibility of gaining the union objective than what the pickets had actually done.

A pair of cases involving political parties offers a significant comparison of the availability of alternatives. In *Rice* v. *Elmore*[49] the Democratic party in South Carolina was ordered to admit Negroes to its primaries despite fears of the party leadership that they might take over the party. Shortly thereafter in *Ray* v. *Blair*[50] the Democratic party leadership in Alabama was upheld in its effort, in effect, to keep Dixiecrats out of its primaries. In the latter case the Court observed that if the Alabama Dixiecrats did not like the terms on which they could participate in the Democratic party, they might organize a party of their own. But the same answer could have been given to the South Carolina Negroes. Is this not gross inconsistency? Resisting the temptation to quote in full the aphorism about equal rights of rich and poor to sleep on park benches, one needs only a casual acquaintance with the facts of political life to know that the alternative apparently available for each is genuine for the Dixiecrats and almost fanciful for the Negro.

In the balancing of these equities the judiciary usually is confronted with one important fact: the state has already thrown its weight in one side or the other of the scales. How much should this weight count for? Equity from its beginnings has been sensitive to the bearing of public policy. Yet if public policy as expressed by executives or legislators were wholly determinative of the issues, there would be nothing for the Court to do in most of these cases except bow to it. In fact the Court sometimes instances and expounds public policy as an additional reason for its decision; it sometimes utilizes public policy to tip the scales of justice, but not to dispense with them. Thus in the cases involving group discrimination against the Negro, the Court has analogized the public policy against governmental discrimination imbedded in the Constitution itself.

If the rights which an association claims stem from the Constitution itself, how can the Court justify their limitation on the ground of public policy formulated in a mere statute? The answer lies in the fact that the Constitution although a higher source of public policy is also the source of more general policy. The statute although a lower source often expresses a more specific public policy. To ascertain the bearing of public policy in such cases is not a mechanical process of subordinating the lower to the higher source; it requires that the more general policy be interpreted by reference to the more specific policies which elaborate it, qualify it, and clarify it. Two examples will illuminate the Court's approach to this task.

In the Giboney case[51] the Court restrained picketing even though it holds

[48] Carpenters and Joiners Union of America, Local No. 213 v. Ritter's Cafe, 315 U.S. 722 (1942).

[49] 165 F. 2d 387, certiorari denied, Elmore v. Rice, 333 U.S. 875 (1948).

[50] 343 U.S. 214 (1952).   [51] 336 U.S. 490 (1949).

that picketing involves speech which is entitled to First Amendment protection. But freedom of speech is not absolute. The pickets here admittedly sought to induce the company to act in violation of a state antitrust law. Now the common law had been treating monopoly as against public policy centuries before the policy was repeated in statutes and centuries before the First Amendment was adopted. The policy is about as settled as any public policy can ever be. Under these circumstances not a single member of the Court thought that it was sensible to suppose that free speech necessarily includes the right to create monopoly.

The Prince case[52] was more difficult and evoked division. In sustaining the conviction of a woman for taking her niece with her to sell religious tracts on the street at night over the plea that freedom of worship was thereby abridged, the Court gave great weight to public policy against child labor. But this public policy is new and had been disregarded and even attacked by the Court within memory. Its weight as settled policy derives not from its age but from the fact that it has been widely adopted after long discussion and over bitter opposition. The possibilities of evasion of the statutes which embody it are great enough to justify refusal to grant dispensations.

Most complaints against the exercise of group power come from persons who are not members of the organization. But some cases reach the courts in which members of an association seek relief from alleged unfair treatment. These latter cases raise additional questions. The ancient tradition of the common law has been strongly opposed to taking jurisdiction of these internal conflicts. In the present century the pluralists have stressed the importance of a group's right to self-government.

In contrast to these arguments for a large measure of autonomy for associations in their relations with their own members are all the implications arising from the patent fact that in a modern economy membership in the great economic associations becomes dubiously voluntary. Workers in many trades if they wish to draw their wages must be union members; disbarment or expulsion from a medical society will cut off a lawyer's or a doctor's practice and fees; membership in a trade association may spell the difference between business success or failure. Economic pressures aside, the importance of groups in giving men a sense of attachment to the outside world means that a group's sentence of exile on a member or even a self-imposed expatriation can be a traumatic experience. Caught in these crosscurrents the Supreme Court has difficulty in reaching a safe position. It may appear that the Court and its members are sometimes swept along in different directions at the same time.

To reach some opinion on the matter let us begin with a pair of the Court's holdings. In the Case decision[53] individual workers including those who were union members could not maintain advantages they might have under an individual contract against the collective agreement negotiated by the union. Yet in the Burley cases[54] the majority insisted, although far less force-

[52] 321 U.S. 158 (1944).   [53] 321 U.S. 329 (1944).
[54] 325 U.S. 711 (1945) and 327 U.S. 661 (1946).

fully on rehearing, that union members' rights to back pay could not be settled by an agreement that the union had negotiated. How can these decisions be reconciled? One clue lies in the prospective effect of the union action in the former and the retroactive impact of union action in the latter case. In the situation described in the Case opinion members were put on notice that future pay and working conditions would depend upon the collective agreement. Whether or not they had an opportunity to ratify or reject this particular agreement, they could use their influence within the union in regard to further bargaining. But in the Burley cases the union was negotiating about pay that its members had, on their interpretation of a past agreement, already earned. If their interpretation was correct, the new agreement had wiped out their vested rights. It may well be that the obligations of members to accept prospective and retrospective rules of an association should be different.

Consider next the position of Mr. Justice Frankfurter in a pair of opinions. Dissenting in the Burley cases he had argued powerfully that the only proper test of the members' obligation to be bound by the union's new agreement was the customs of the union. These groups, he insisted, have a life of their own which courts must respect unless they wish to create chaos. The life history of this union showed that members had always regarded such agreements as binding upon them. In the Kedroff case[55] he emphasized that the only proper function of the Court was to enforce the canon law of the church as it stood before the dispute between the two schismatic factions began. This amounted to settling the dispute by enforcing a group constitution and disregarding the vast subsequent changes in the organic life of the group and the new customs which had consequently arisen. Are these positions consistent? It deserves note that in the Burley case the group's fundamental law was not clear on the point at issue, but he thought that in the Kedroff case it was. Further, in the Burley case a few members were in opposition to a single action of the group and certainly were not disputing its over-all authority. But the situation in the Kedroff case might be described as religious civil war. The issue raised was basic authority in the association, and neither faction recognized the legitimacy of the basic law, whether written or customary, whether static or dynamic, by virtue of which the other claimed authority. Mr. Justice Frankfurter did not deny the similarities between the two cases, but he discerned the differences between them too, and these he thought controlling. His reasoning may not compel agreement, but it deserves respect, for it is relevant to the problem.

Justice Rutledge wrote for the minority in *United States* v. *Congress of Industrial Organizations*[56] and for the majority in the Burley cases. In the light of his reluctance in the latter to see union members bound by a group decision, consider his position in the former. He thought there that a law forbidding a union to use for political purposes funds collected in dues from its members without their individual consent to use of the money for this

[55] 344 U.S. 94 (1952).
[56] 335 U.S. 106 (1948).

purpose so severe an infringement of a group's right to freedom of speech and press that the Taft-Hartley provision should be declared unconstitutional. But in the Burley cases the union was acting as an agent of the members in regard to their private rights. In the CIO case Justice Rutledge stressed that the union's participation in political affairs, although undertaken by the leadership for the advantage of the members as the leaders interpreted that advantage, was also and importantly the exercise of a public function akin to the functions performed by a political party, not the handling of mere private business. It may be added that union members who disagreed with the union's political stand were still free both to seek to change that stand and to vote as they chose in the elections, whether or not they succeeded in altering the union position. The degree of autonomy which associations should have in the government of their own members is a difficult problem in the growing public law of association and one which will in future tax judicial creativity.

RESTRAINTS UPON SUBVERSIVE ASSOCIATION

The final principle, which is also a limitation on the power of groups, forbids the use of rights of association to injure the whole society or its political institutions. Especially since the beginning of the cold war it is this principle, as it has been applied in the regulation of the Communist party and similar subversive groups, which has captured the headlines. If one remembers only the headlines, it may seem that freedom of association is being severely limited in the United States today and that the Supreme Court has been acquiescing in these limitations. But it is misleading to try to grasp the law of the American Constitution from the newspaper headlines of this or any other decade. One who is familiar with the many cases in which rights of association have been upheld in the past quarter-century and with the exposition of the principles underlying these rights in legislative deliberations as well as judicial opinions and scholarly commentaries will not be so quick to toll the knell of American freedom.

Through our history we Americans have been disturbed, indignant, and even vengeful toward a good many organized groups that rightly or wrongly we have considered menacing. Superficially these groups appear quite diverse and range from the ultrareactionary to the wildly radical. But they all have had or have had attributed to them one or more of several characteristics. Put another way, each of these groups has been seen as a threat to one or more of several deeply and widely cherished values.

One of these values is equality. Groups suspected of having an elitist spirit, especially if they have had an element of secrecy about them, and even more if they have also appeared ambitious to exert political influence, have fallen foul of that value. An elitist spirit embraces, in American eyes, a multitude of sins—an authoritarian form of organization, or a claim to exclusive possession of "the one true way" to religious, economic, or political salvation, or simply social hauteur. Even with George Washington as a member the Order of the Cincinnati were not spared from harsh attack as long as they seemed to desire political influence. (It may be an effect of our equalitarian spirit that the veterans' organizations arising from our later wars have been open to former enlisted men as well as officers.) The Federalist party went down under the weight of an unwise boast of being the representative of the rich, the well-born, and the able. The Know-Nothings expired under their definition of Americanism, which as Abraham Lincoln observed would by logical extension exclude most Americans. Surely no small part of the hatred toward "the trusts" stemmed from the feeling that their sponsors agreed with George F. Baer that they had been chosen by God to look after the interests of everyone else.

No doubt the American passion for equality has sometimes swelled into absurdity and sometimes degenerated into bigotry. Even the Masons and college fraternities have not escaped mistrust on the score of elitism, and the Catholic Church has had to defend itself against bitter denunciation. Yet out of all the clamor the American people have reached a seasoned and a reasoned judgment. The only groups whose elitism has led to a legal verdict of subversion have been the Klan, the Bund, and similar rightist groups, and of course the Communists and their leftist fronts.

Closely linked to the value of equality is tolerance of religious, racial, and ethnic difference. Groups which refuse to honor this value may also be regarded as subversive by many. The religious bigotry of Jehovah's Witnesses has provoked such charges. College fraternities, no longer suspect because of their secrecy, now come under attack if they practice racial and religious discrimination. But the neo-Fascist groups have aggressively challenged this American commitment. So have the Communists; although posing as the protectors of racial minorities, their chief interest has been to exploit these groups, and their opposition to all religious faith and ethics is well known.

Americans likewise value highly their economic welfare and economic status. Groups whose programs threaten or have seemed to threaten the property rights and more broadly the economic status of others not unnaturally have been regarded as subversive by those who saw themselves cast in the role of the victims. Early in our history it was the Jeffersonian Democratic-Republican societies, later the Abolitionist societies, later still the "trusts," and today the labor unions. The Jeffersonians and Abolitionists won acceptance; monopolies of capital and of labor have had to submit to regulation. Again it is the Communists, however, whose radical attack on the economic system raises against them the hand of every man in a way that none of the other groups has felt.

Finally, Americans place high value on national patriotism. Especially in time of war or crisis groups which deny this value must expect harsh treatment, for the average citizen regards them often with fear and always with loathing. Passion at such times has often led to unjust assaults upon groups, not least religious sects. The Quakers early and the Witnesses lately have been denounced as subversive for holding pacifist beliefs. The Catholic Church, which has been a vital agency in aiding millions of immigrants to become Americans in spirit, has nevertheless had to reply to bigoted charges of "allegiance to a foreign prince." But putting these false fears aside, it is clear that no other group has so overtly and violently denied the value of national loyalty as the Communists.

No other group has ever been pursued so relentlessly as subversive of American society and government as the Communists and their satellite organizations. But no other group has ever threatened or denied all of these values of equality, tolerance, economic welfare, and national loyalty as do the Communists. Instead of repeating the frequent query, why are the American people so concerned about internal subversion, should we not ask if there would not be something wrong if we did not recognize this association as a menace to American society?

The question remains: why do other Western democratic states appear less disturbed than we? At least it should not be assumed as self-evident that superior wisdom inheres in those who are least concerned. More than one Western state could not be unduly excited about the Nazis and their fifth columns until disastrous consequences were visited upon them. Still, it is said, it is paradoxical that although some peoples may not be vigilant enough, America, where the appeal of communism is least effective, should be the most excited. Let it be admitted—a happy admission—that the power of the indigenous Communist groups, in contrast to their desire, to overthrow the government of the United States is very small.

The plain truth is, however, that the diverse and burgeoning legal measures taken against communism in the United States, which were examined in the preceding chapter, can never be understood if they are conceived as a coolly rational program to avert the menace. Seen only as that, it can easily be argued that some of them at least are unnecessary and others are ineffectual or worse. Such criticisms in making one point miss another.

A large part of the contemporary legal drive against subversion in the United States may best be understood as a great symbolic rite rather than as a practical policy. Negative in expression though it may be (and this may be one of its weaknesses) it is a pledge to defend the values threatened. As symbolism is it to be condemned out of hand? No doubt there are dangers, frequently noted. The ritual of investigating, legislating against, and prosecuting Communists may become a cheap emotional binge. Unlike spending the winter in a damp and frigid dugout to fight the Communists in Korea, or suffering the heat, the insects, and the diseases of tropical swamps to fight them in Indochina or Malaya, fighting Communists in the United States is usually a rather painless campaign which might qualify one for a good-conduct ribbon but hardly merits the Congressional Medal of Honor (even for Congressional combatants). If ritual becomes a substitute for effective action at home or distracts our attention from situations abroad that no amount of ritual can correct, then it is dangerous. If it harms or intimidates many innocent persons, then it is also dangerous. But it is not dangerous simply because it is a ritual.

The symbolic side of the anti-Communist effort in the United States cannot be baldly contrasted with a program of effective action, for it is part of a larger policy. In the short run and for the long pull Americans are called upon to make and are making not only symbolic gestures but real sacrifices to prevent Communist triumph. It is not easy for men to screw their courage to the sticking point ,and certainly logic alone does not usually provide sufficient motivation. No social scientist would expect a community chest campaign or the March of Dimes or a bond drive or a union organizing fight or a religious revival or a civic reform movement to be conducted without manifold appeals to symbols. Why should he suppose then that, if men must bring themselves to face sacrifices including death, they can succeed without resort to emotion, or insist that they must? Nor should one assume that government has created the anti-Communist campaign to manipulate public opinion and to engineer consent to sacrifices. There are many bits of evidence which suggest that government officials have responded cautiously to popular demands for these symbolic gestures.[57]

Legal action against subversion, it was suggested, can be classified as security, publicity, or outlawry measures. Security measures constitute the bulk of practical action against subversion. It is significant that little of the libertarian criticism has been leveled against them. There has been objection to the use of wire-tapping in our counterespionage. There are criticisms of certain aspects of the security program for government employees. One of these is directed at the limited disclosure of the evidence against him to the employee concerned. Another questions the necessity for extending the program to nonsensitive positions. But the truth again is that this extension is a symbolic rather than a practical measure. The third attacks loyalty oaths as ineffective. Again, as a practical security measure they have quite limited effectiveness, but they are essentially part of the symbolic side of anticommunism.

The bulk of the symbolic program, on the other hand, is expressed through the use of publicity and outlawry techniques. Publicity in so far as it demonstrates the nature of Communist operations and thus alerts the public, in distinction to investigations aimed at exposure of individuals to public condemnation, can properly be described as a security measure. This aspect of publicity thoughtful liberals have not censured and have even approved in strong terms.[58] Outlawry measures in so far as they are enforced so as to cramp the style of Communist leaders can also be regarded as security measures. But the mass of outlawry measures on the statute books clearly has a symbolic rather than a practical significance.

When libertarians fail or refuse to recognize the distinction between the practical and the symbolic side of the antisubversion effort and denounce symbolic measures because they are not practical, they are adding to the general confusion, wasting their ammunition, and accomplishing little in averting the dangers inherent in the program. For the symbolic ritual in the

---

[57] Samuel A. Stouffer, *Communism, Conformity, and Civil Liberties: A Cross-Section of the Nation Speaks Its Mind* (New York, 1955).

[58] Cf. Robert K. Carr, *The House Committee on Un-American Activities, 1945–1950* (Ithaca, N.Y., 1952), pp. 449–55.

program is not going to disappear, however distasteful ritual of any kind may be to persons with a matter-of-fact turn of mind. But too much ritual may finally bore even those who like a bit of it.

Our precise question is: what can legal procedure and particularly judicial process do to avert these dangers? The candid answer must be, not very much. It cannot prevent reliance on symbolic measures as an inadequate substitute for practical measures at home. But there is no good reason to believe that we are guilty of this mistaken reliance and that our practical security measures are now a failure. It cannot prevent rituals at home distracting people's attention from practical necessities in international affairs. It can do little to alleviate the intimidation of innocent people from organizing, speaking, and acting in behalf of what they believe is right. How great this danger is no one really knows; it is possible to exaggerate it as well as to underestimate it.[59]

In describing the world-wide movement of which American communism is a part, Morton Grodzins has said: "At no previous point in the short history of national states has an alternative to national loyalty been so widely advertised or seemed to promise so much."[60] In Arnold Toynbee's language this is the challenge to which Americans and others must make an adequate response if their civilization is to survive. The prevention of internal subversion in this country alone holds little promise of being an adequate response, although it is vital to an adequate response.

An international challenge must be met by an international response. That international response must find, and to some extent is already finding, expression in international law. For it must not be forgotten that international law is also a law of associations. One of the grave weaknesses of international law is, in Karl Llewellyn's phrase, that it is "barebones law," which is still too much limited to the settlement of violent disputes.[61] The analogy between the principles of public law of association growing within the United States and the principles of an international law adequate to meet the challenge is striking.

International law has long recognized the first principle. "The equality of states" is a way of saying that each national association has a right to exist free from unjust abridgment of its rights by any political superior. The fifth principle struggles for support: no national association has a right to subvert the peace and to destroy other societies and their political institutions.

But an adequate response will require the building of "a jural order of the world"[62] which can maintain the principles in between these two. In the

[59] Stouffer, op. cit., pp. 78–83.

[60] In a forthcoming book, *The Loyal and the Disloyal: Social Boundaries of Patriotism and Treason.*

[61] Cf. the discussion of Professor Llewellyn's article, "The Normative, the Legal and the Law Jobs: The Problem of Juristic Method," 49 *Yale Law Journal* 1355 (1940), in Julius Stone, *The Province and Function of Law* (Cambridge, 1950), pp. 717–21.

[62] The phrase is the late Charles E. Merriam's. For an indication of the central role which he assigned to groups in political theory cf. his *Systematic Politics* (Chicago, 1945), especially the Preface.

interest of all peoples some strong national states must be granted legal powers commensurate with their responsibilities, and others which are weak must be given aid in accordance with their needs if they are to fulfill their functions adequately in the society of nations. The third principle will also have to be recognized. Private parties below the dignity of national states cannot be allowed to block the freedom of any national state association; private imperialisms are just as hateful as public ones, and like the private infringements upon freedom of association within a national community, they can hardly exist unless they receive support from governmental power. Finally, but not least, states must accept the fourth principle, in practice as well as in principle. They must recognize that limitations on their power cannot be confined to a prohibition against subverting the peace. In some sufficient ways they must admit that in the exercise of their otherwise legitimate powers they may infringe the rights of multitudes of private persons, and that therefore they have a responsibility to consent to fair mediation, arbitration, and adjudication of these conflicts. In so far as their action may injure only their own members they may rightly claim a large measure of autonomy, even as they allow it to the voluntary associations within their own boundaries. But if justice is to be done, they cannot claim complete immunity from disinterested judgment even here. If the greatest challenge the national state system has ever faced finds its successful response, the response must be an adequate public law of international association.

TABLE OF CASES

Schneiderman v. United States, 320 U.S. 118 (1943), 130, 137, 150 n.
Senn v. Tile Layers' Protective Union, 301 U.S. 468 (1937), 71.
Shapiro v. United States, 335 U.S. 1 (1948), 125.
Shelley v. Kraemer, 334 U.S. 1 (1948), 167.
Smith v. Allwright, 321 U.S. 649 (1944), 109–10, 170.
Steele v. Louisville and Nashville R.R. Co., 323 U.S. 192 (1944), 88, 164, 170.
Stromberg v. California, 283 U.S. 359 (1931), 132–33, 158, 159.
In re Summers, 325 U.S. 561 (1945), 29–30, 164.
Taylor v. Mississippi, 319 U.S. 583 (1943), 33.
Terry v. Adams, 345 U.S. 461 (1953), 110 n.
Texas and N.O.R. Co. v. Brotherhood of Railway and Steamship Clerks, 281 U.S. 548 (1930), 67 n.
Thomas v. Collins, 323 U.S. 516 (1945), 35 n., 73–76, 80, 159, 160.
Thornhill v. Alabama, 310 U.S. 88 (1940), 71–73, 160.
Truax v. Corrigan, 257 U.S. 312 (1921), 67 n., 70–71.
Trumbo v. United States, 339 U.S. 934 (1950), 132.
Tucker v. Texas, 326 U.S. 517 (1946), 41 n.
Tunstall v. Brotherhood of Locomotive Firemen and Enginemen, 323 U.S. 210 (1944), 88 n.
United Mine Workers v. Coronado Coal Co., 259 U.S. 344 (1922), 122 n., 67 n.
United Public Workers of America (C.I.O.) v. Mitchell, 330 U.S. 75 (1947), 111–12.
United States v. Ballard, 322 U.S. 78 (1944), 59–60.
United States v. Bland, 283 U.S. 636 (1931), 28 n.
United States v. Brims, 272 U.S. 549 (1926), 67 n.
United States v. Bryan, 339 U.S. 323 (1950), 132.
United States v. Classic, 313 U.S. 299 (1941), 109.
United States v. Congress of Industrial Organizations, 335 U.S. 106 (1948), 91, 114–17, 160, 174–75.
United States v. Fleischman, 339 U.S. 349 (1950), 132.
United States v. Harriss, 347 U.S. 612 (1954), 121 n.
United States v. Lovett, 328 U.S. 303 (1946), 134, 156.
United States v. MacIntosh, 283 U.S. 605 (1931), 28 n.
United States v. Rumely, 345 U.S. 41 (1953), 113, 118–21.
United States v. Schwimmer, 279 U.S. 644 (1929), 28 n.
United States v. United Mine Workers, 330 U.S. 258 (1947), 91–92.
United States v. White, 322 U.S. 694 (1944), 125.
Valentine v. Chrestensen, 316 U.S. 52 (1942), 76 n.
Ex parte Vallandighan, 1 Wallace 243 (1864), 127.
Vidal v. Girard's Executors, 2 Howard 127 (1844), 50–51.
West Virginia State Board of Education v. Barnette, 319 U.S. 624 (1943), 30–32, 160.
Whitaker v. North Carolina, 335 U.S. 525 (1949), 86–87, 167.
Whitney v. California, 274 U.S. 357 (1927), 128, 145 n., 157
Wieman v. Updegraff, 344 U.S. 183 (1952), 149.
Wolff Packing Co. v. Court of Industrial Relations, 262 U.S. 522 (1923), 67 n., 81.
Worcester v. Georgia, 6 Peters 515 (1832), 50 n.
Youngstown Sheet and Tube Co. v. Sawyer, 343 U.S. 579 (1952), 81.
Zorach v. Clauson, 343 U.S. 306 (1952), 64 n., 65–66, 160–61, 164.

INDEX

Abolitionists, 176
Aliens, 28–29, 133, 141, 145–46
American Federation of Labor, 13, 85, 159
American Political Science Association, 97
Anarchism, 127, 154
Anomie, 153
Anti-Saloon League, 166
Aristotle, 83
Australian ballot, 99

Barker, Sir Ernest, 1 n., 10 n., 11, 18 n., 69, 117
Bill of Attainder, 134
Black, Justice Hugo, 29, 40, 46, 51, 64, 65, 74, 86, 88, 109, 112, 115, 119, 135, 136, 138, 139, 141, 148n.
Brandeis, Justice Louis D., 70, 71, 87, 157
Brewer, Justice David, 50, 63
Buchanan, President James, 87
Bund, 176
Burke, Edmund, 97
Burton, Justice Harold H., 65, 135–36
Business corporations, 9–10, 115, 125, 154
Butler, Justice Pierce, 157

Cannon, Speaker Joseph, 96
Cardozo, Justice Benjamin N., 65
Catholic church, 13, 26, 36, 52, 61, 157, 159, 167, 170, 176
Chafee, Zechariah, 15, 28 n., 123, 128 n., 132 n., 142 n., 158
Charisma, 152, 155
Child labor, 173
Citizenship, 3–4, 141
Civil Rights Acts, 73–74, 109
Civil service, 110–12, 146
Clark, Justice Tom, 65, 134, 135
Clay, Henry, 162
Clayton Act, 67, 70, 76
"Clear and present danger," 72, 139
Cleveland, President Grover, 113
Closed shop, 86–89
Coercion, 65, 73, 79–80
Cole, G. D. H., 9
Collective bargaining, 80–81, 90–91, 171, 173–74
College fraternities, 176
Commission on Freedom of the Press, 169
Committee for Constitutional Government, 119

Common law, 173
Communist Control Act of 1954, 150–51
Company towns, 40–41, 168
Compulsory arbitration, 81
Concession theory, 6, 130
Congress of Industrial Organizations, 73, 114, 159
Conscientious objectors, 27–30, 164
Conventions, political party, 96
Coolidge, President Calvin, 157
Corrupt Practices Acts, 108, 112–17
Corwin, Edward S., 158
"Countervailing power," 164

Debs, Eugene V., 67
Democratic party, 103, 107–10, 114, 159, 170, 172
Democratic-Republican Societies, 17, 155, 176
De Tocqueville, Alexis, 10, 14, 103, 154
Dicey, Albert V., 102
Disclosure of: "official records," 125; political contributions and expenditures, 112–13, 117–21
Dixiecrats, 172
Douglas, Justice William O., 29, 35, 37, 46, 56, 59, 65–66, 74, 105, 109, 112, 115, 119–21, 136, 138, 139, 141, 144
Durkheim, Emile, 153

Eisenhower, President Dwight D., 150
Electoral College, 96, 105
Elitist groups, 175–76
"Employers' free speech," 79–80
Equal protection of the law, 129
Erdman Act, 77, 167

Fair employment practices laws, 88, 166, 168
Family, 3, 4, 6, 8–9, 154
Federalist party, 17, 176
Figgis, Neville, 10, 12
Finer, Herman, 114
Flag salute, 30–33, 37, 132–33, 160
Frankfurter, Justice Felix, 30–32, 35, 38, 41, 46–48, 59, 65, 74, 87, 90, 92, 115, 118, 134, 136, 140, 148 n., 156 n., 170, 174
Ford, Henry, 108
Ford, Henry Jones, 94–95
Fraternal orders, 4, 13, 123, 176